Eleanor and W[illegible]

Thank you so much for your support and encouragement. Am proud to be in your collection.

Heartfully yours,

Priscilla A. Phifer

03/15/21

Printed in the United States of America

First Edition, 2020

ISBN - 978-0-578-77276-9

Designed and Produced by: Andrea Designs Studio

Artwork Photographs: Gary Washington, Professional Photographer

First Printing

FOREWORD

ARTIST PRISCILLA A. PHIFER DEMONSTRATES A RATHER OPEN, FREE-SPIRITED APPROACH TO HER ART.

She states that she is self-taught, however, there is an early history of her creativity in visual art activities that include design, decoupage, floral arranging, and decorating. This early engagement with processing materials seems to be a forerunner to her enthusiastic painting practice.

Thematically, Phifer organizes many of her works into groups. They include overlaying colors resembling plaid patterns; some grid-like compositions with varied applications of paint delineating pathways; some with surfaces that are built with pigment and palette knife. This variety of imagery is enhanced by the artist's investigative process and visual art influences and exuberant painting style. Geometric forms become stabilizers punctuating her visual poetry. She produces brightly colored canvases that are joyful and inventive, leading the viewer to high expectations which are immediately fulfilled.

Priscilla is a prolific painter whose visual repertoire reveals the exciting path before her.

Shirley Woodson, Painter
2020

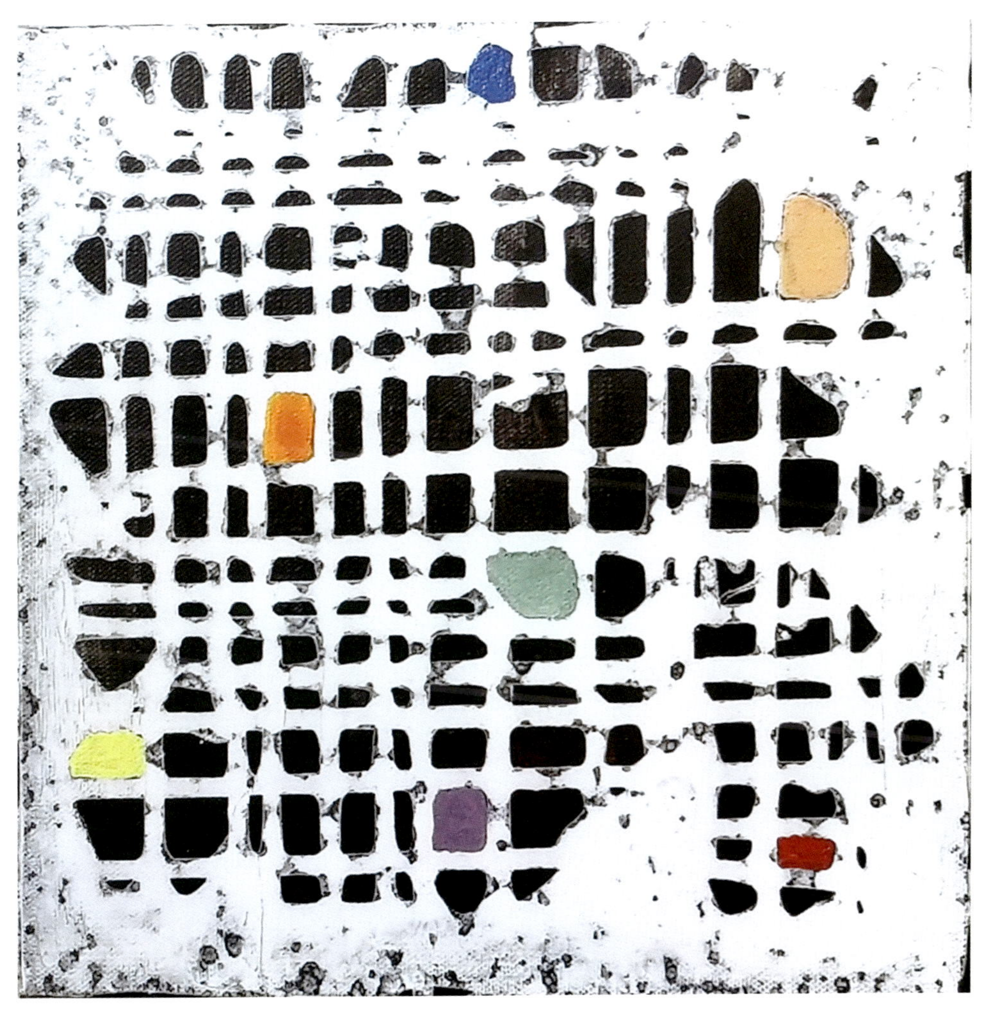

COLLECTOR:
SHIRLEY WOODSON

STAY IN YOUR OWN PANE #5 (10" X 10")
2019

PREFACE

This book is important because it documents not only my art but helps establish my legacy in the art world while recognizing my collectors. Creating the book, however, was bittersweet. A project originally conceptualized by son Drake and bonus daughter in 2018, Monique passed suddenly in August of that year, and the project saw several starts and stops. Delayed also by the Corona virus-19 pandemic, it was a challenge for Drake to continue sending professional photographer Gary Washington to homes of collectors, relying instead on the collectors, themselves, to send their best selfies! Now, that's creativity! It seemed the book was destined for another delay or shelved forever.

This book also highlights some of the collectors who were instrumental in shaping my career. They are featured in the approximate order that they collected my work, to show the progression or evolution of my work. Collectors help motivate and inspire me. A listing of all collectors is in the back of the book. It is exhilarating when friends become collectors and collectors become friends. I am forever grateful to those who have played a part in this wonderful journey of unexpected pleasures.

As I reflect, it seems creativity and my flair for the arts run through my veins. There are vocalists, photographers, visual artists, and musicians in my immediate family. I grew up with a mother who had lots of fabric and skeins of yarn around the house. My mother sewed, knitted, crocheted, painted walls, and hung wallpaper. The girls in the family would receive embroidery kits, and I would also make terrycloth dolls. Recalling a sixth-grade barn-scene project, I embellished the barn using twigs for the façade, sand for the roof, and construction paper for the grass, water, and cows.

Although creativity has been lifelong, my professional career as a visual artist began five years ago, debuting as an intuitive abstract expressionist, and I can certainly see some of the influencers and inspiration for my work. In addition to textile influences, especially of lines, early works by Charles Burwell and works by Mark Rothko influenced the "You Are Here" and "Dot Dash" series, the only two series painted with a brush. Sam Gilliam and Jackson Pollock show up in the "Woven," "Syncopation," "Stay in Your Own Pane," "If Women Ruled," and "Color My World" series, all a form of action painting without using a brush. All paintings are original, except for a limited edition of 20 each of "Tribal," the first painting in 2015, and "If Women Ruled," the first painting in 2020. "If Women Ruled" was an experiment in controlled acrylic pouring, requiring hours of layering and iterations.

The "Syncopation," "You Are Here," "Stay In Your Own Pane," and "If Women Ruled" series were unintentional as they were collector driven or made popular by demand. "Syncopation" was initially created for the Detroit Chamber Winds and Strings, and grew to over 20. A "You Are Here" was positioned just outside the elevator where my beloved bonus daughter, Monique Parnell Phifer, held her 50th birthday party. As guests arrived, the painting indicated that they were at the right place! Perhaps they reflected on other aspects of their lives as well. Four more were created after the celebration. This painting will always have extra special meaning. Monique passed August 30, 2018. "If Women Ruled" was first created for the NCA Michigan's March Women's exhibit at the Detroit Public Library in 2020. Eight originals in various sizes were created. The Covid-19 pandemic caused a shutdown of all the art institutions around this time, so the public did not see this exhibit.

This book is as much about my collectors and people behind the scenes as it is about my journey. Please see acknowledgments on page 160-162.

Priscilla A. Phifer
2020

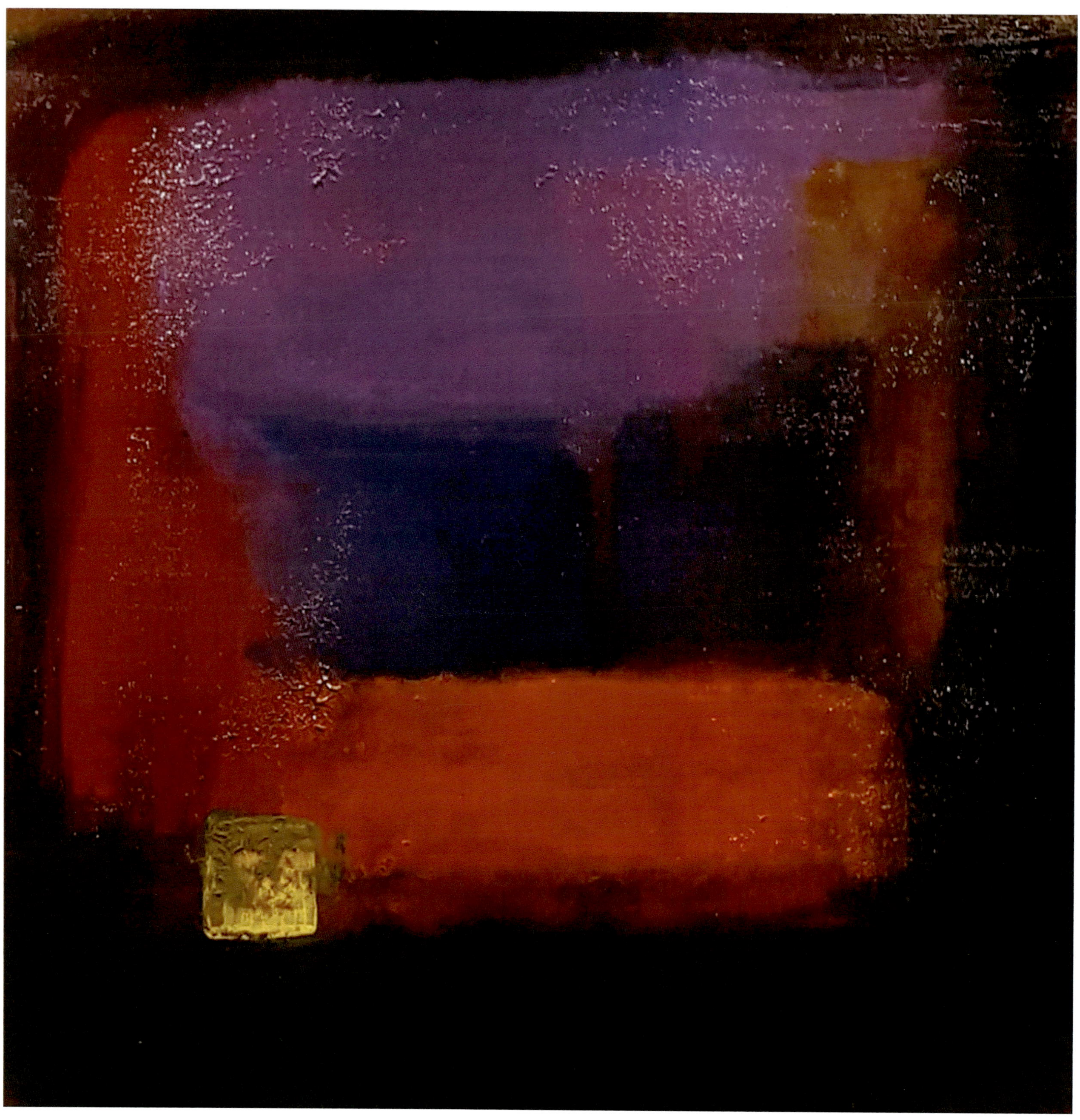

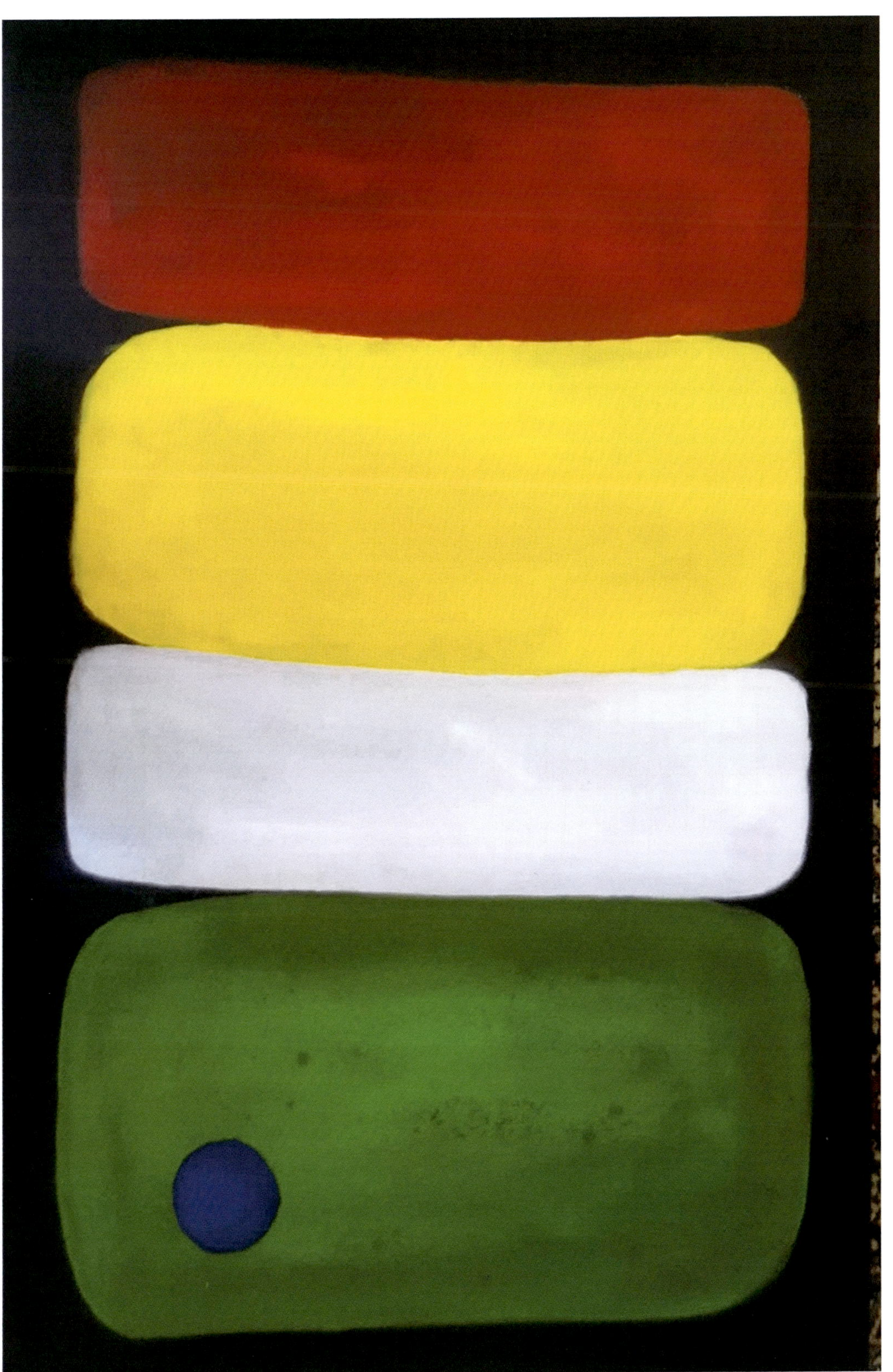

COLLECTOR:
MONIQUE AND DRAKE PHIFER

LEFT:
SOUL SEARCHING (24X24)
2015

RIGHT:
YOU ARE HERE #4 (24X36)
2016

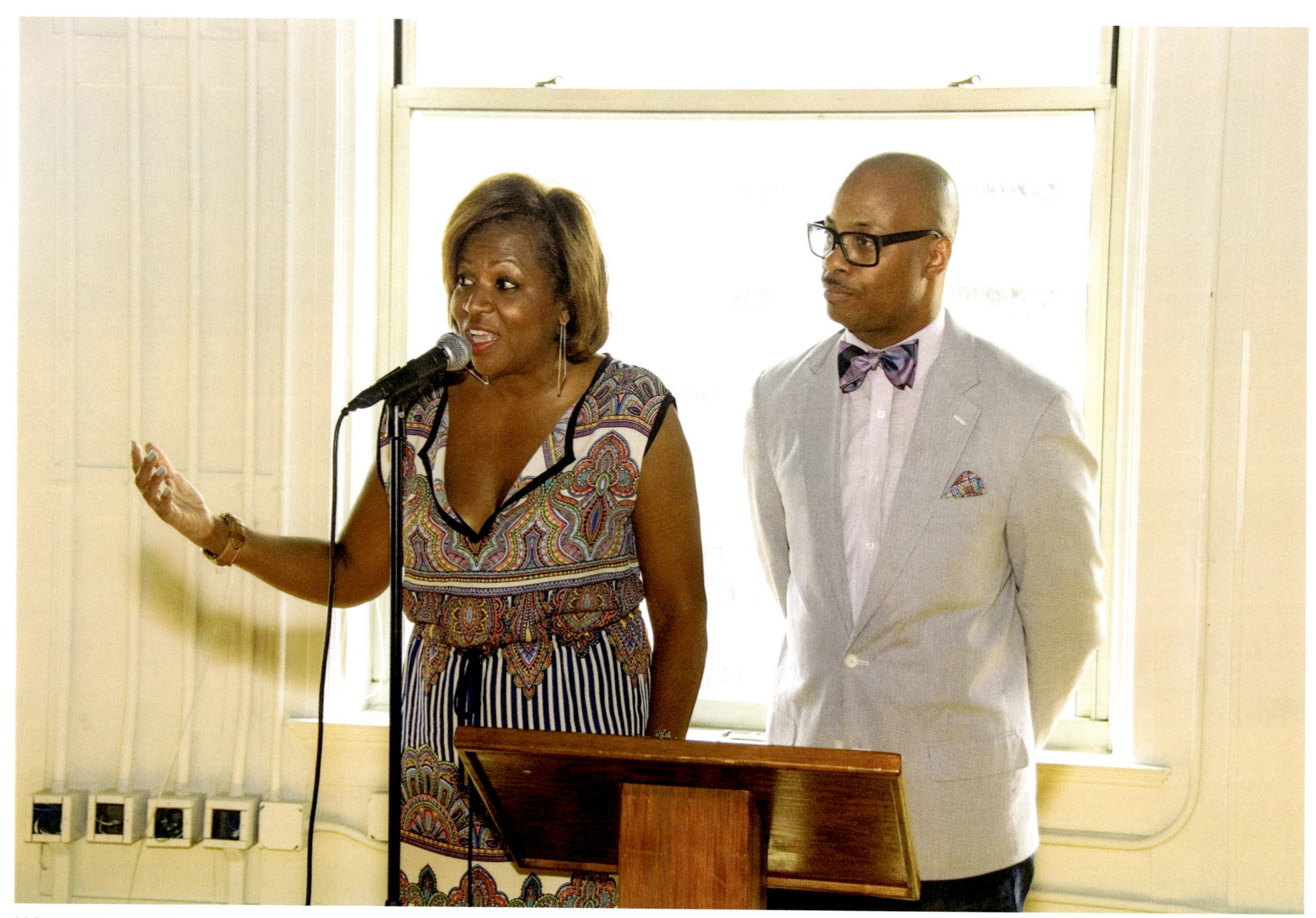

MONIQUE + DRAKE PHIFER AT FIRST SOLO SHOW

KENNETTE LAMAR OF ANNISTIQUE PHOTOGRAPHY

GALLERY STATEMENT

Over the last few years since Priscilla embarked on her mission to become a full-time artist, it has been my pleasure to watch her development and to provide her with ideas and insights that I have learned along the way. One of them is to "keep your family and friends out of your studio" and to "do you!" I tell her all the time to not let anyone get in the way of her vision, which I think is important to any artist. Another one is not to set your prices too low or too high, of which I think she had done a fine job. I am amazed by her moxie and the success she has had since she began. I am happy to see her accomplish her goals as an artist, opening up new vistas of freedom and creativity as she continues her art expedition.

As a longtime gallerist, a common refrain I hear from new and sometimes established collectors, especially those more partial to figurative illustrations, is that anybody can do abstract. When I hear this I cringe because I just don't see it that way and I don't think that the collectors of Priscilla's works see it that way, either. In fact, what I believe they and I see is someone who is in touch with her primal impulses and her desire to communicate her feelings in a visceral way. I applaud her on the creation of Hue:::Intuition and hope that she continues evolving and growing as an artist. Additionally, I truly hope that this book helps Priscilla to continue to enlarge her view of herself as a full-time artist and take on new challenges.

For posterity's sake, it is important to let the world know that you can switch gears at any point in life and that creating yourself anew is part of the fun. But, more importantly, this thing of art is about community and history. I am delighted to support Priscilla in her endeavors as an artist as she documents her journey, tells her story. I am excited to see the ongoing process of becoming for PRISCILLA A. PHIFER as advocate, as mentor, and, of course, as artist.

George N'Namdi
N'Namdi Center for Contemporary Art
2020

INTRODUCTION

When I first met Priscilla in 1965, she had a love for the arts and the creative world. Over the years, she and I together became tentative, and then more serious, collectors. We would buy an artwork wherever we traveled. As the years rolled by, I observed Priscilla's increasing interest in developing art herself. She began with exotic floral arrangements, became an expert in decoupage and, ultimately, turned to canvas to evolve into the accomplished artist that she is today.

While Priscilla did not study in an accredited fine arts program, she had formal studies under local artist/teachers, and she learned techniques through experimentation and from artists on the Internet, primarily on YouTube. She spent many hours of self-enhancement of her raw talents.

Years before Priscilla's art career, she was introduced to many notable artists at a Wayne State University Introduction to Art class, where she first learned about Mark Rothko and Jackson Pollock. In her early art career, she acquired an appreciation for other artists such as Sam Gilliam and Charles Burwell. Priscilla's works are also informed and influenced by geographical history of her life, having spent her developmental years in the hills of Fairmont, WV; her adolescent and young adult years in the pristine atmosphere of Glastonbury, CT; and her later years in the urban excitement of Detroit, MI. In Detroit, Priscilla operated for a few years a small boutique which included the sale of original and limited-edition art. She, along with some of her fellow tenants, would sponsor an annual art exhibit in the lobby of the building where her shop was located. The exhibit was open to members of the National Conference of Artists, Michigan Chapter, without charge to them, and the exhibit would occur during Black History Month.

Priscilla did not begin serious work on canvas until she had reached the age of 70, thus bringing a lifetime of experience to her work. She infrequently uses a brush, but instead employs techniques using hardware and household items which she describes to "drip, drag, scrape and splash." Her works are primarily abstract, and she considers herself an intuitive abstract expressionist. That intuition, to me, demonstrates that she has a deep reservoir of spirituality that is transmitted to the canvas. One of her most amazing abilities is demonstrated though her use of color, especially since she is somewhat color-blind. Her special relationship with color is readily apparent by the way in which she can choreograph the colors so that, whether the colors are harmonious or discordant, they evoke a sense of intrigue or mystery.

Most artists in new endeavors initially lack confidence in their work and are hesitant to immediately display their works to the world. Priscilla was no different as she opened her first solo exhibit with an inventory of 30 pieces. Expecting sales of two or three works of her moderately priced works, she was delightfully surprised when collectors left with 26 works. Since then, her works have been in exhibits, some of her own and others at far-flung venues. To mention some, her works have been in group exhibits at the Artists of Colour in Windsor, Canada; the N'Namdi Center for Contemporary Art, Detroit; Dell Pryor Gallery, Detroit; the Allee Willis-sponsored exhibit at her home in Los Angeles for Detroit Fine Arts Breakfast Club members; the Detroit Artist Market, Detroit; the Charles Wright Museum; the Ellington White Contemporary Gallery and Rosenthal Gallery-Fayetteville State University, both in North Carolina; the Carr Center, Detroit; NCA Michigan Gallery, Detroit; and a two-year public art program, Farmington Hills, MI. Her art hangs in private collections and public places from coast to coast, including the Ambassador Fine Arts Permanent Collection at Mack Alive in Detroit.

This compilation is for the purpose of publishing the variety of Priscilla's works and to acknowledge and thank all collectors. Some of the collectors have been included in the photographs alongside her works collectors, while others are listed. Priscilla appreciates them all as demonstrated by her collectors' appreciation event in June 2019. Priscilla had planned her fourth solo show in April 2020 to coincide with her 75th birthday, but the Corona virus pandemic made short shrift of those plans.

Randolph Phifer
2020

HOMAGE

CULTURAL REVOLUTIONARY

Fabulous mother and wife, compassionate, culturally courageous, community conscious, fine art collector, artistic and avant-garde are heartfelt words that describe Priscilla. I first met this cultural revolutionary and Delta Sigma Theta Sorority sister in the early 1980s at her business on Meyers and Six Mile in Detroit. I have always loved her mother wit, loyalty, vision, and energy. My son, Khalid, lights up when he sees Priscilla, because of her endless youth and vitality, remarking, "Wow, she's always witty and exciting."

One day, Priscilla visited the Sherry Washington Gallery, and I had just read an article in the Homestyle section of the Detroit News about her being an artist and decorating with decoupage. She was oh so happy and humbled that I had the article in SWG. I knew then that she was creative and moving to her artistic zenith. As a painter, Priscilla has honed her gifts, explored, and dedicated her life to pursuing her inner vision and love of art making, thus creating coveted abstract images that bespeak her mind, passion, and history.

Sherry Washington & Khalid Raheem Haywood
Sherry Washington Gallery
2020

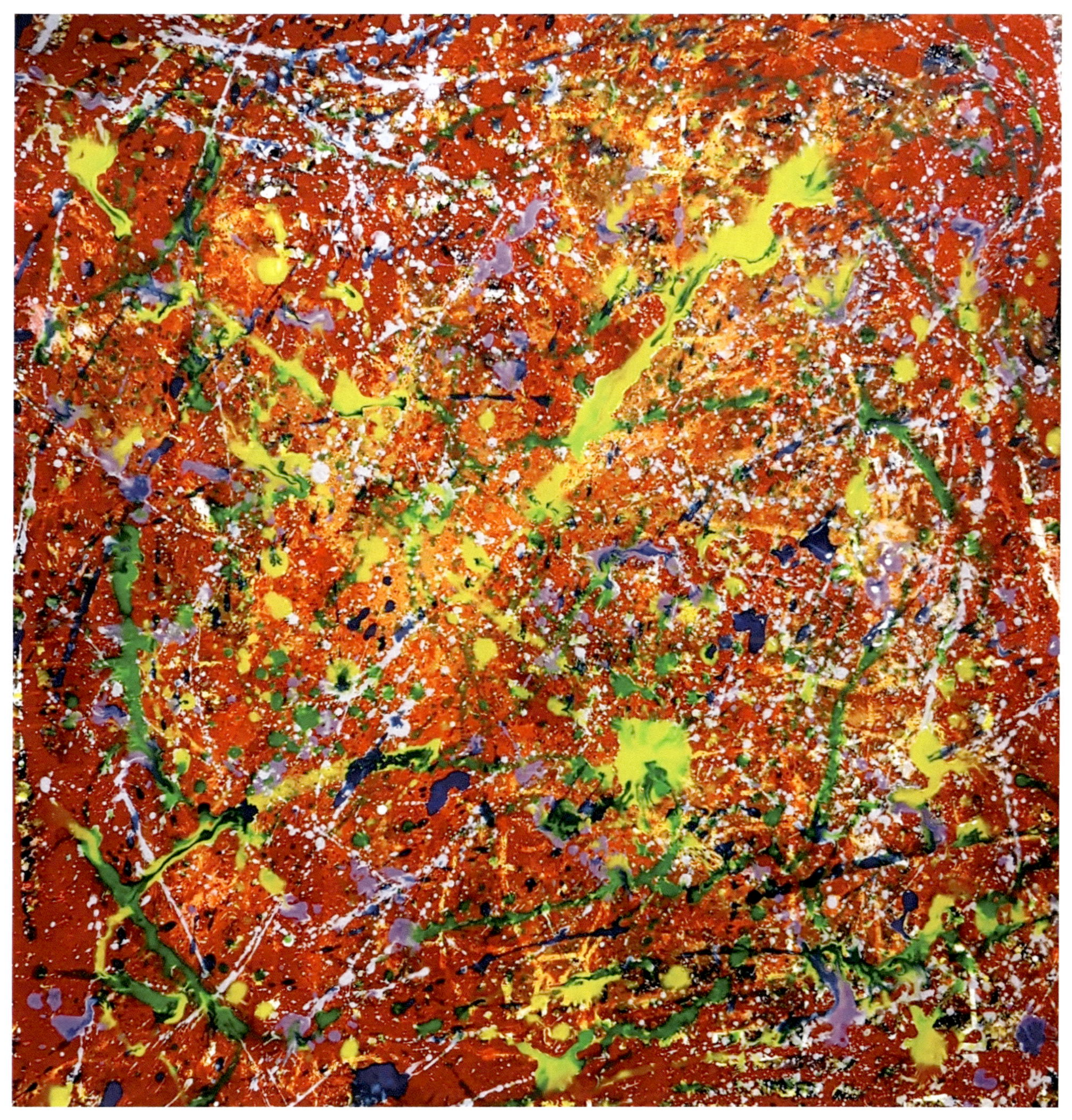

COLLECTOR:
STEPHEN AND JACQUI LEWIS-KEMP

RED (36” X 36”)
2016

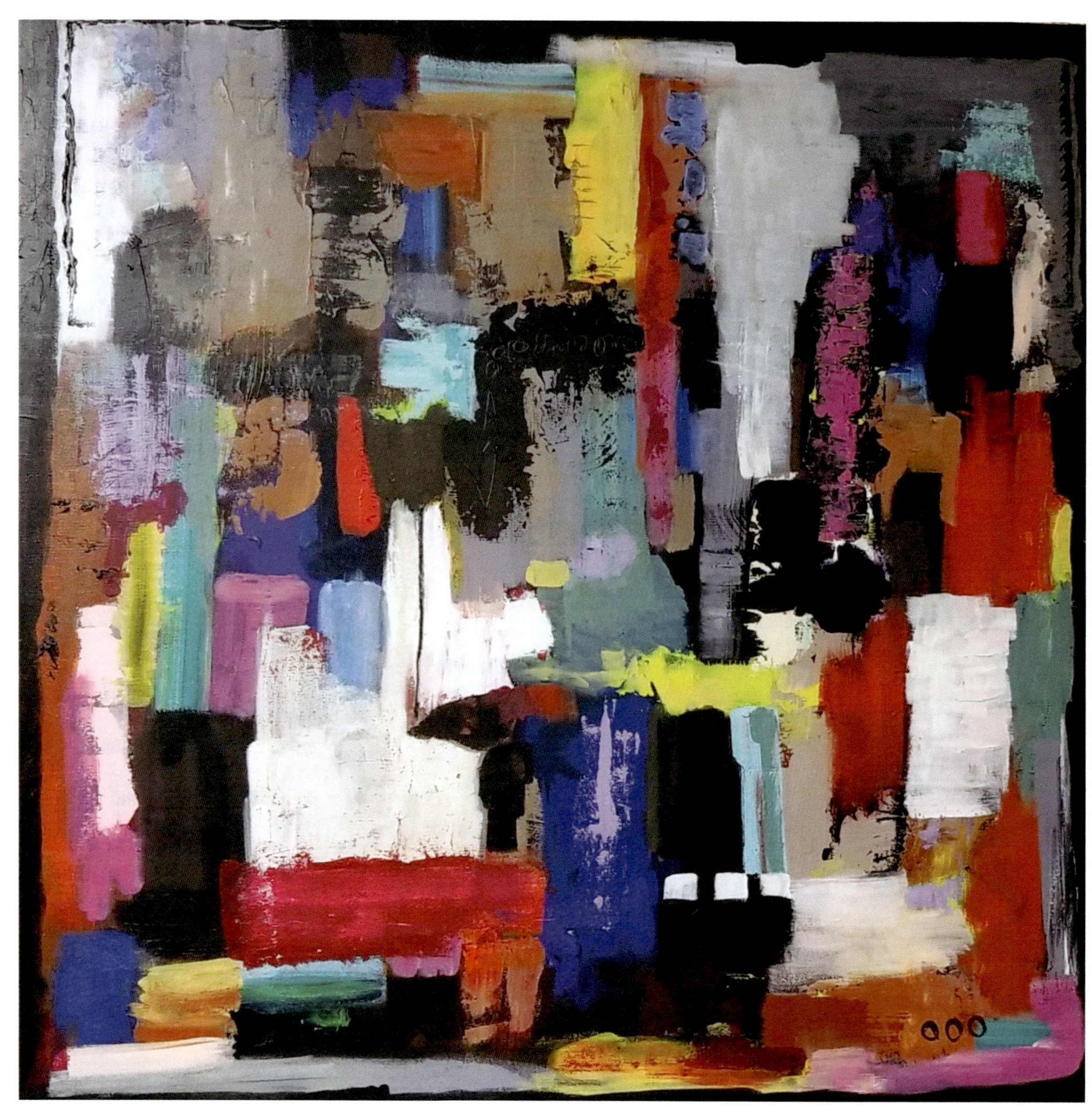

COLLECTOR:
HAROLD AND JOANN BRAGGS

FOR GILDA (36" X 36")
2018

ADVICE FROM A COLLECTOR

ADVICE FROM A COLLECTOR (COLLECTOR OF 'FOR GILDA')

Don't just buy what you like, but buy what moves you, such as the "For Gilda" painting now in our collection. Art that moves you is more enduring, and as you develop your eye it will remain long lasting in your collection. We primarily look for original artwork or very limited editions that are, of course, in our price range. You develop your eye by seeing art. The more you see the more your eye will develop. Spend lots of time at artist studios, museums, galleries, gallery shows, artist talks, etc. If possible, meet those artists whose work you enjoy. Learn about the different mediums. Research what interests you and learn what real fine art is. Art is not always pretty. And, please, please, please, make sure that all your acquisitions are signed by the artist before you purchase.

Joann and Harold Braggs
Co-Founder, Detroit Fine Arts Breakfast Club
2019

A BEAUTIFUL FRIEND

About four years ago, I had the distinguished privilege of meeting Mrs. PRISCILLA A. PHIFER during a tour of the eclectic, multi-disciplinary, fine art collection of David and Linda Whitaker of Detroit.

Robbie Best invited her and her "art posse" to a meeting of my Detroit Fine Arts Breakfast Club. Priscilla found a group she felt comfortable with, and she jumped in headfirst to further aid and encourage emerging artists, like herself, both young and senior to be the absolute best they all could be.

Sometimes, I call her "Lady P" out of full respect and admiration for her gutsy Chutzpah! Priscilla seems silent, but behind the scenes is very headstrong and determined, with a great love for her fellow mankind. She has the natural ability to make fellow artists and people in general feel comfortable and want to push forward to succeed, contributing to everyone's journey and overall greatness of The Breakfast Club. She holds no official title due to the loose structure of the group, but Priscilla is undoubtedly an asset to its operations.

Priscilla invited our art group to the Torch of Wisdom Foundation. Later, she nominated the DFABC for the organization's Honoring Local Heroes event where The Breakfast Club received the Cultural Arts Award at its banquet at Plum Hollow Country Club in 2017.

Borne from the award ceremony, Priscilla silently egged on a joint venture to keep over 50 artists working , hosting a charity benefit art auction, now in its third year, raising thousands of dollars and placing most of it in the hands of Detroit's underserved artists of color.

Priscilla is exceedingly rare, considerate, selfless, and loving of her community and its advancement. I am honored, pleased and proud that our paths crossed the way that it did. My life has not been the same since meeting this great soul!

Henry Harper, Co-Founder
Detroit Fine Arts Breakfast Club
2020

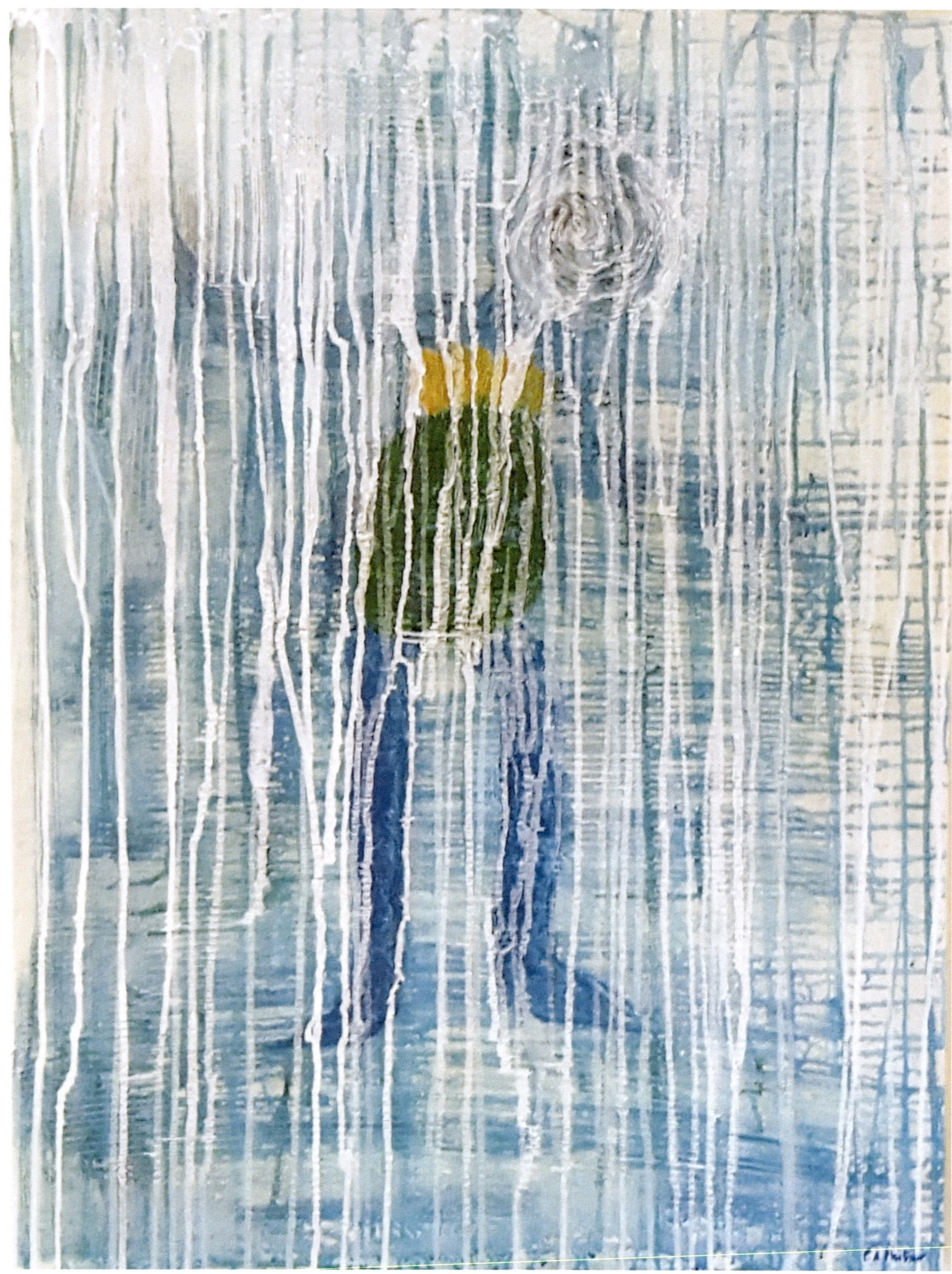

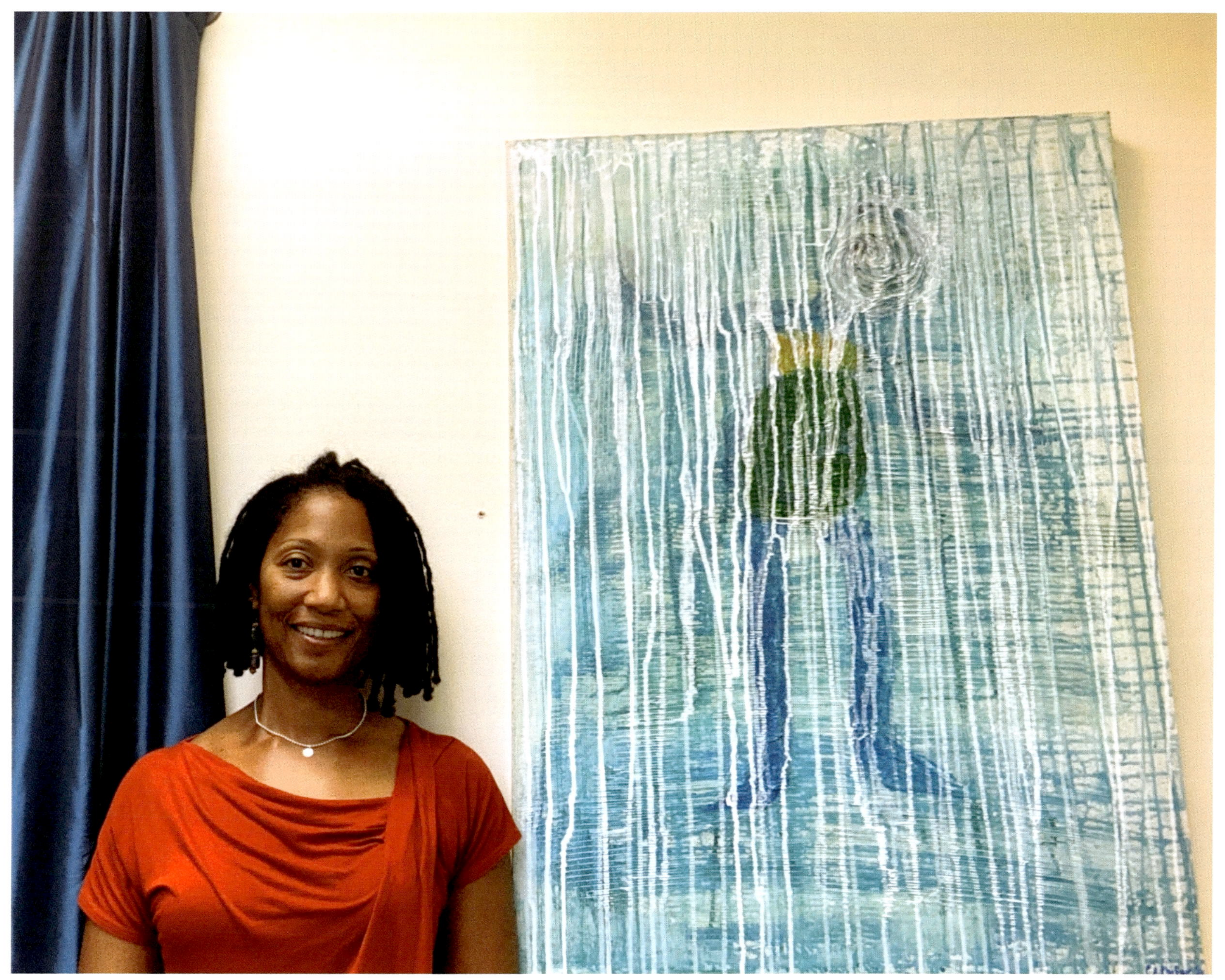

COLLECTOR:
TARA BLACKSHEAR (BALTIMORE, MD)

WHEN IT RAINS IT POURS (30" X 40")
2016

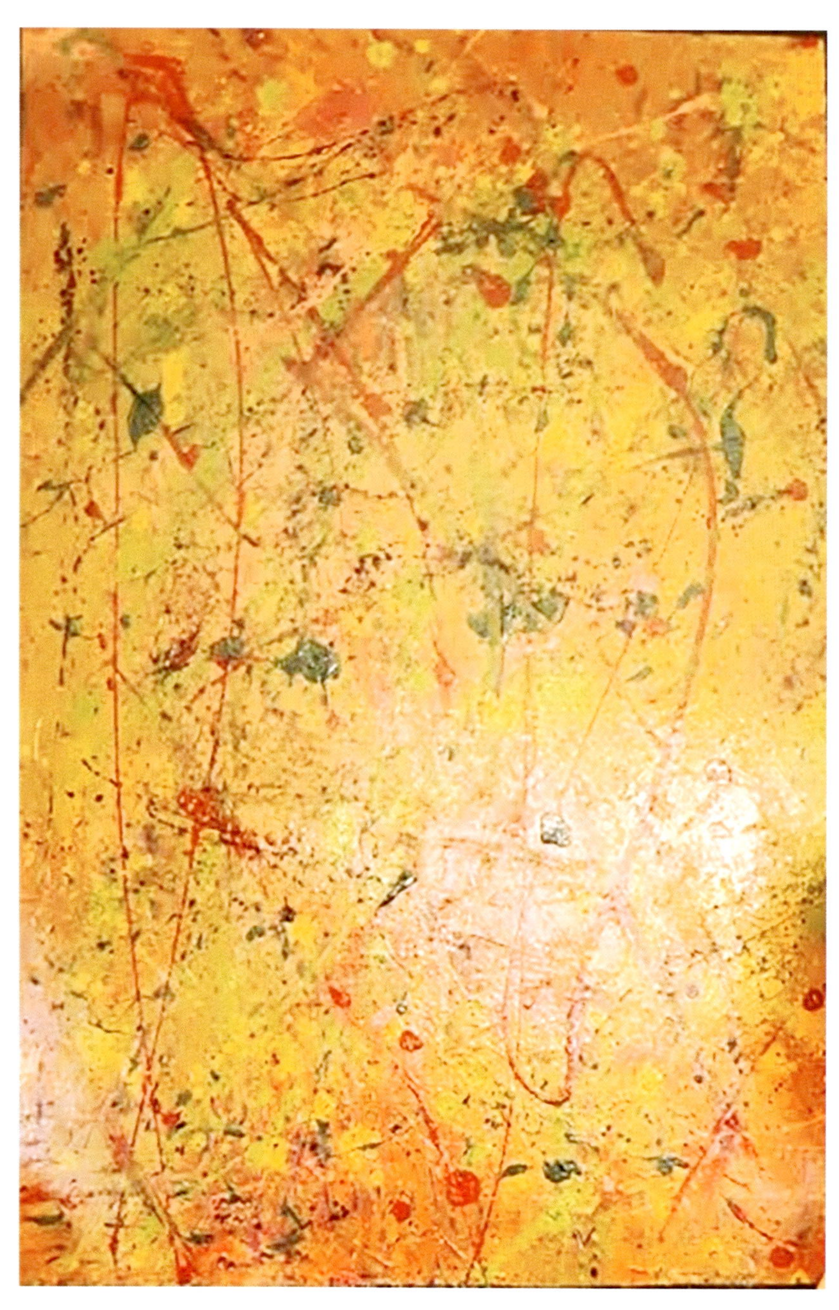

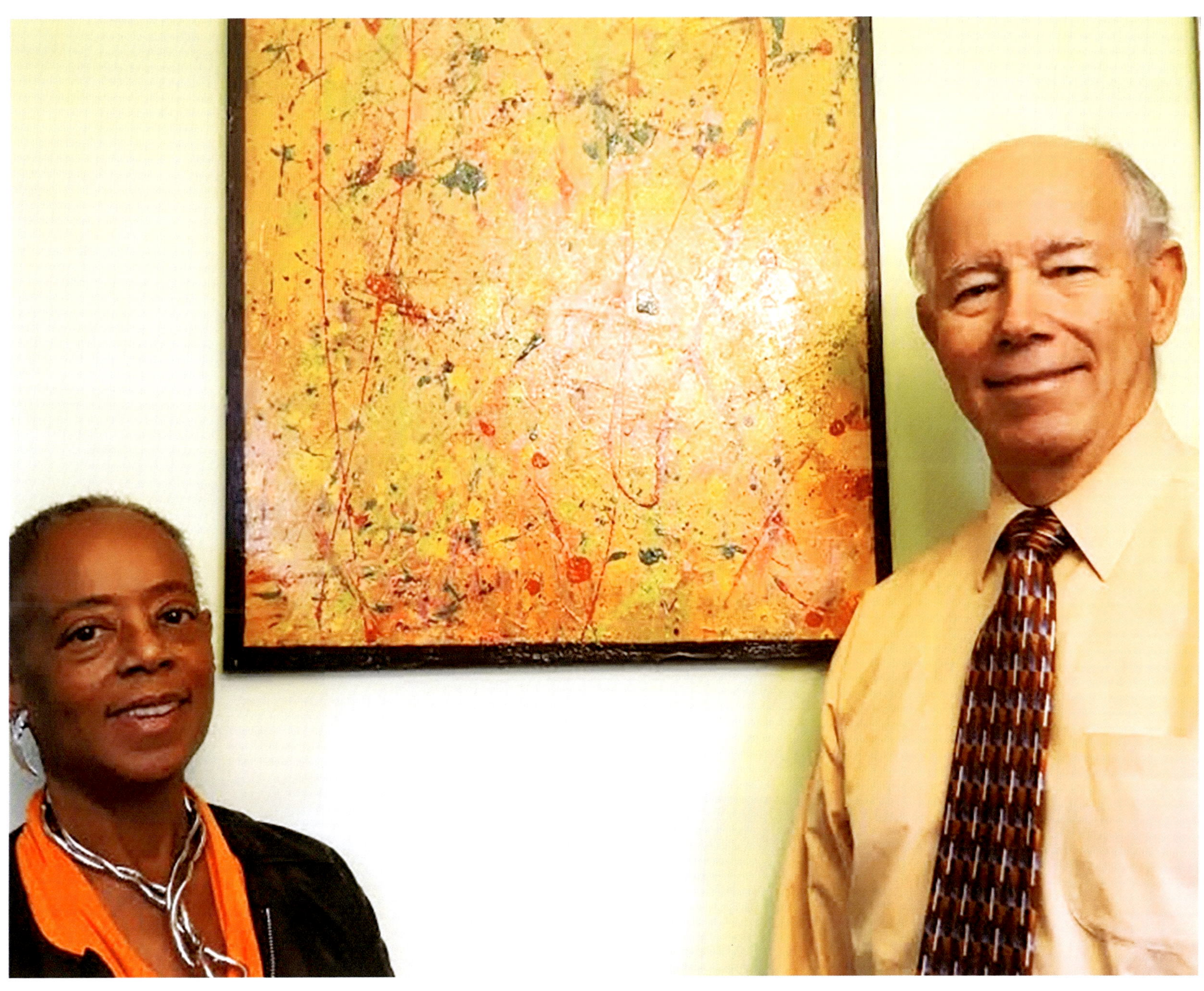

COLLECTOR:
SIDNEY + LINDA JONES
CHICAGO

UNEXPECTED (24" X 36")
2015

I THINK MY MEDICINE IS ART,
MY LANGUAGE IS ART"
- SABRINA NELSON

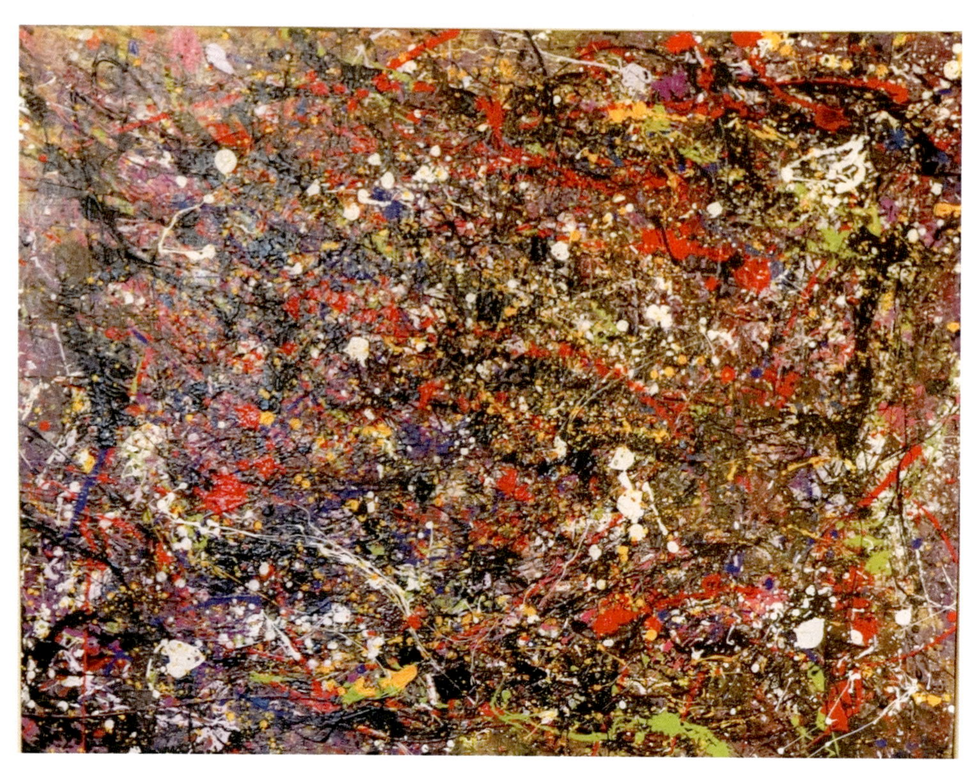

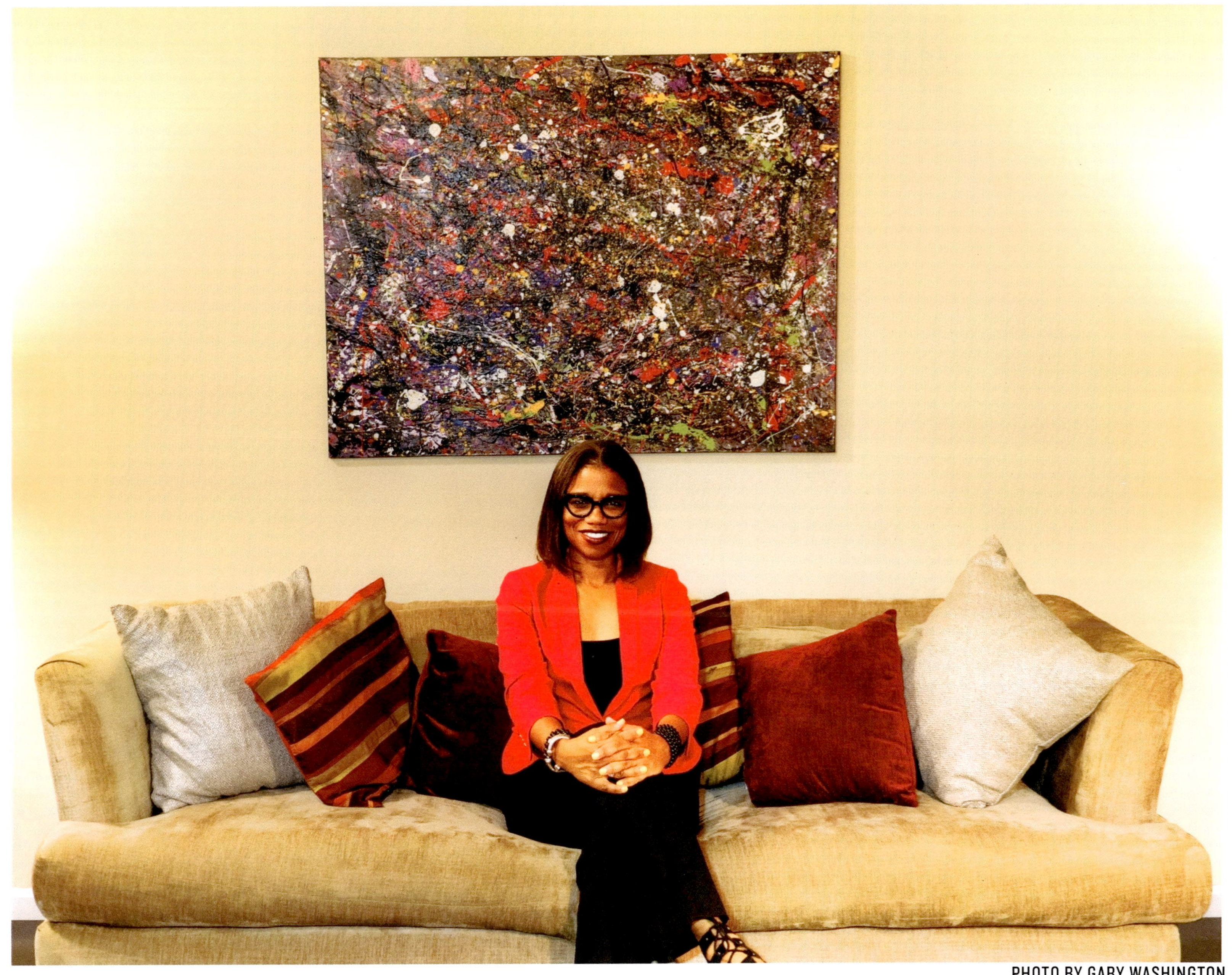

PHOTO BY GARY WASHINGTON

COLLECTOR:
KIMBERLY DANTZLER

NIGHT SQUALL (48" X 36")
2014

PAINTING IS SELF-DISCOVERY. EVERY GOOD ARTIST PAINTS WHAT HE IS. - **JACKSON POLLOCK**

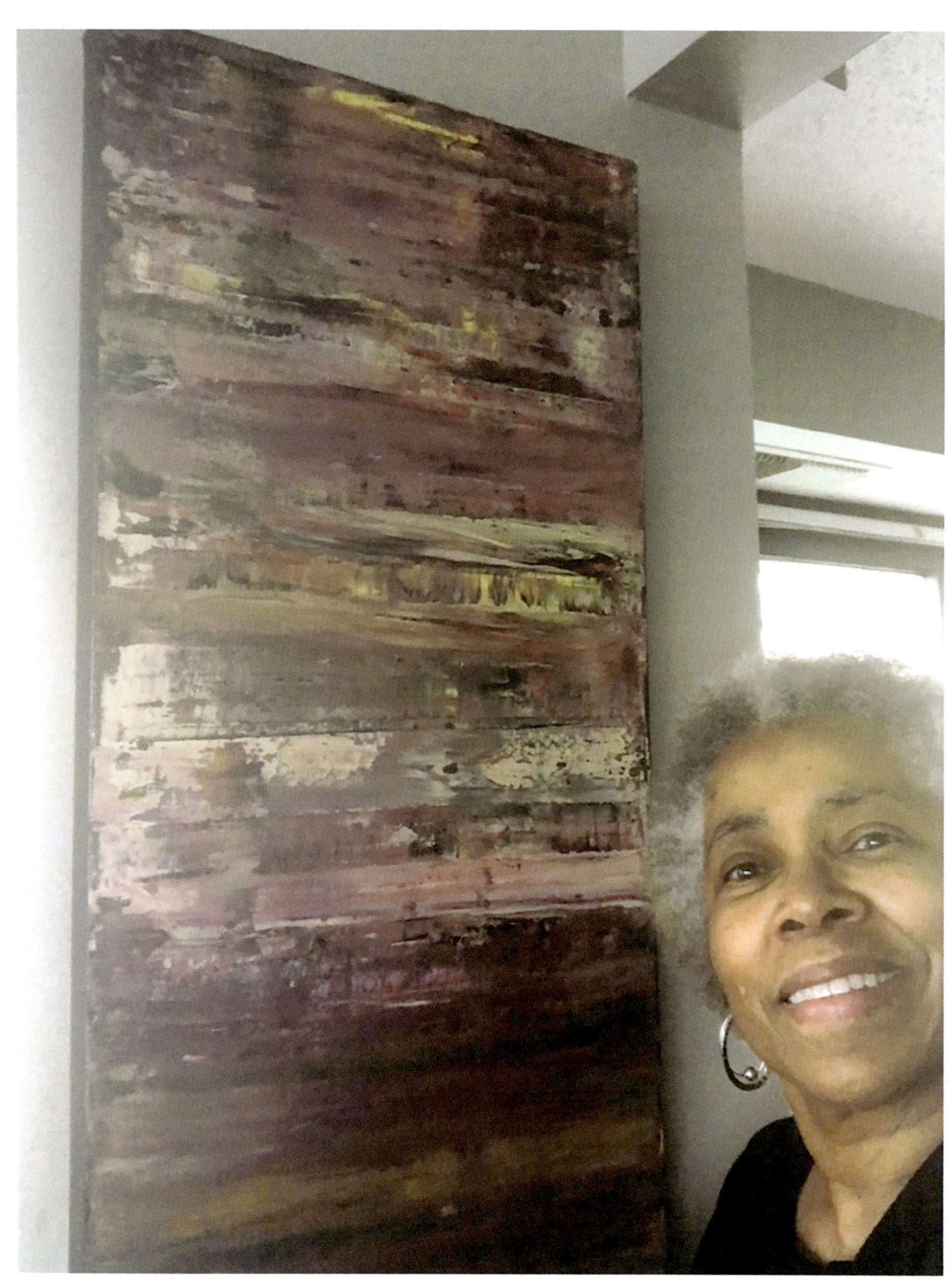

COLLECTOR:
RAYNONA PATRICK +
THE LATE LAWRENCE C. PATRICK JR

THE QUARRY (16 X 40)
2015

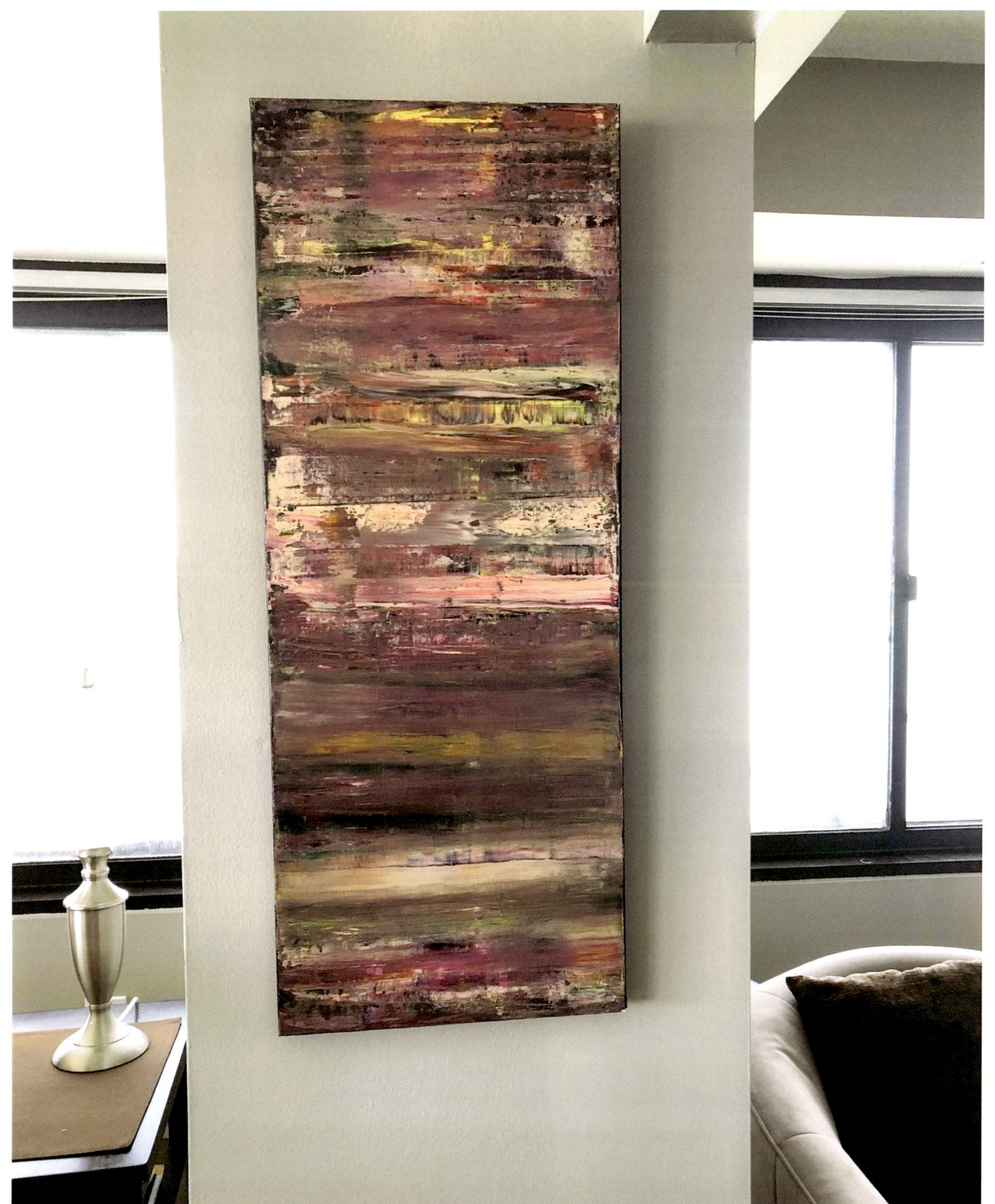

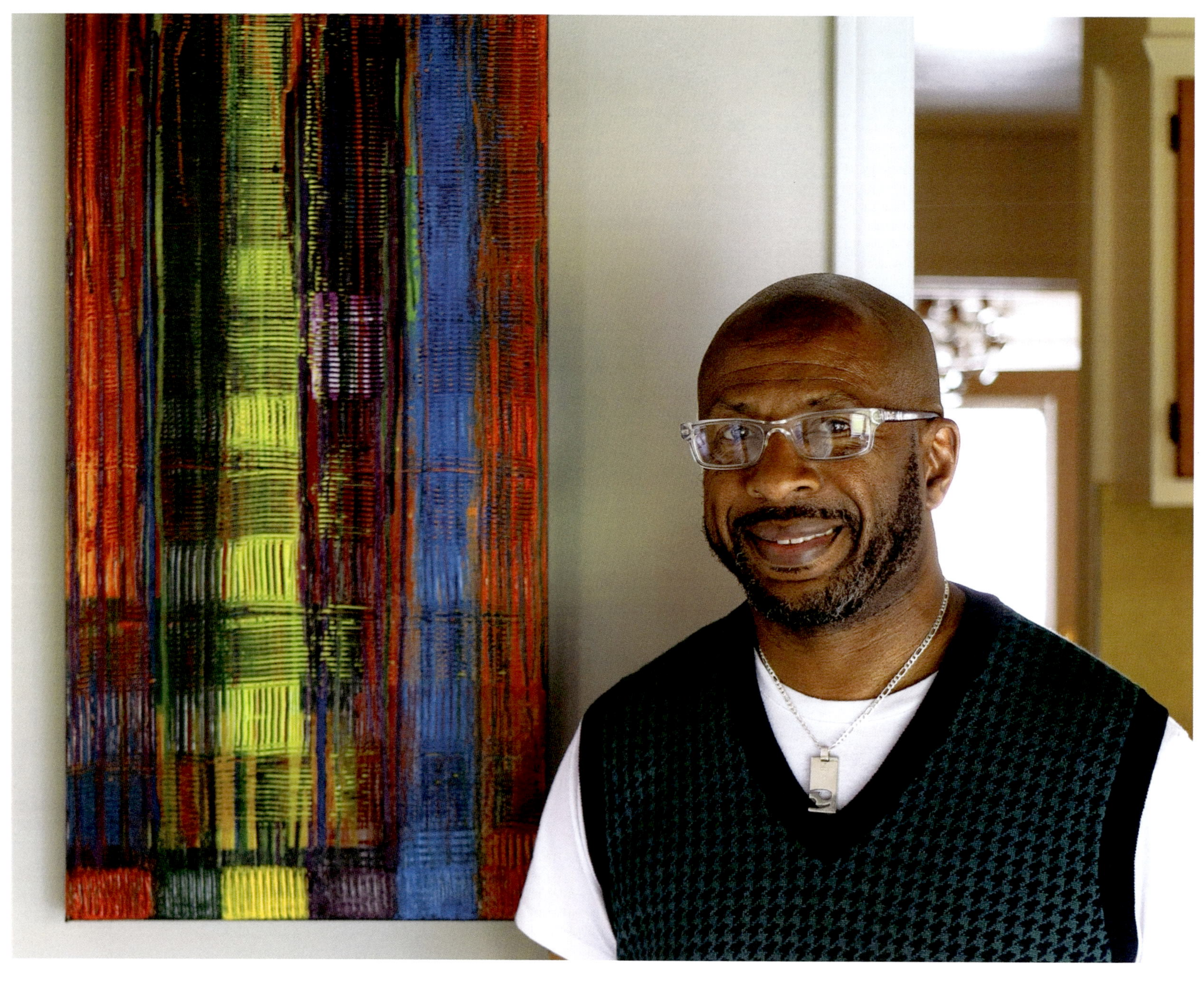

PHOTO BY GARY WASHINGTON

COLLECTOR:
KEVIN THOMPSON

COLOR BLOC (16" X 30")
2014

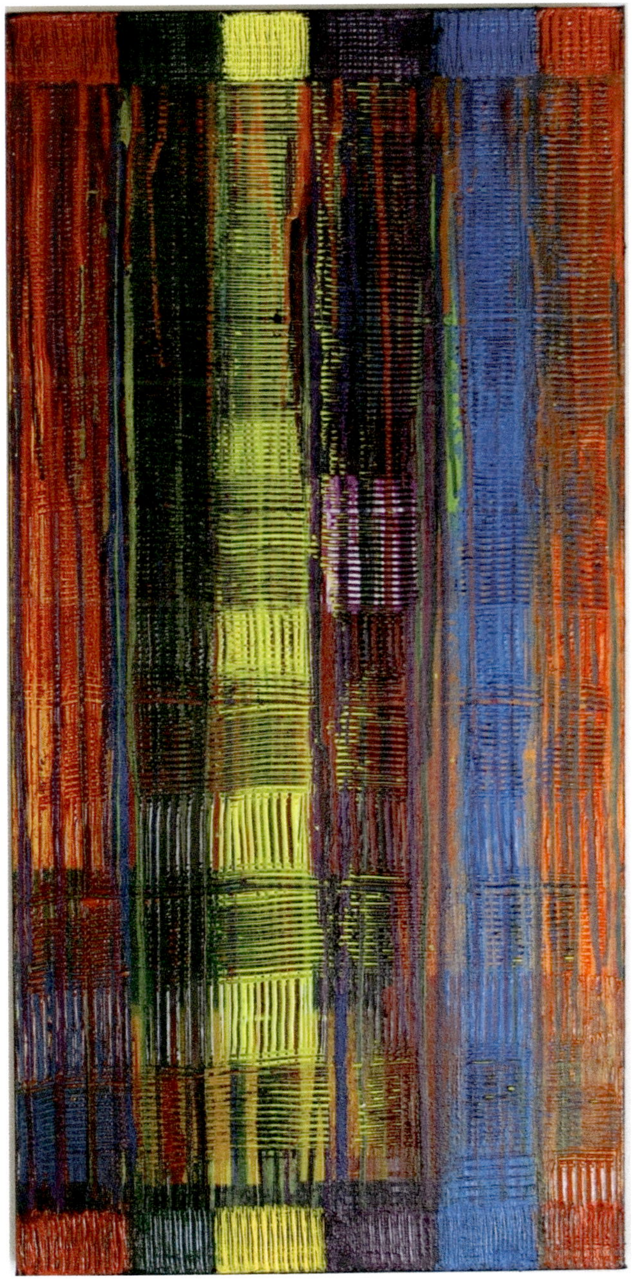

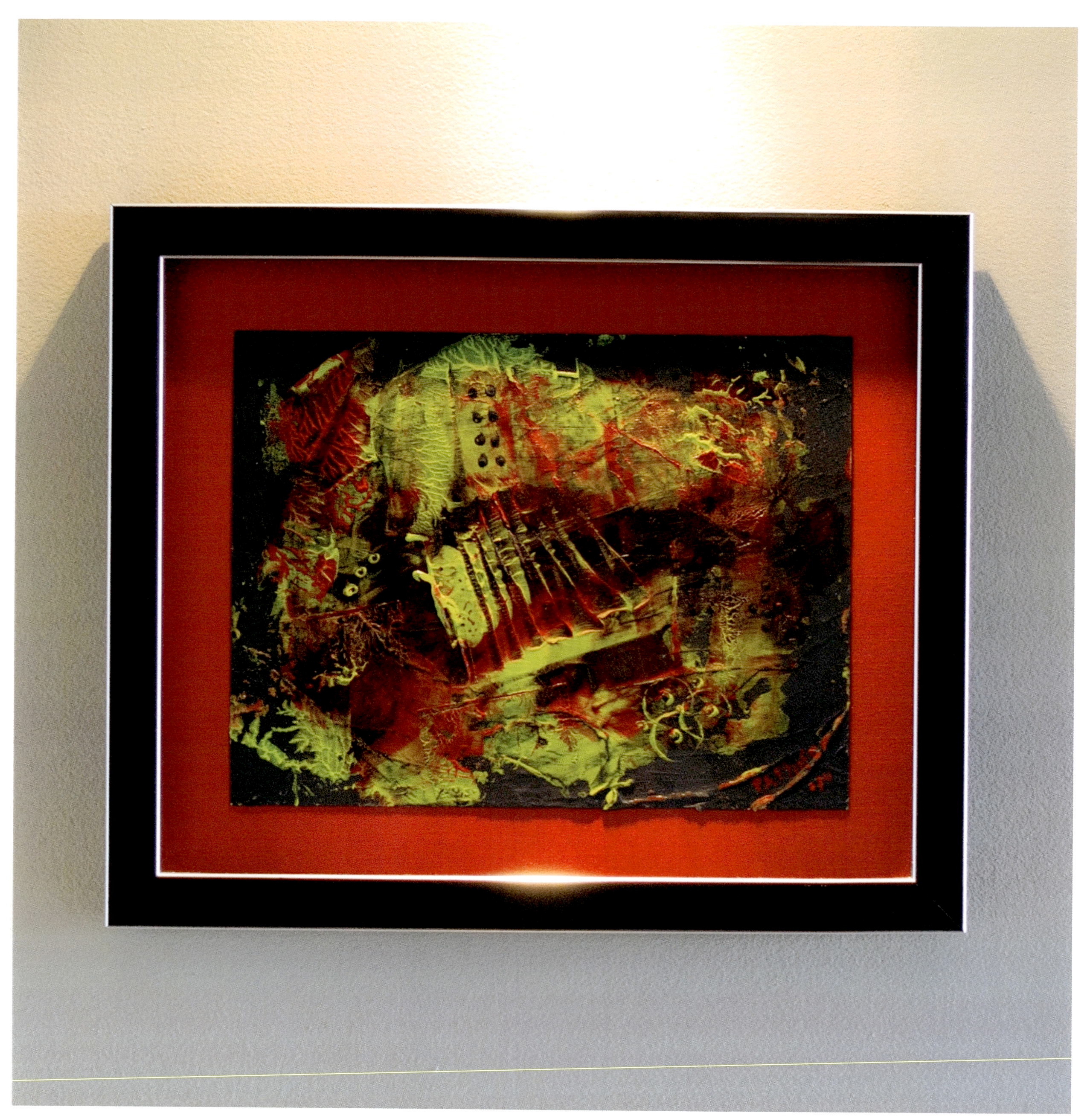

PHOTO BY GARY WASHINGTON

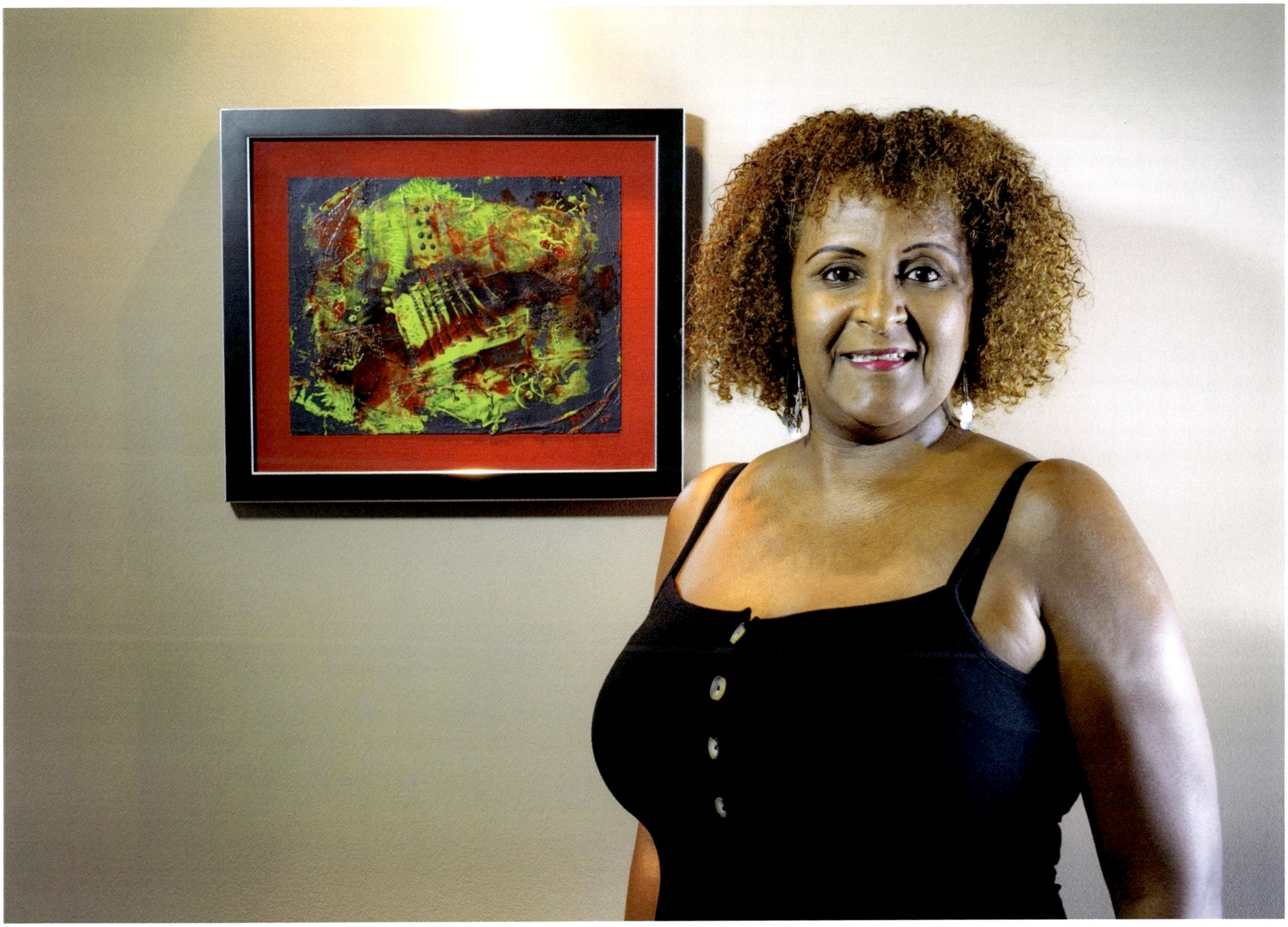

COLLECTOR:
TSEDENIA TEDLA

UNTITLED (14"X 11")
2015

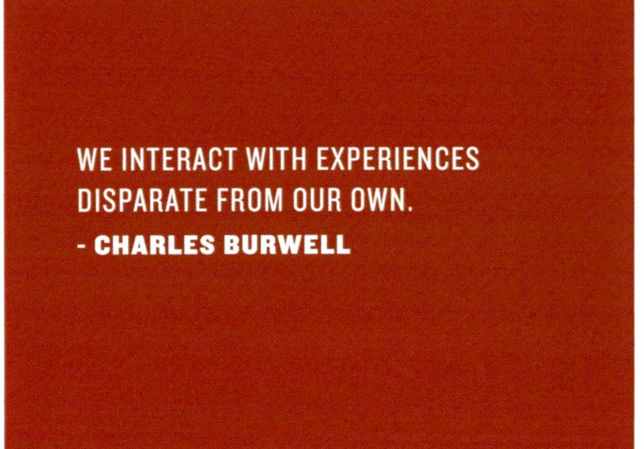

WE INTERACT WITH EXPERIENCES DISPARATE FROM OUR OWN.
- CHARLES BURWELL

COLLECTOR:
DERRICK HARPER

BOUNDARIES (33" X 43" FRAMED)
2015

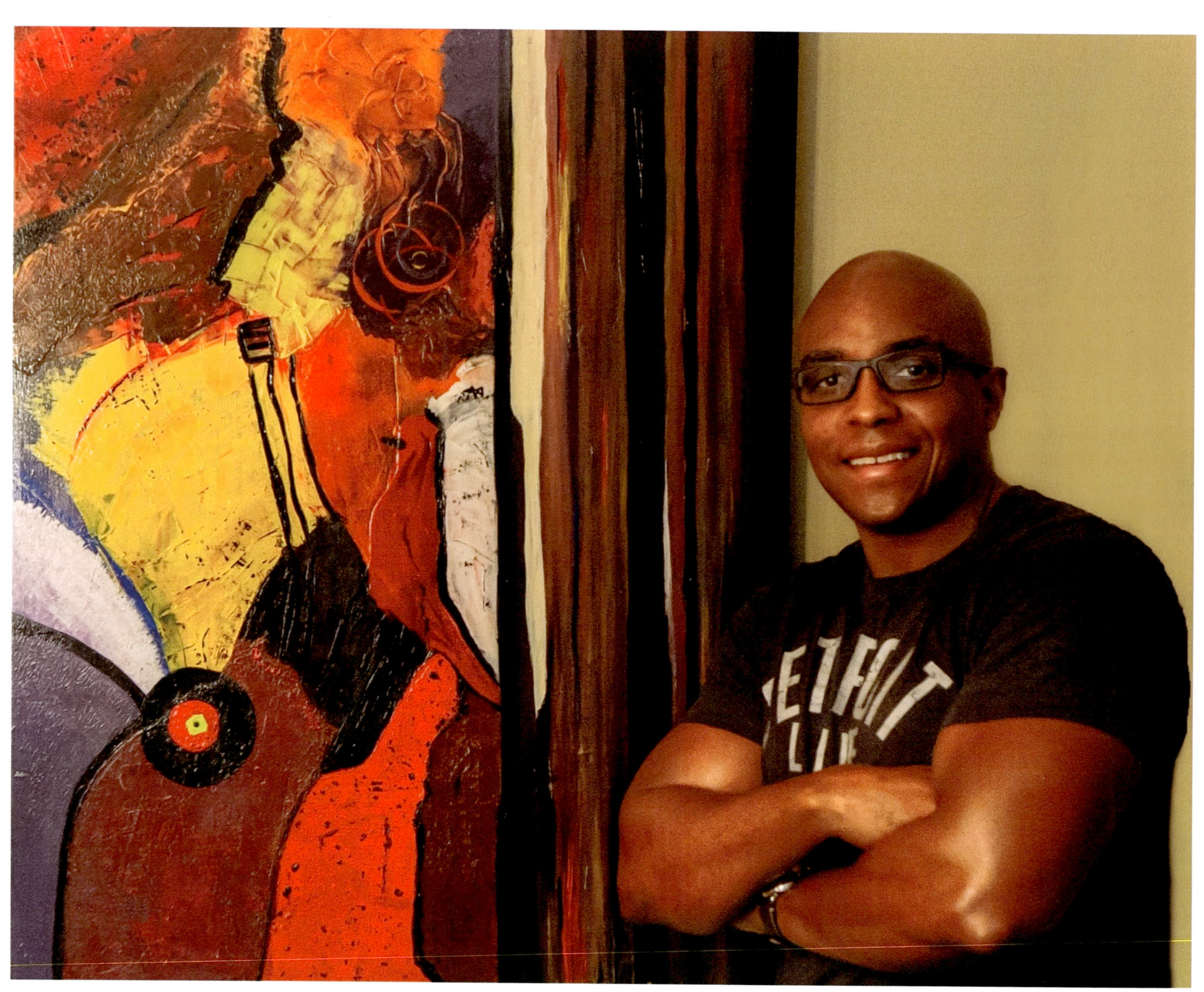

PHOTO BY GARY WASHINGTON

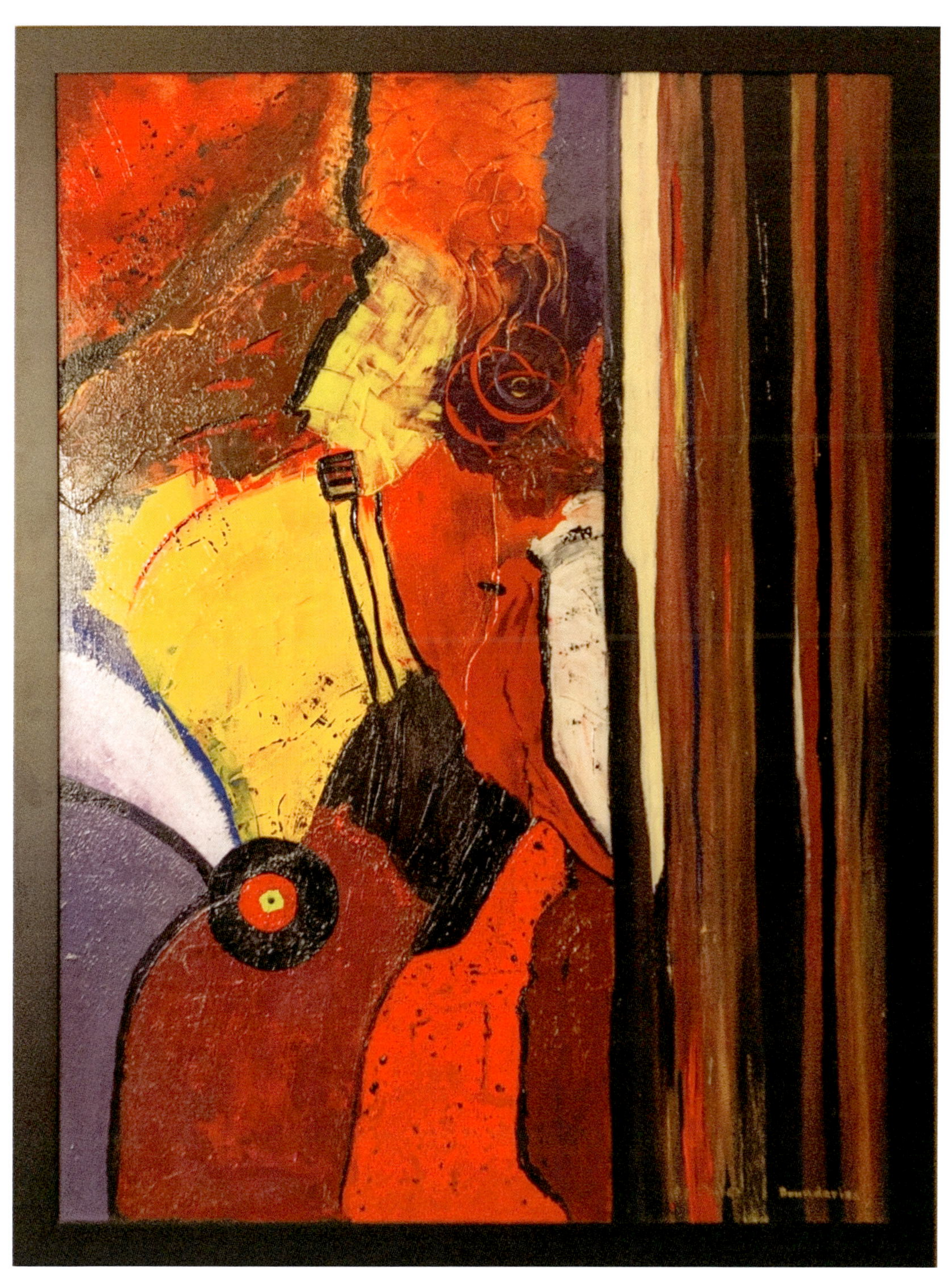

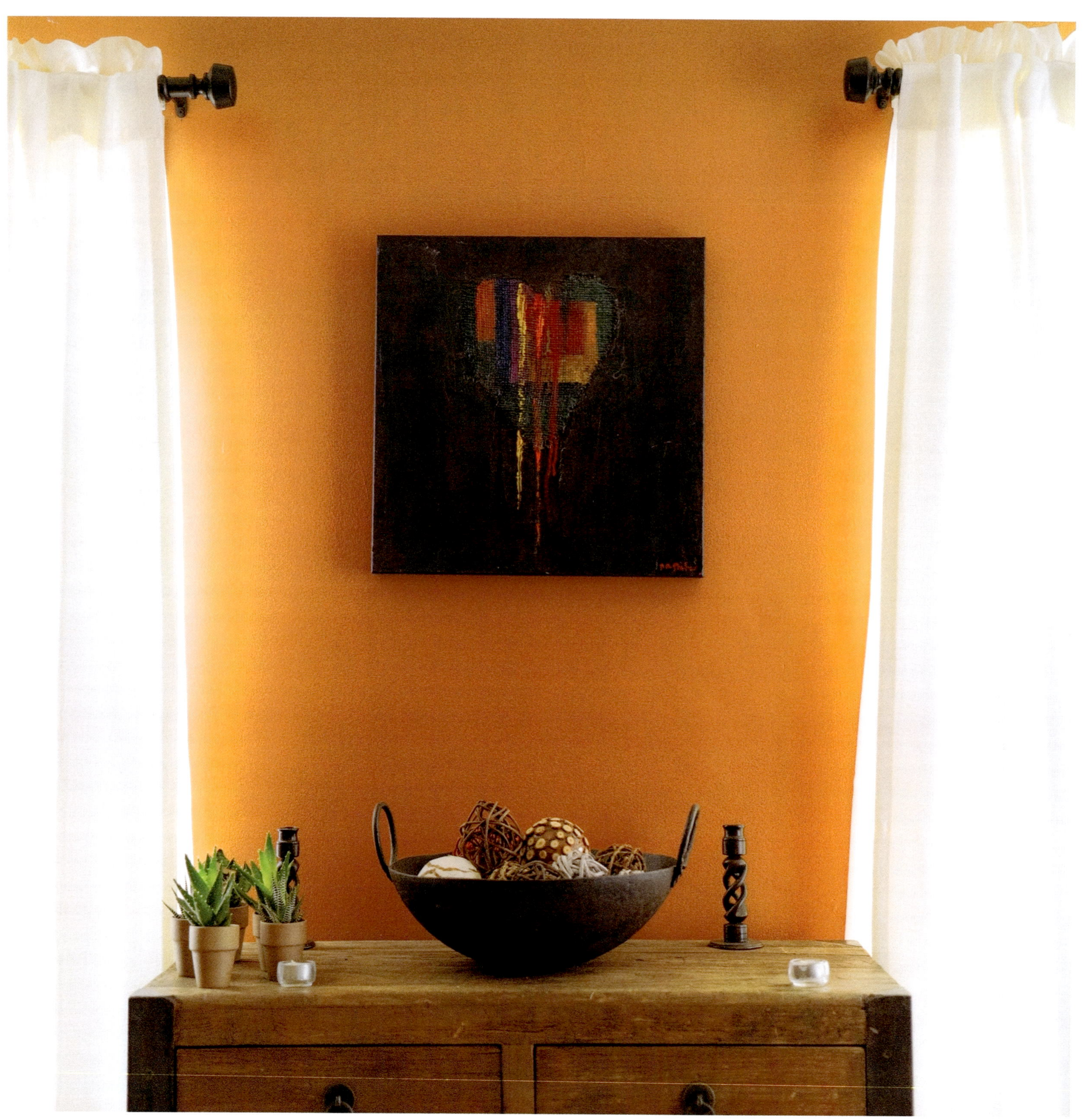
PHOTO BY GARY WASHINGTON

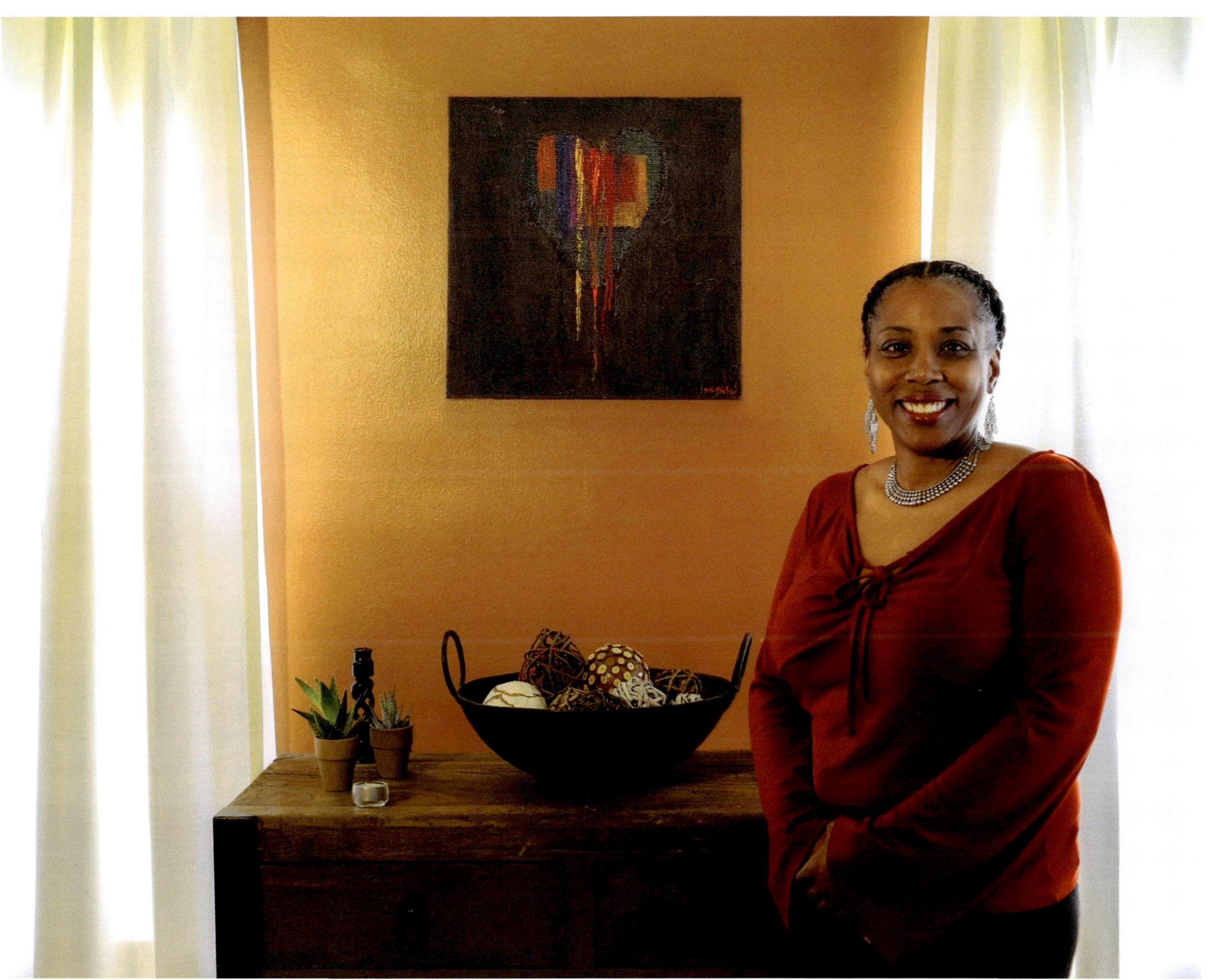

COLLECTOR:
DAWN LAWS

EMOTIONS (20" X 20")
2015

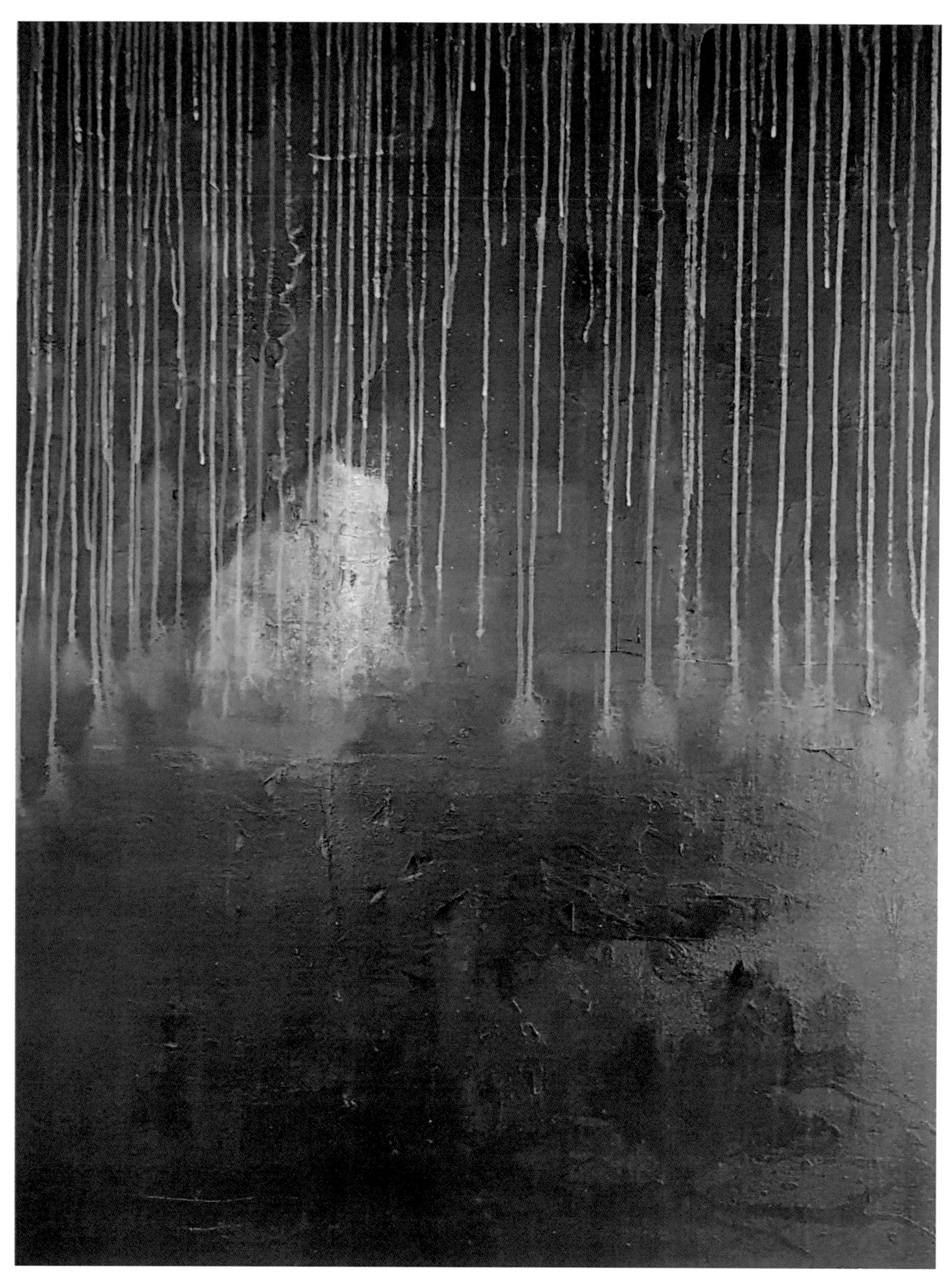

MYSTIC VOYAGE (36X48)
2017

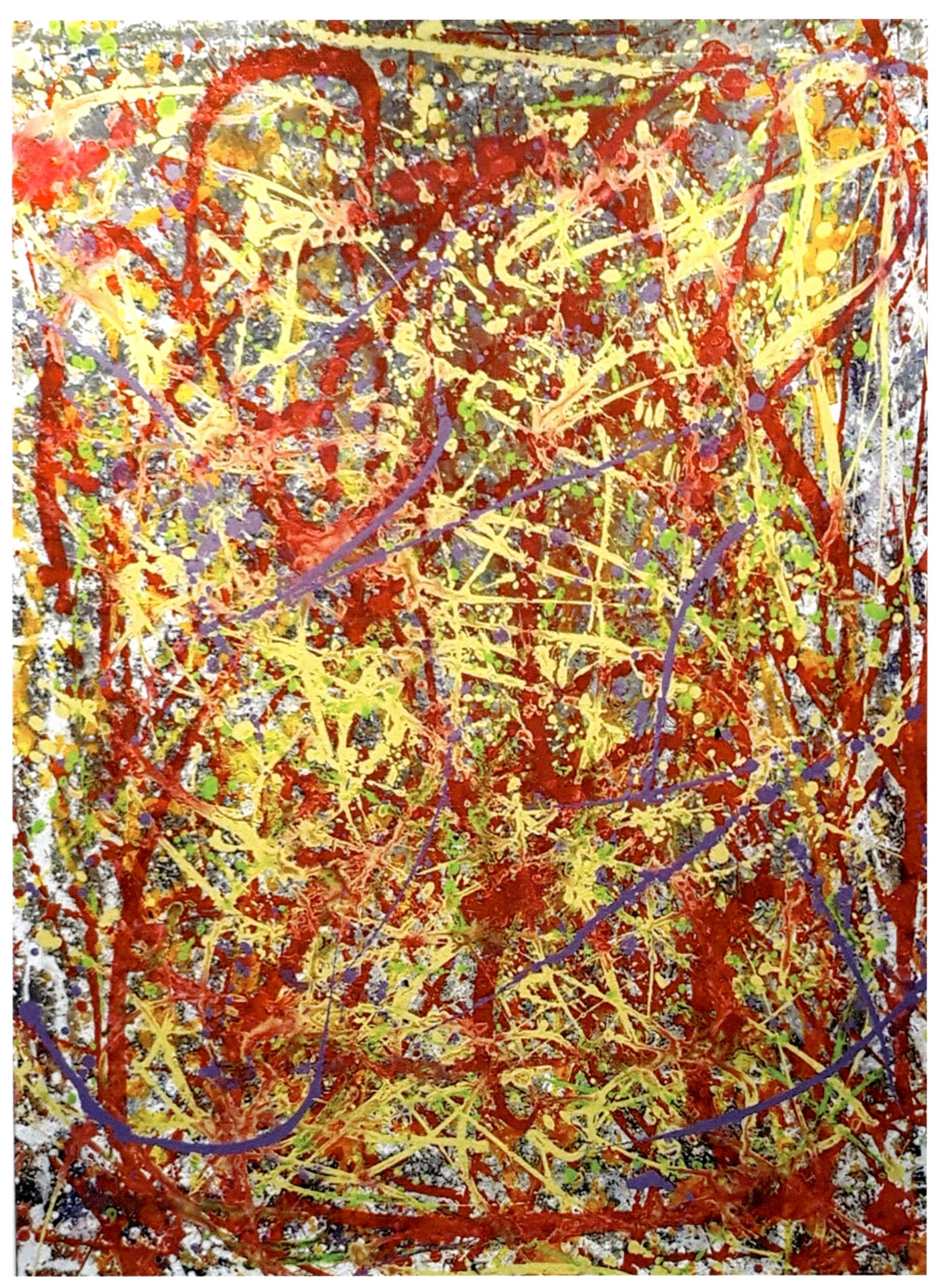

CELEBRATION
(30" X 40")
2016
SOLD AT
TCH OUR TOWN

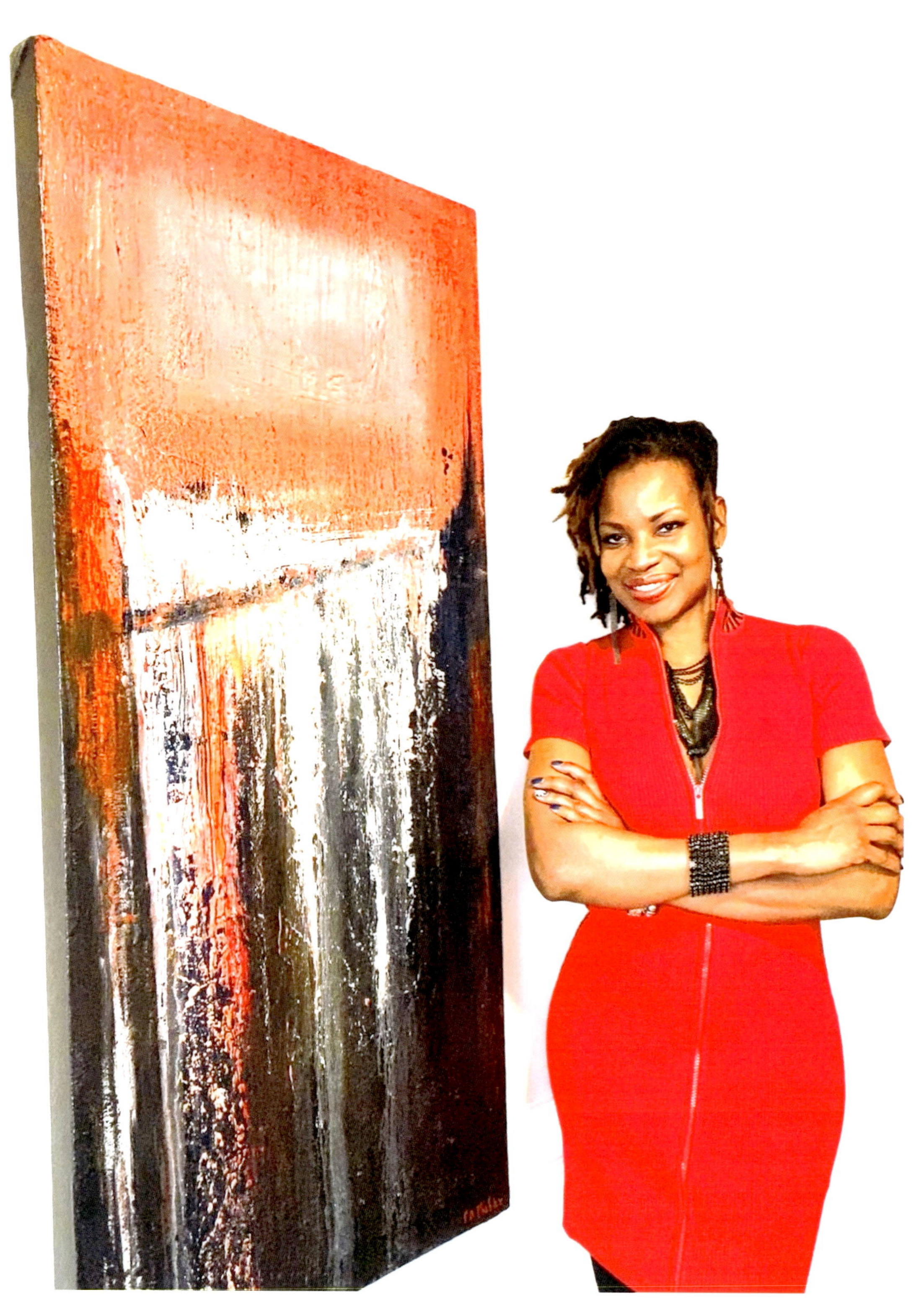

COLLECTOR:
CALLIE BRADFORD

WATERFALLS
(24" X 48")
2015

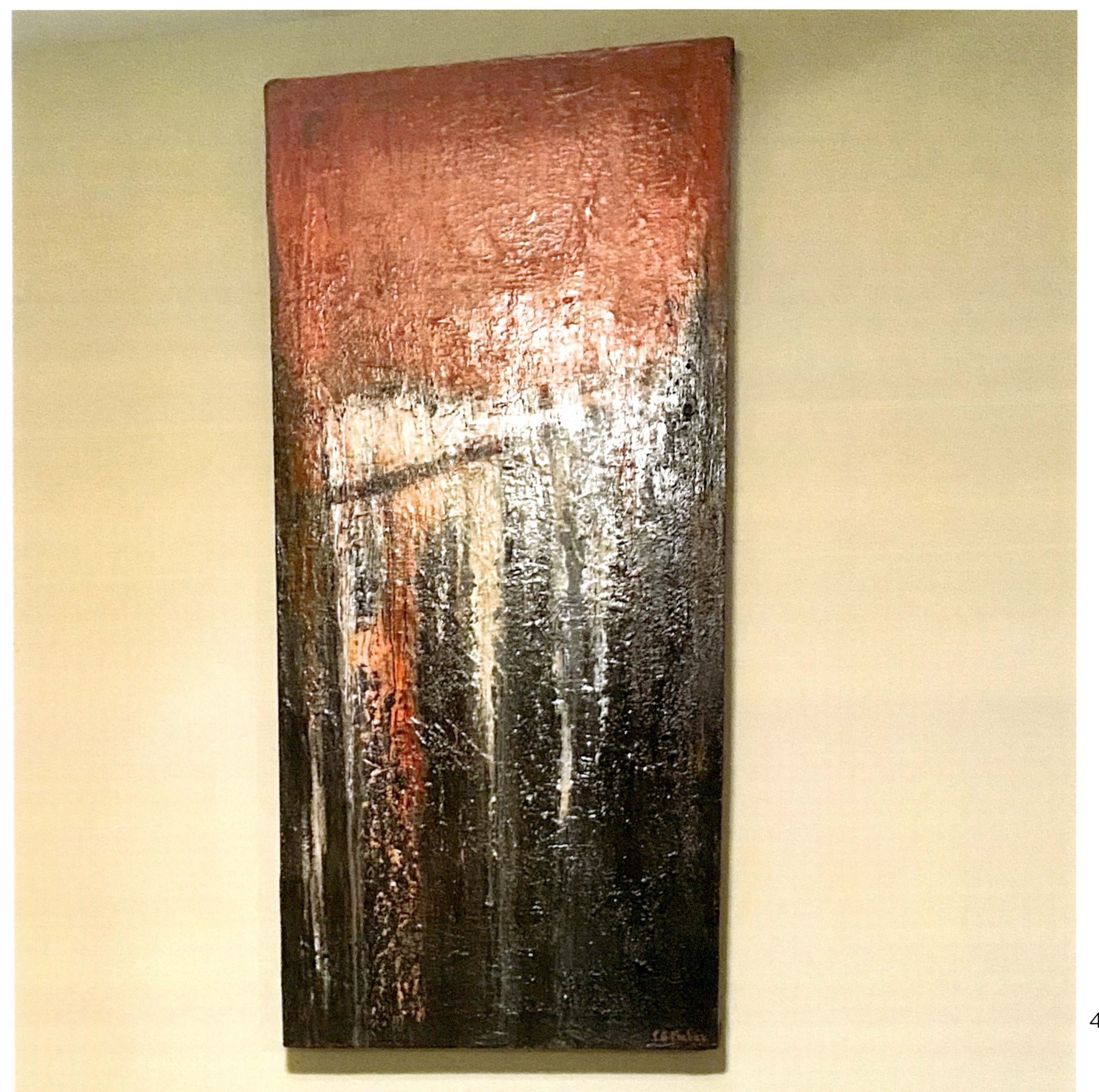

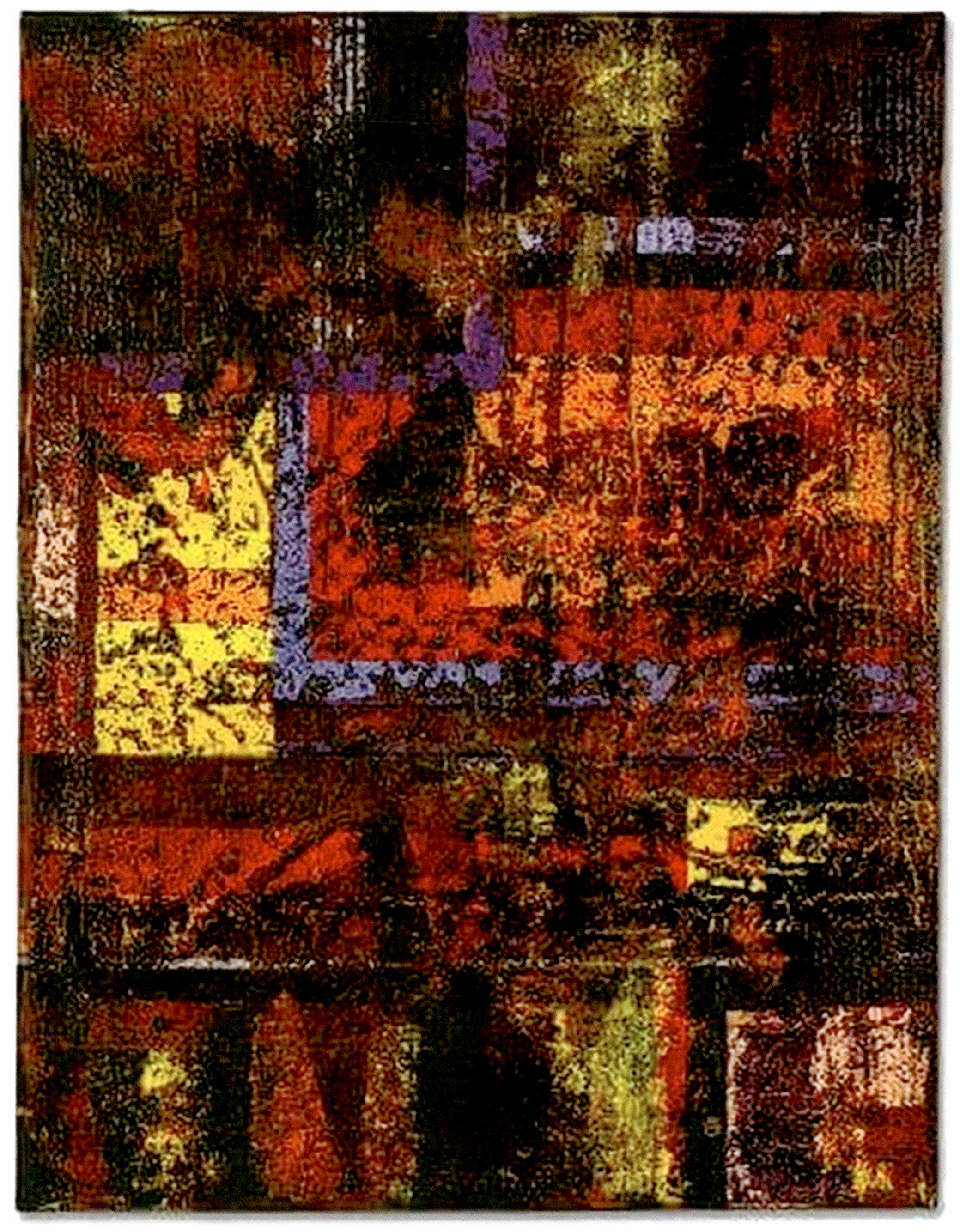

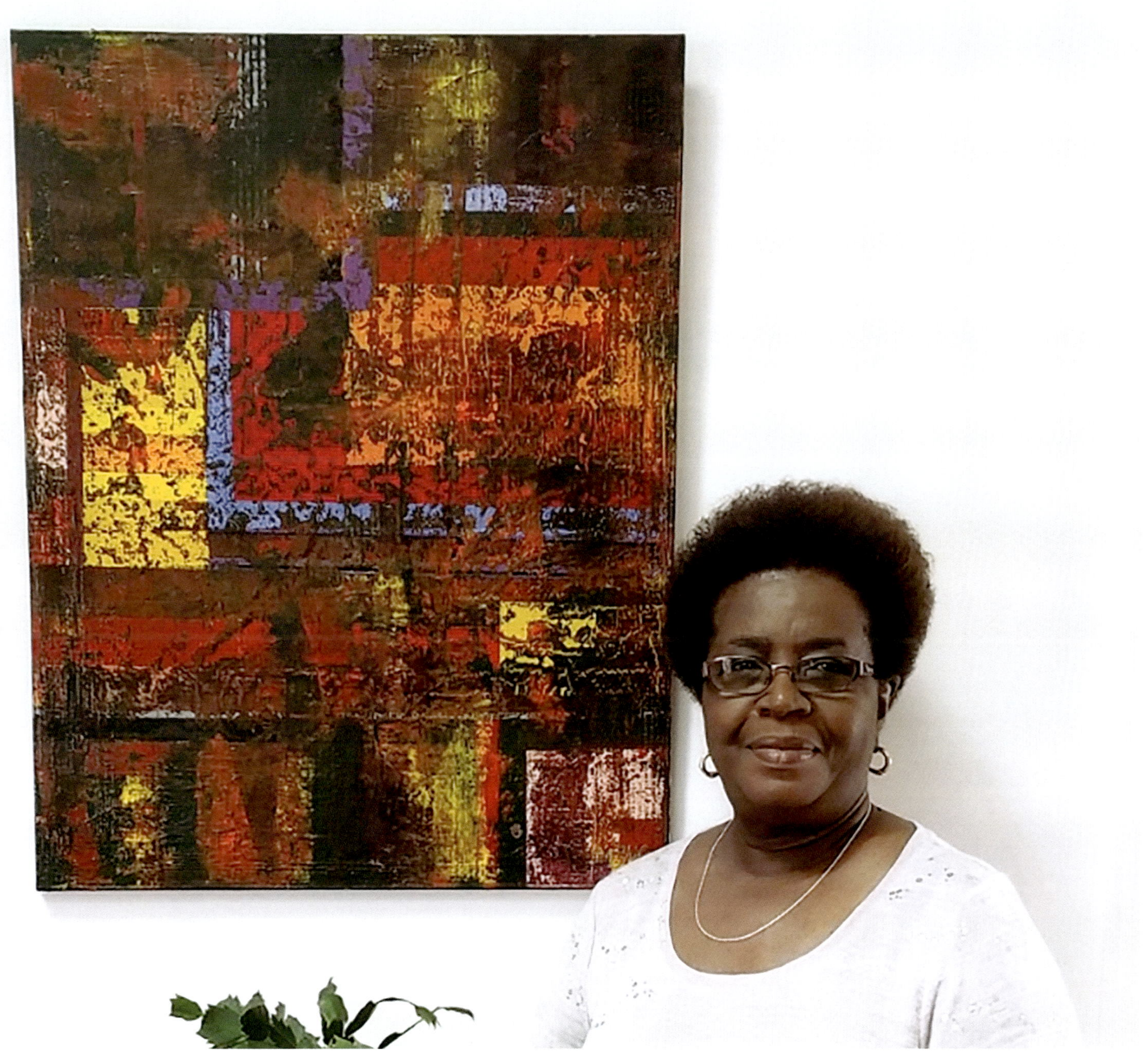

COLLECTOR:
ROBERT + VELAROSE CLAY

RELIC (24" X 30")
2015

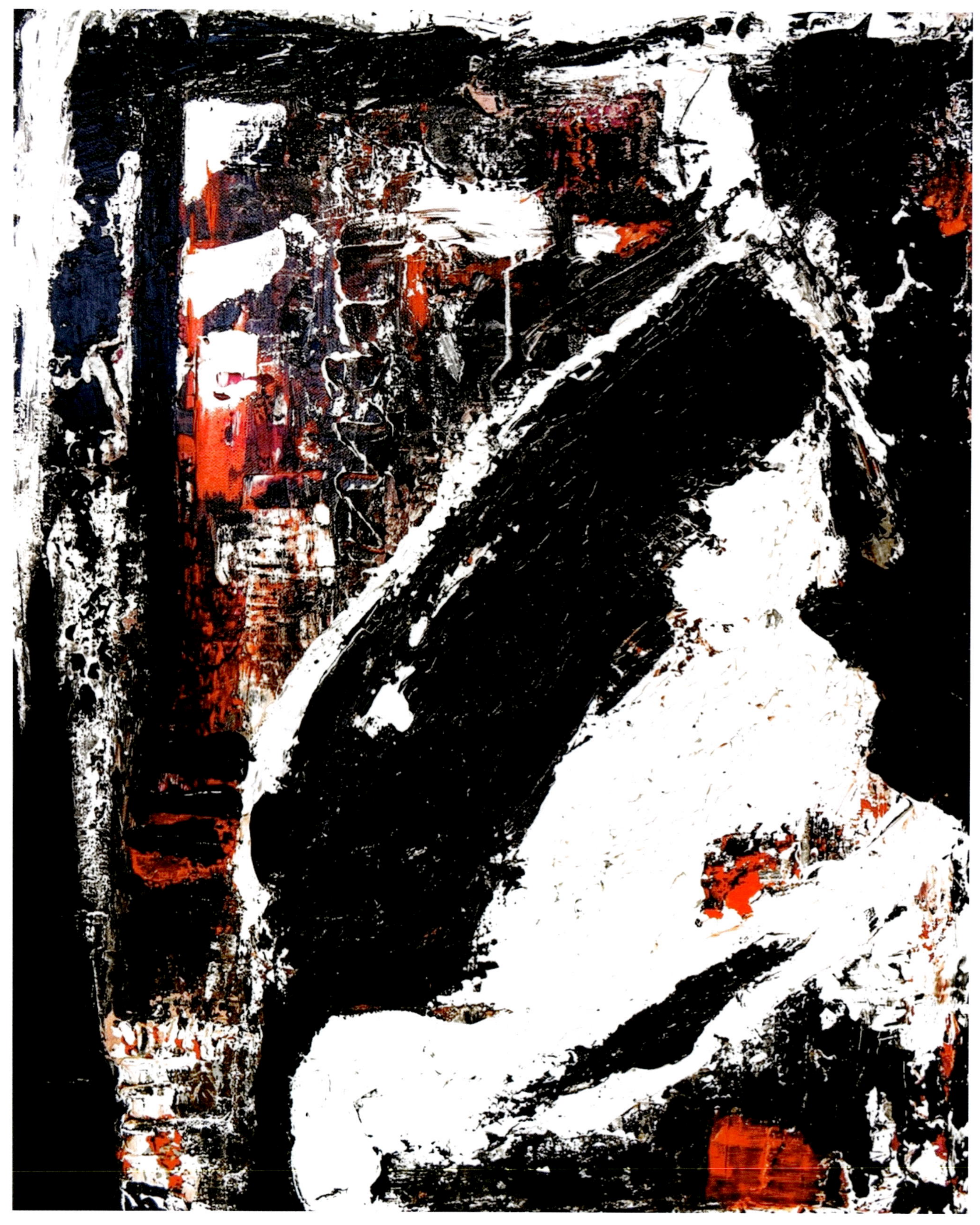

LEFT:

COLLECTOR:
JOAN + EVERETT HOWARD
LOVE (24" X 30")
2015

RIGHT:
LOOSE WEAVE
(36" X 48")
2016

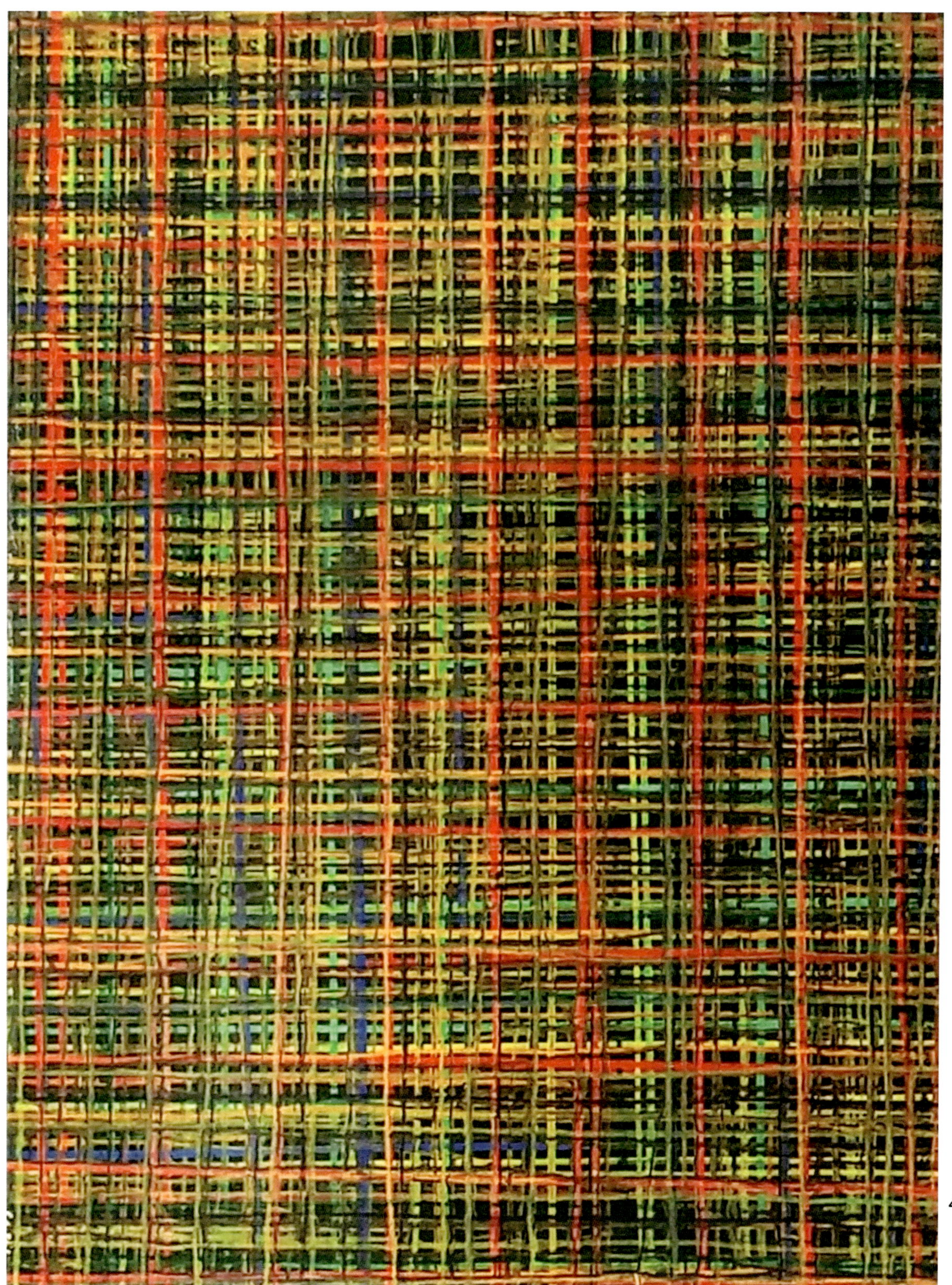

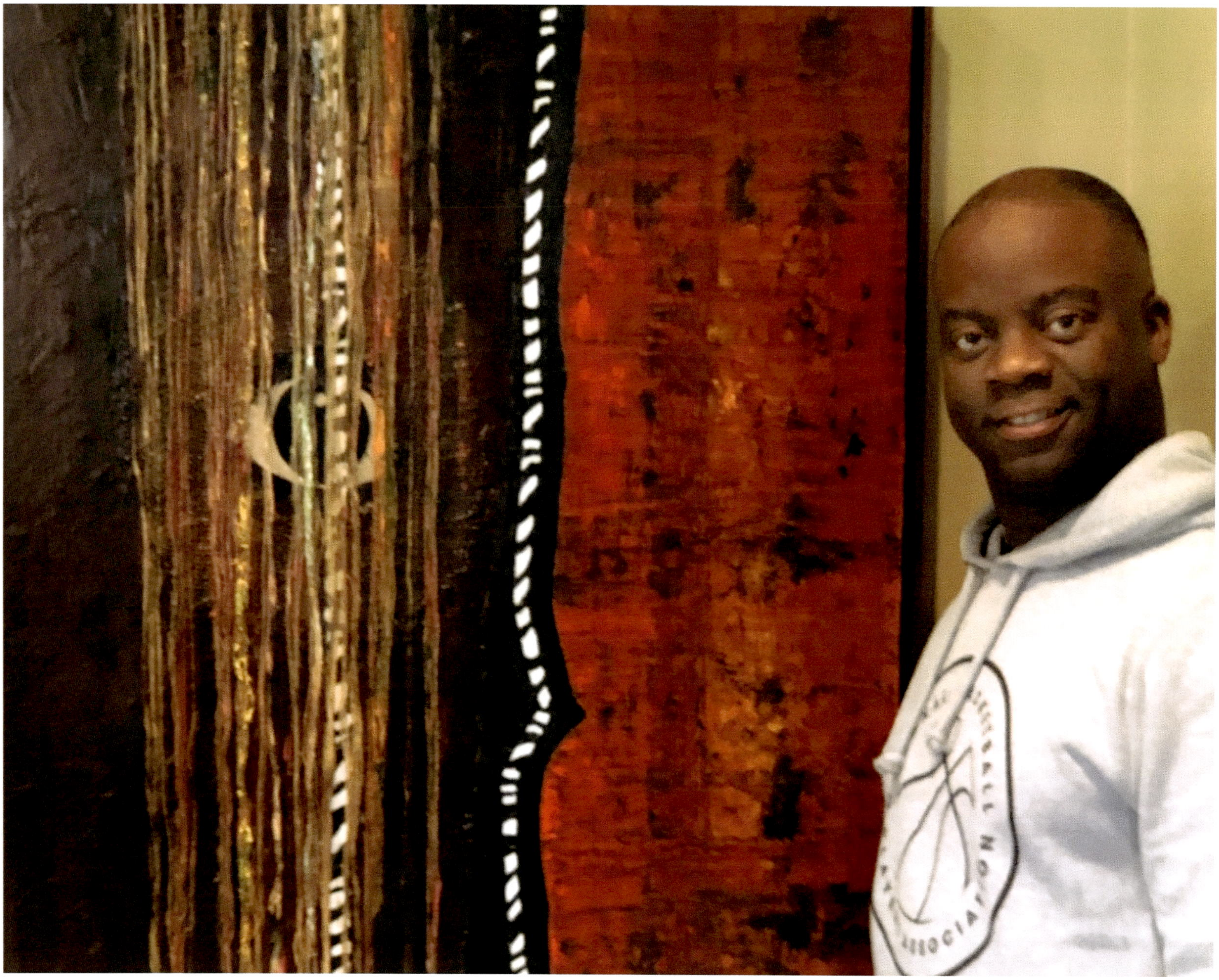

COLLECTOR:
CHARLIE LEWIS
NEW YORK

ALWAYS WATCHING (33" X 43")
2015

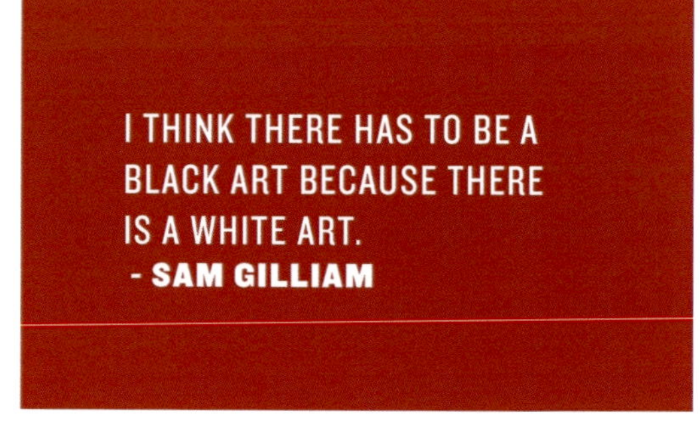

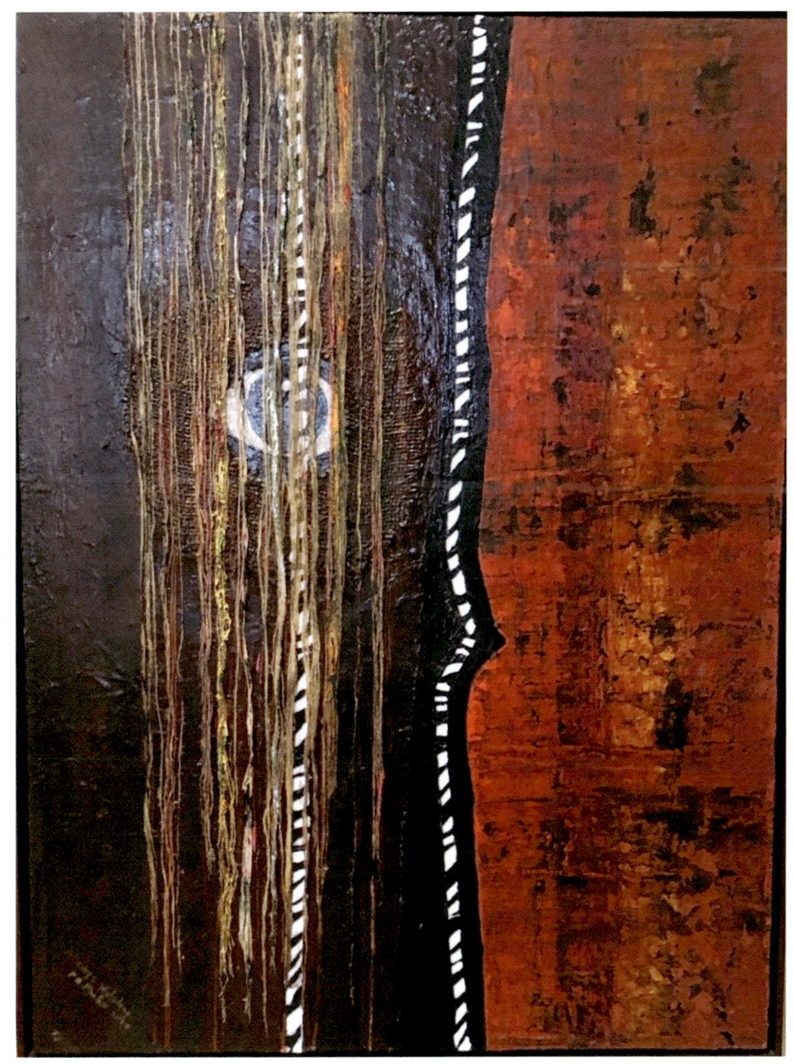

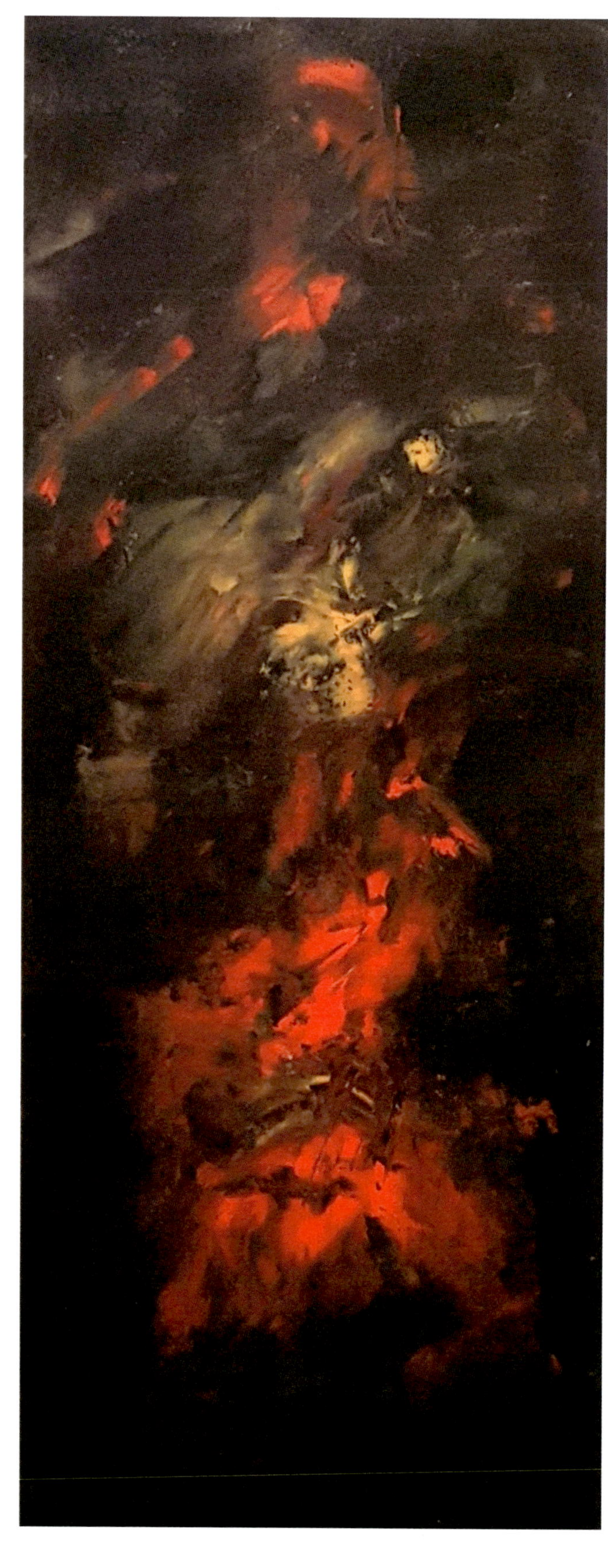

CALYPSO LADY (16" X 40")
2015

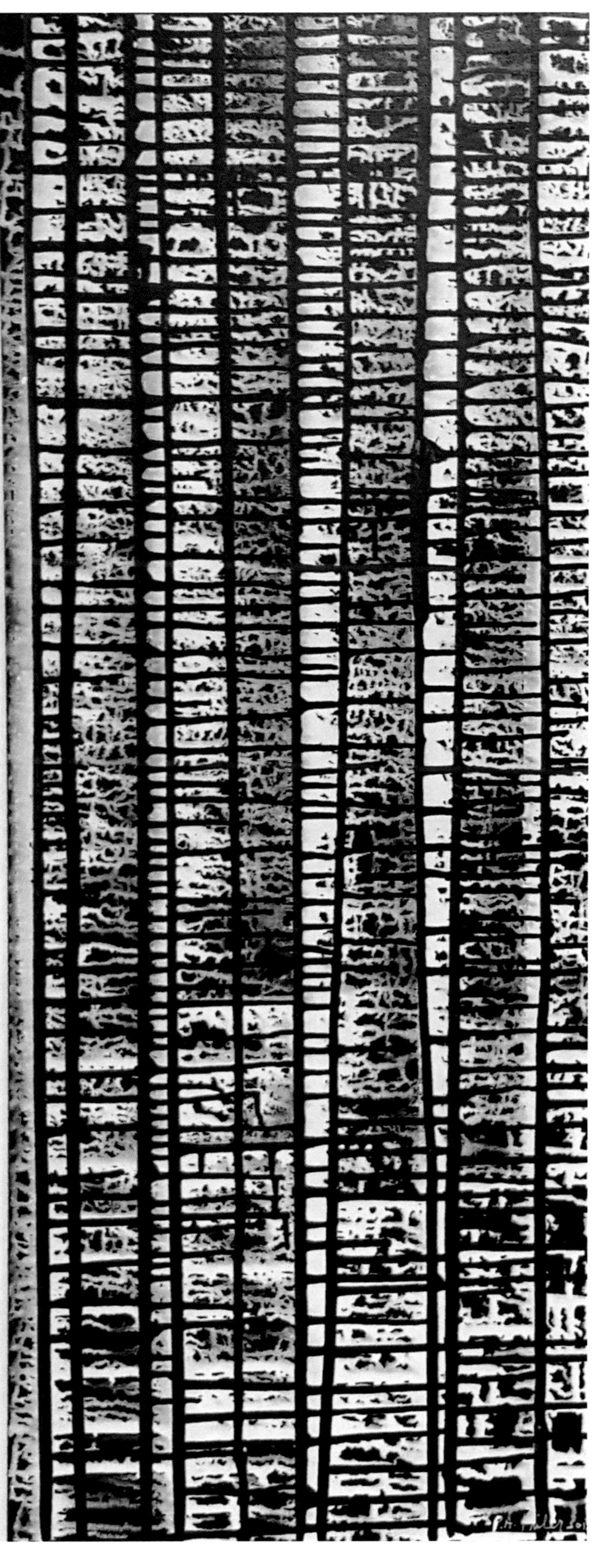

CELLULAR (16" X 40")
2016

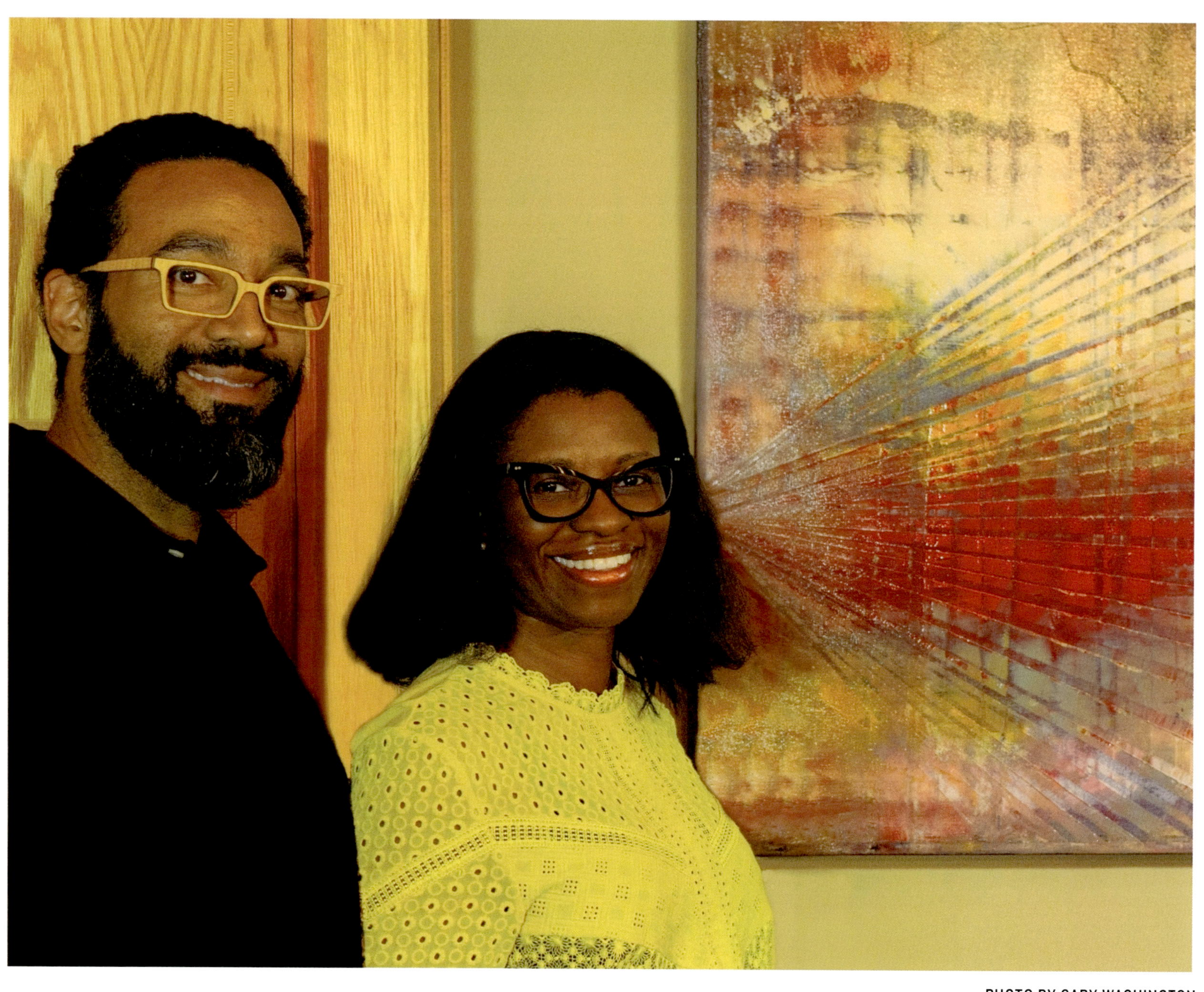

PHOTO BY GARY WASHINGTON

COLLECTOR:
TAFT + SHERIDA PARSONS

THE STATION (24" X 36")
2015

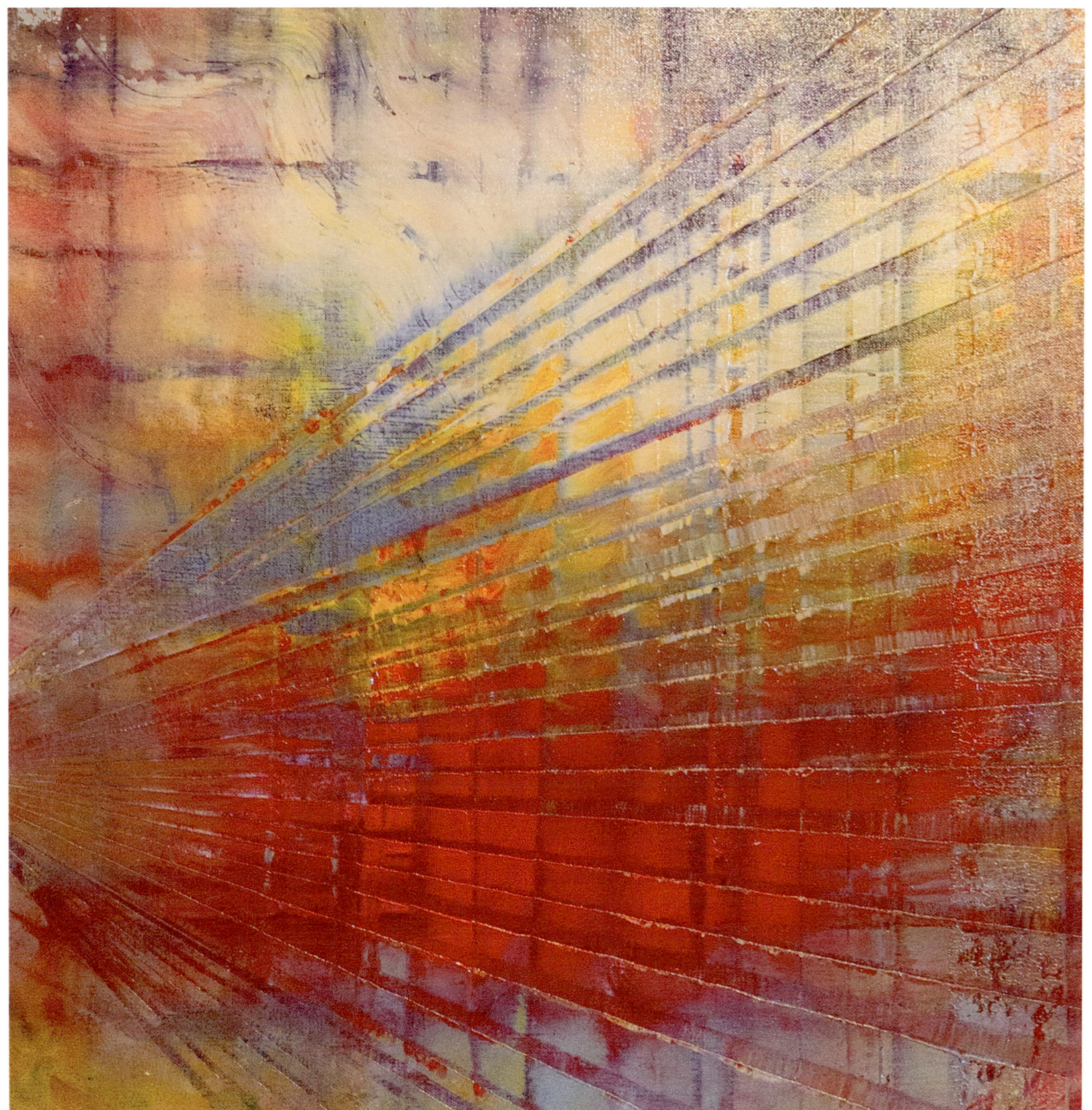

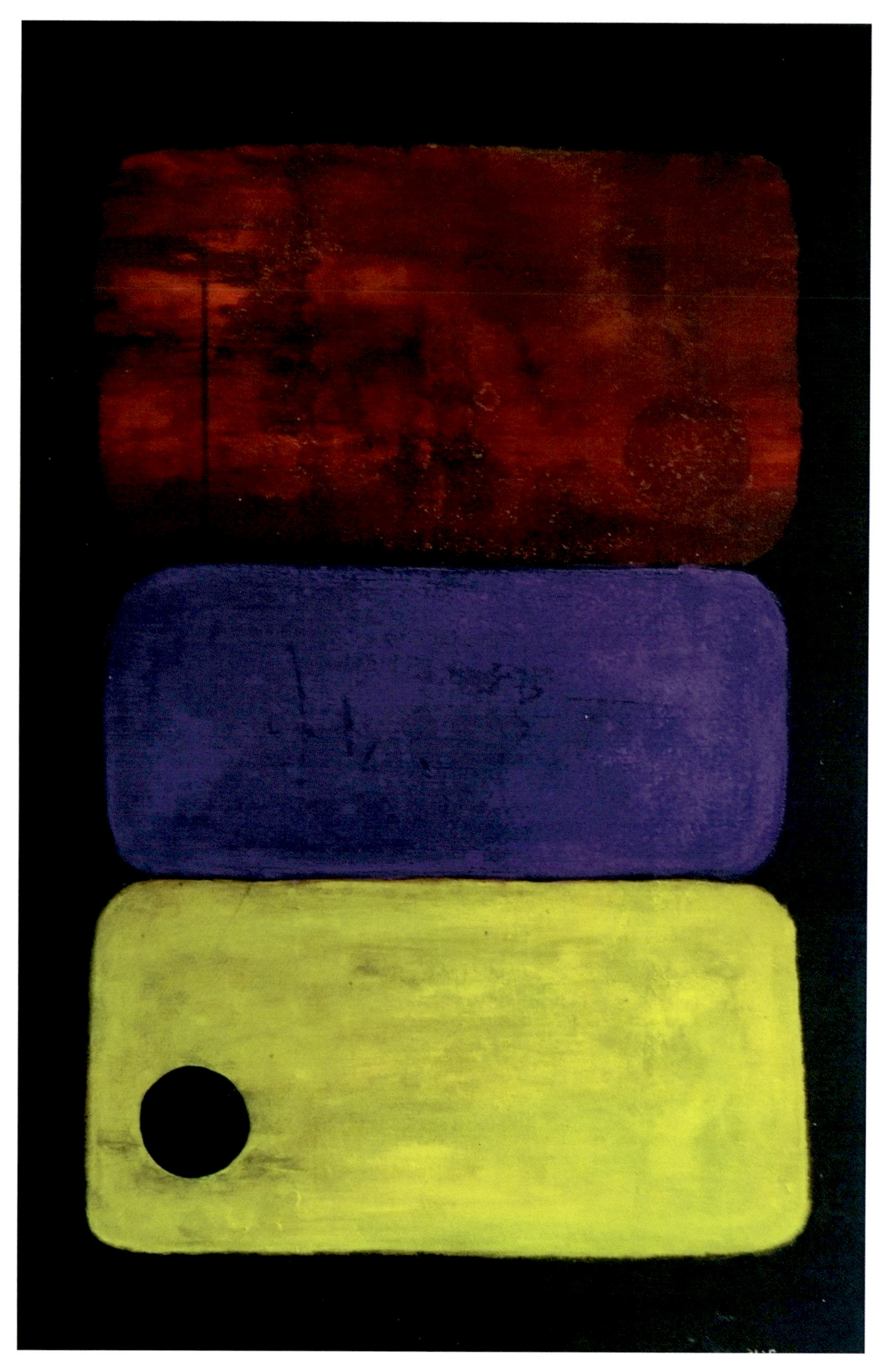

YOU ARE HERE #7(24X36)
2016

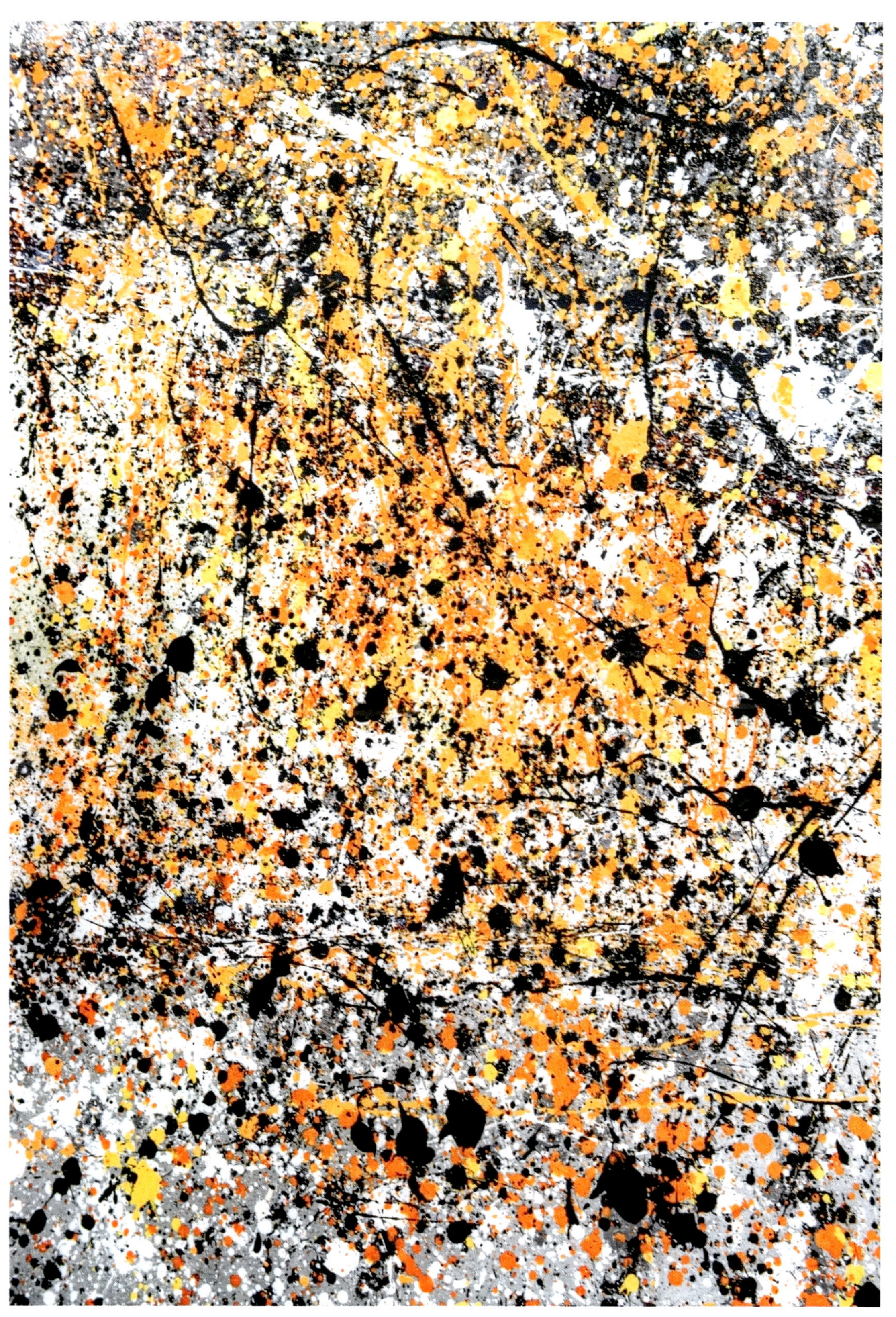

COLLECTOR:
PAUL ROGERS (NY)

ORANGE BANG (36" X 48")
2014

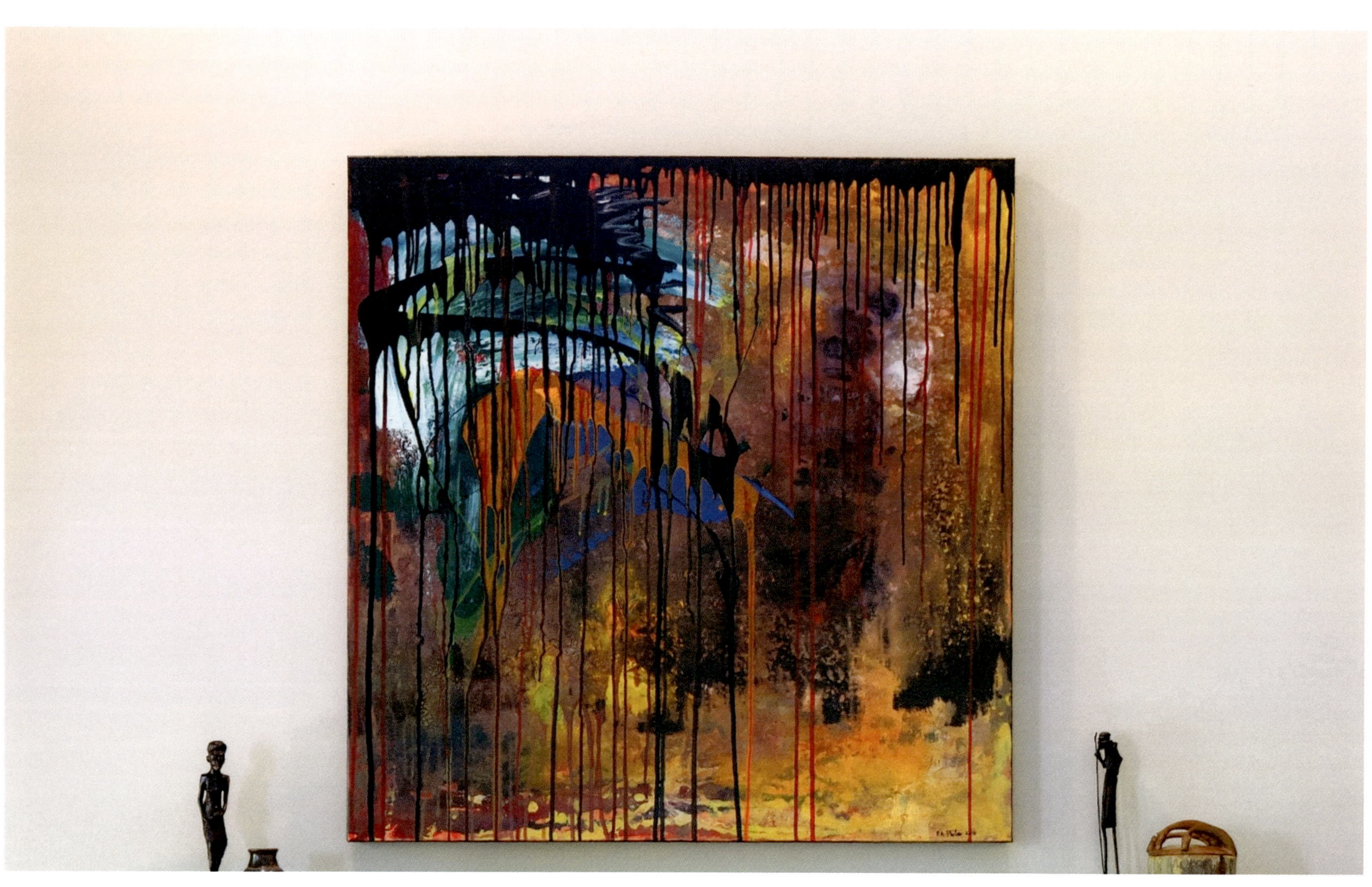

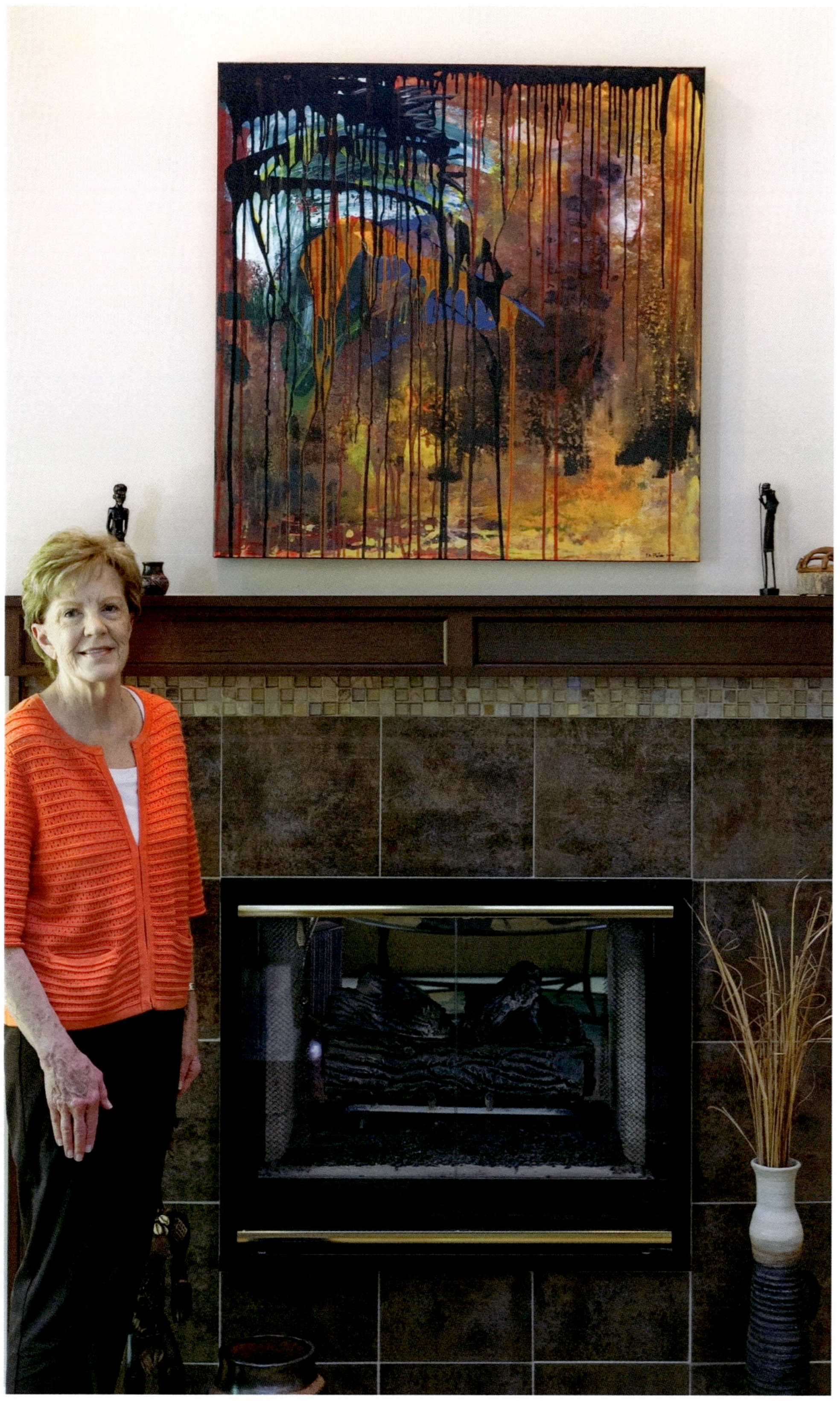

PHOTO BY GARY WASHINGTON

"AN ARTIST'S WORK IS TO REARRANGE EVERYDAY PHENOMENA SO AS TO ENLARGE OUR PERCEPTIONS OF WHO WE ARE AND WHAT GOES ON ABOUT US."
- FELRATH HINES

COLLECTOR:
LYNN MYERS

JUNGLE JOURNEY (36" X 36")
2016

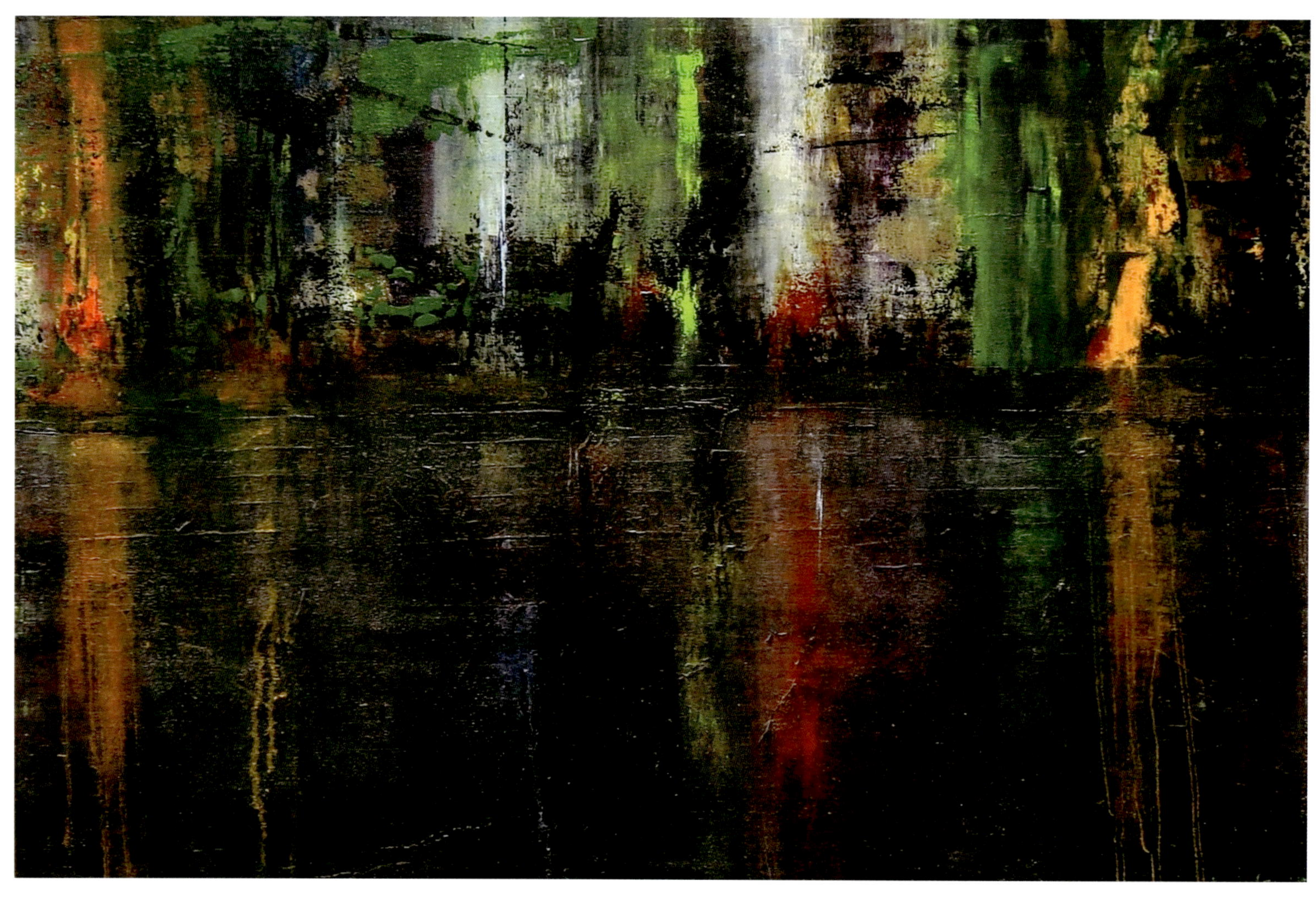

COLLECTOR:
DEBRA DEBOSE

TAKE ME TO THE RIVER (36X24)
2015

MY PAINTINGS ARE NOT LANDSCAPES, THEY ARE MINDSCAPES. THEY ARE BASED ON EMOTIONAL INTERPRETATION– A FEELING, USING LANDSCAPES AS A METAPHOR TO EXPRESS THAT

- RICHARD MAYHEW

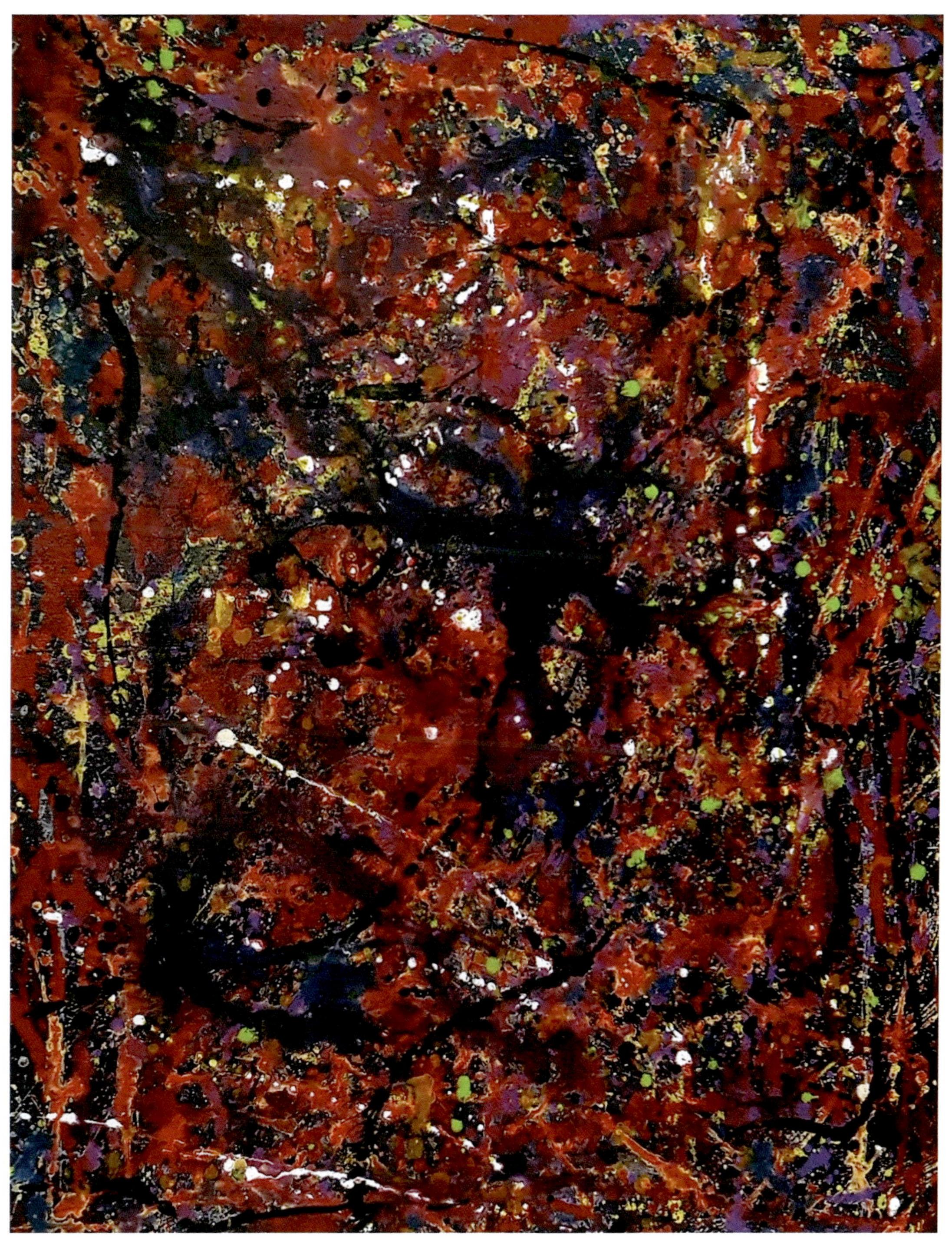

COLLECTOR:
PATRICIA SOLOMON

SPOT ON (30X40)
2016

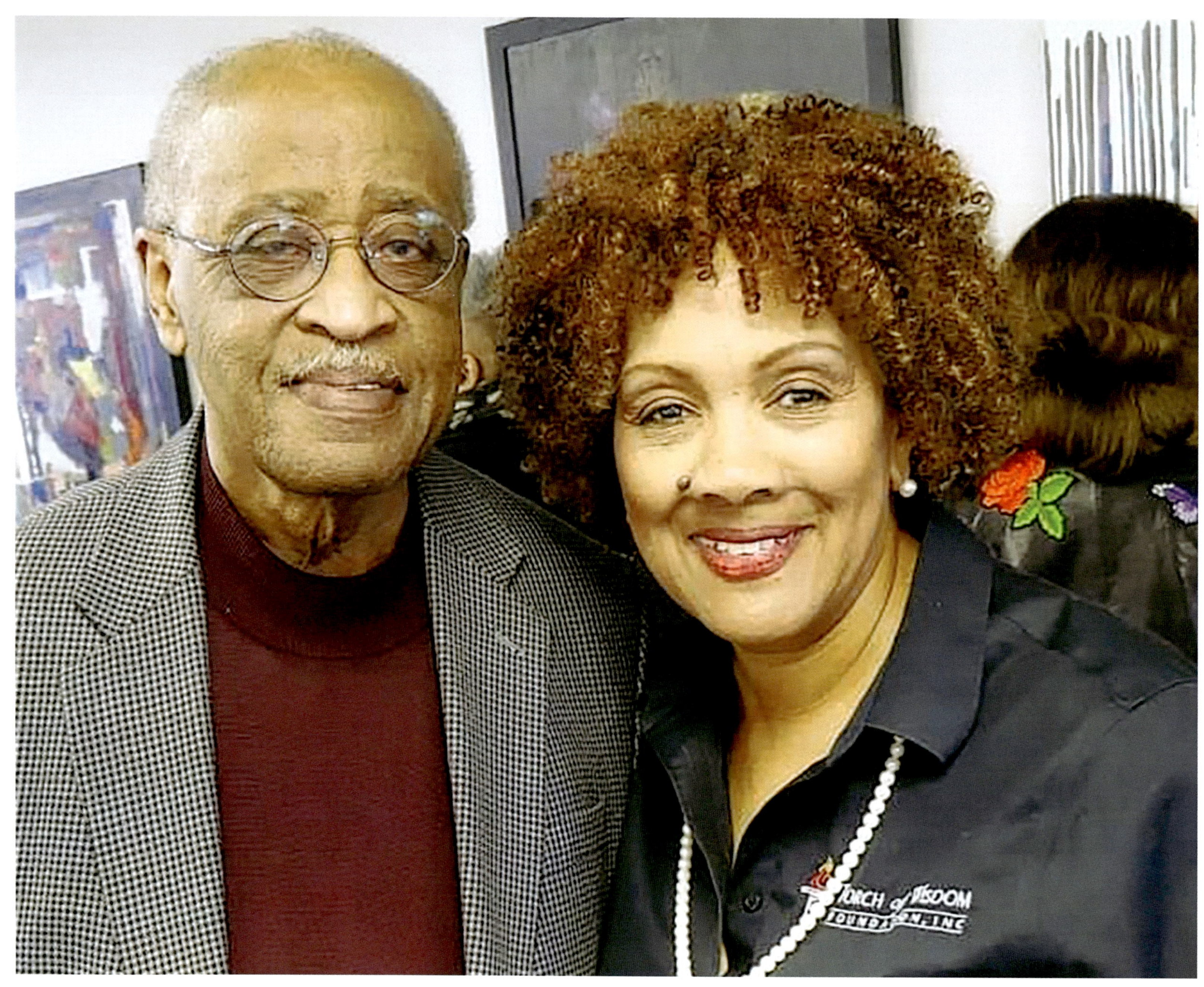

COLLECTOR:
ANDREW + LORETTA BROWN

KALEIDOSCOPIC (36" X 24")
2015

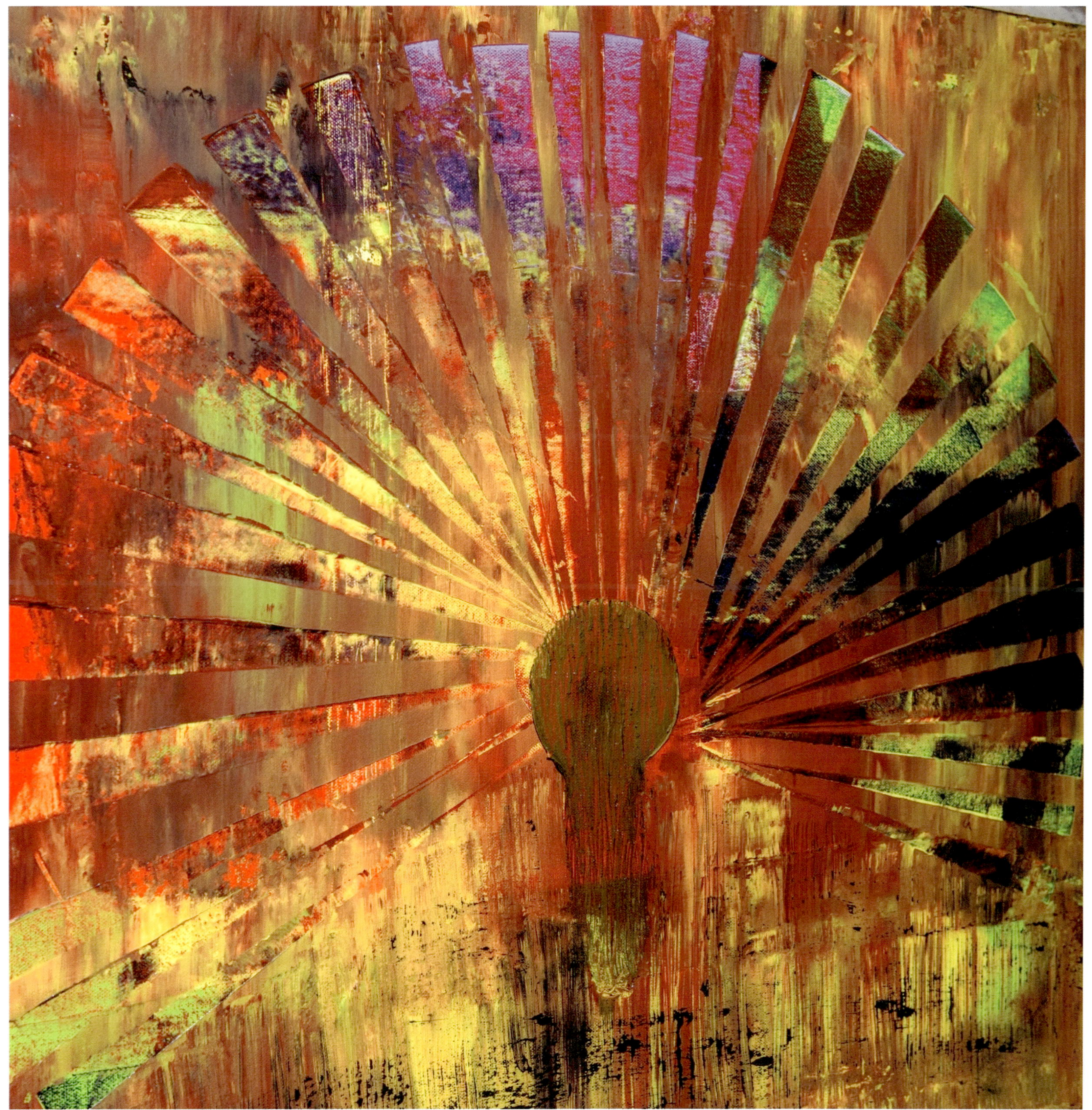

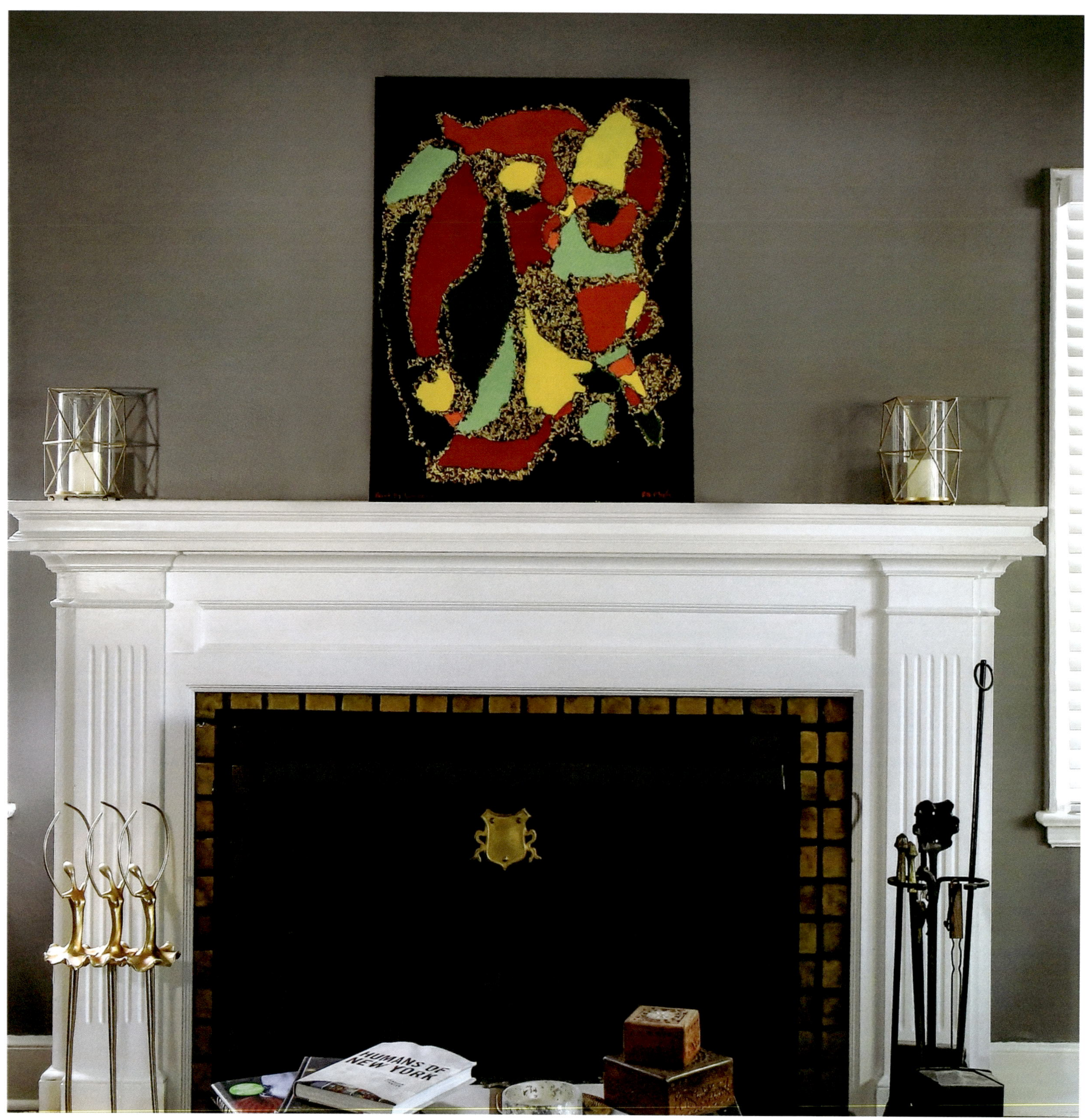
HUMANS OF
NEW YORK

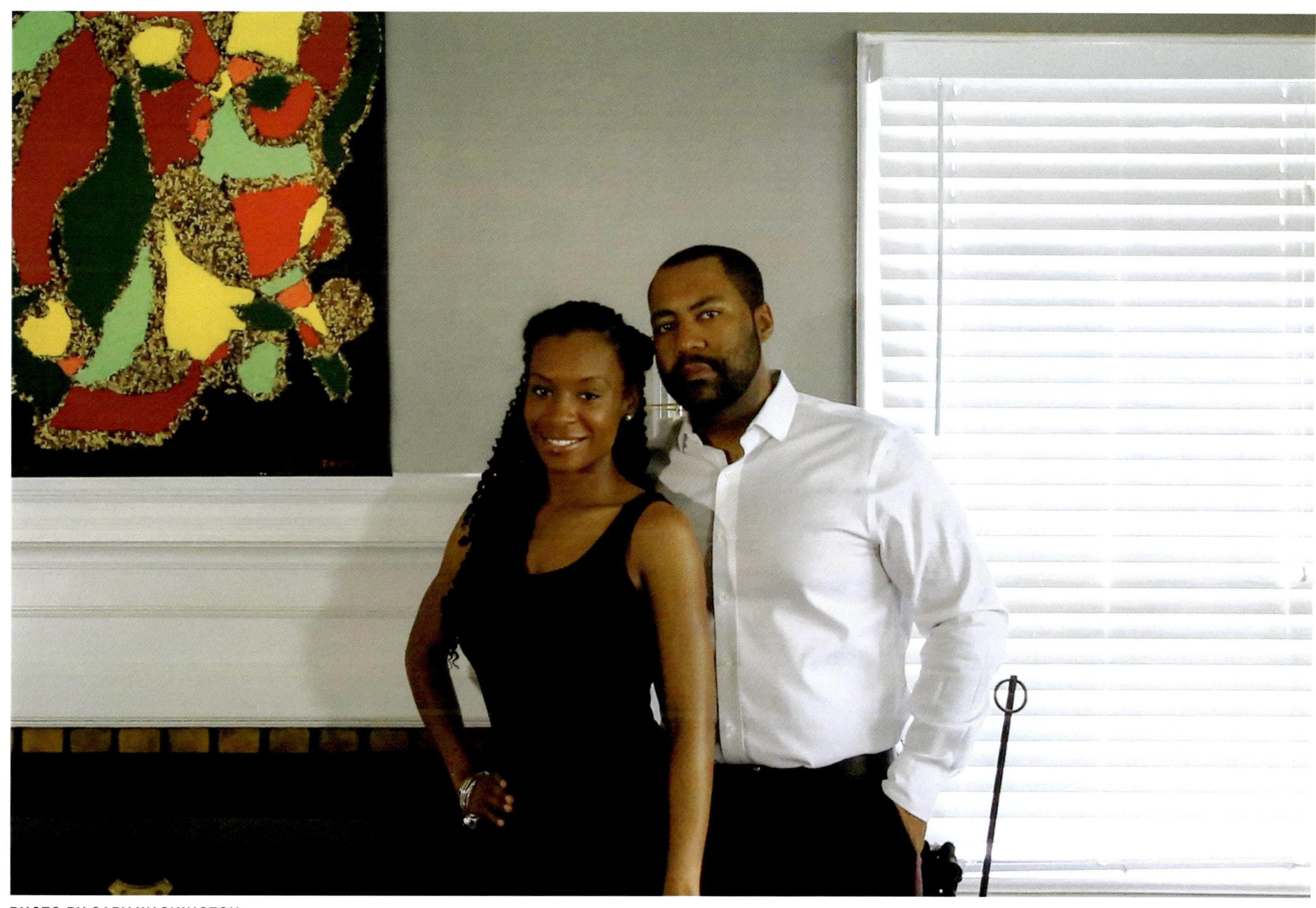

PHOTO BY GARY WASHINGTON

COLLECTOR:
JEREMY + WHITNEY LEWIS

UNTITLED (30" X 40")
2015

ART COMES FROM THE IDEA OF INVERSION, FROM THE CHANGE YOU WANT TO MAKE TO WHAT YOU SEE AND WHEREVER YOU FIND IT.

- **SAM GILLIAM**

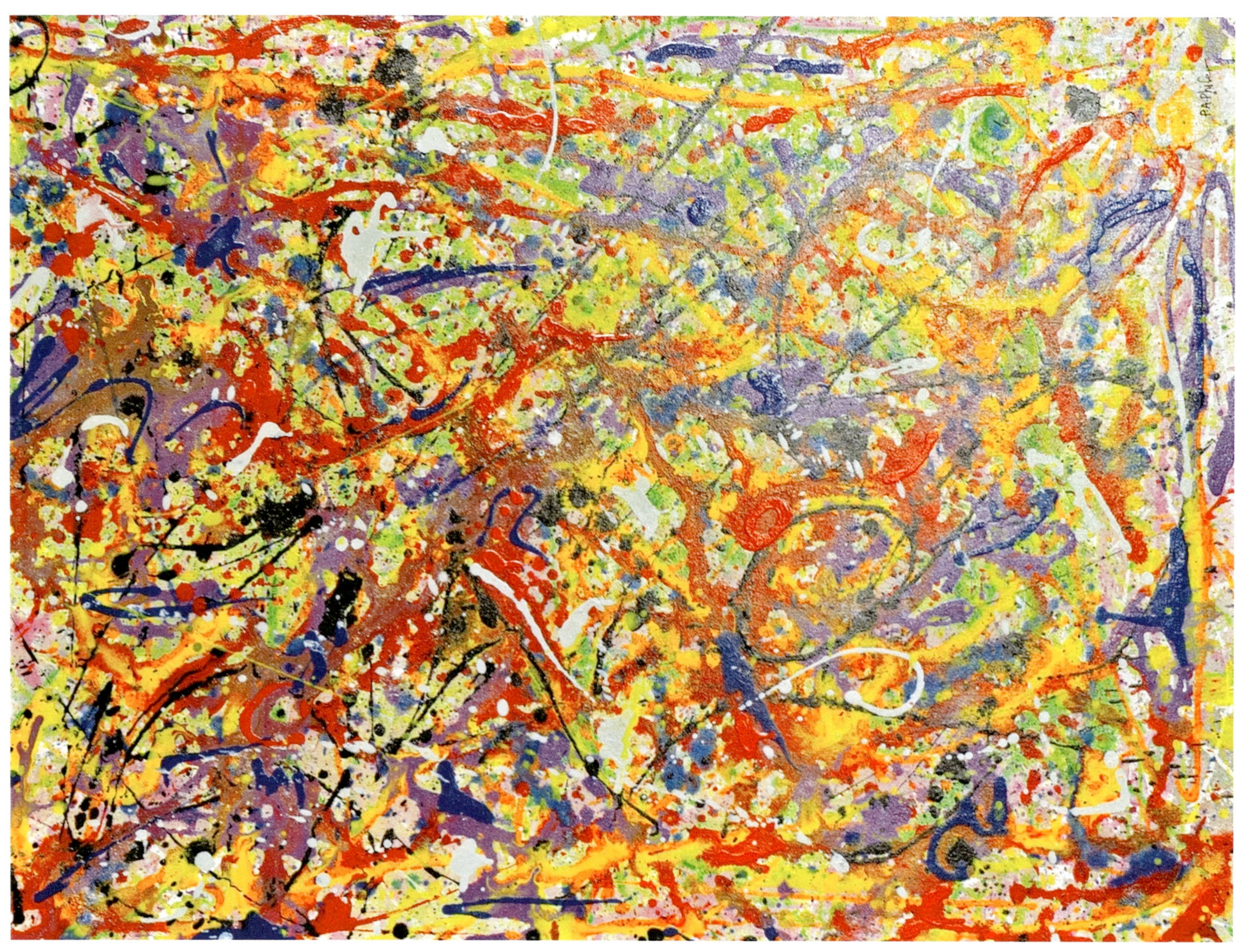

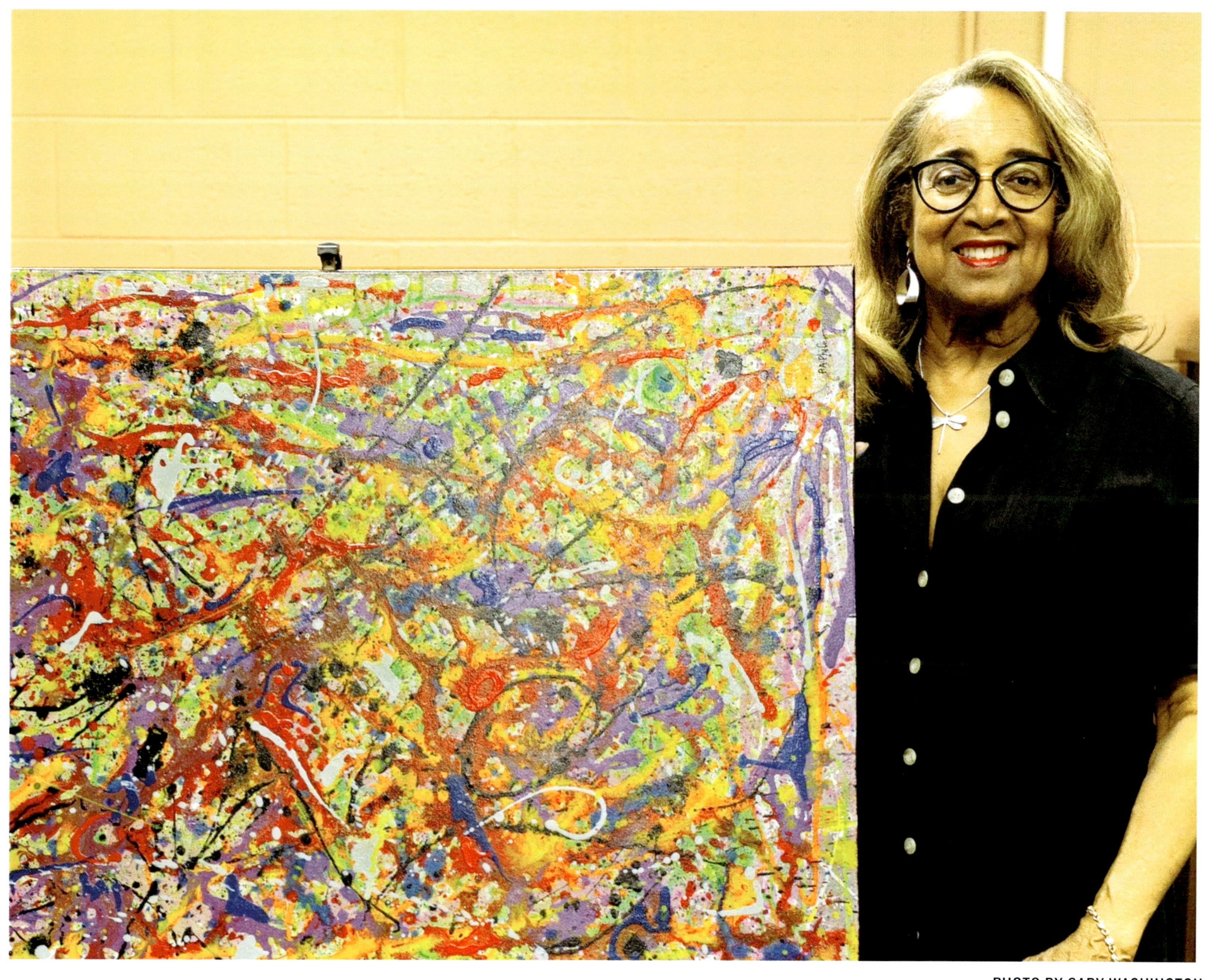

PHOTO BY GARY WASHINGTON

COLLECTOR:
GLORIA + BRIAN RHODES

CELEBRATION 2 (48" X 36")
2016

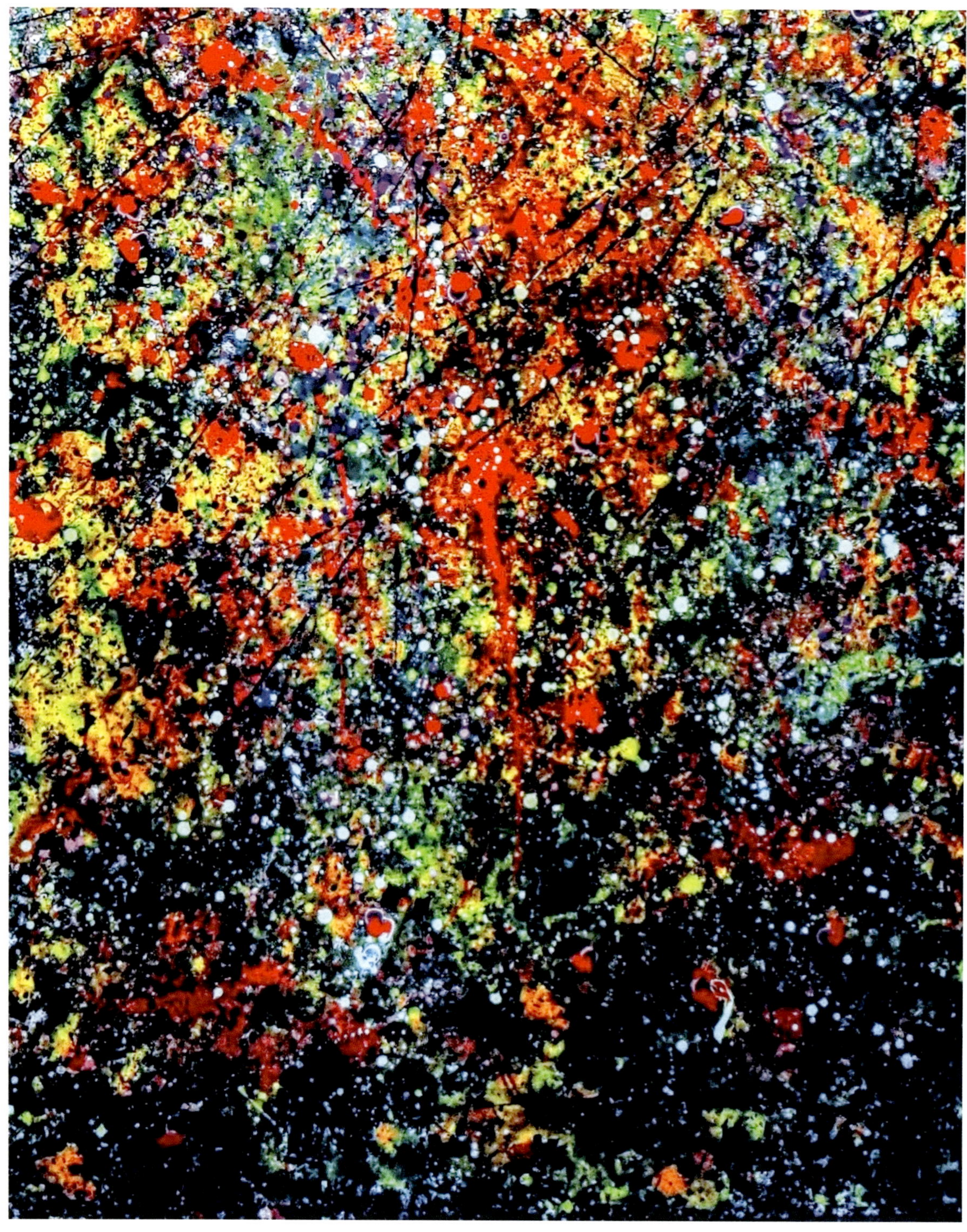

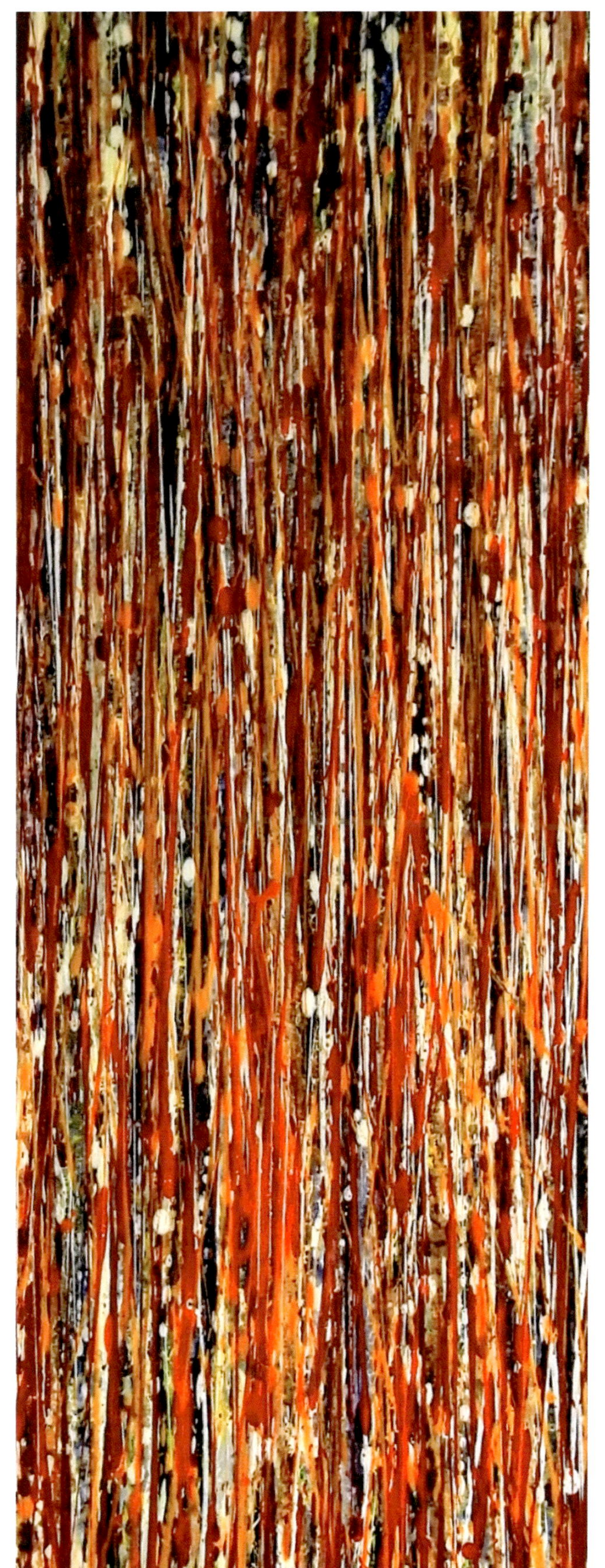

LEFT:
MY GARDEN
(36 X 36)
2019

COLLECTOR:
EDDIE AND CAROLE LENTON

COLOR MY WORLD #3
(16 X 40)
2018

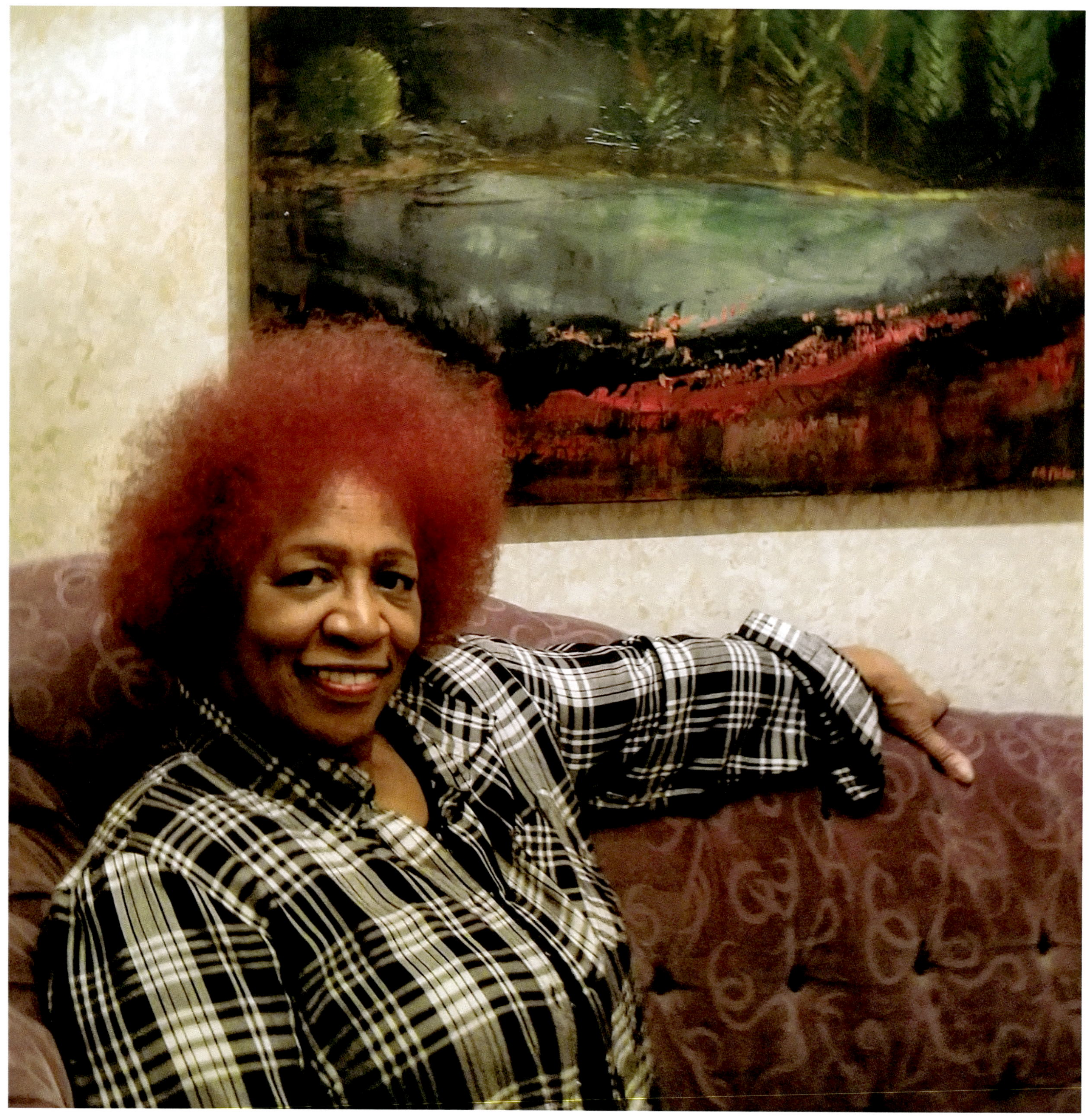

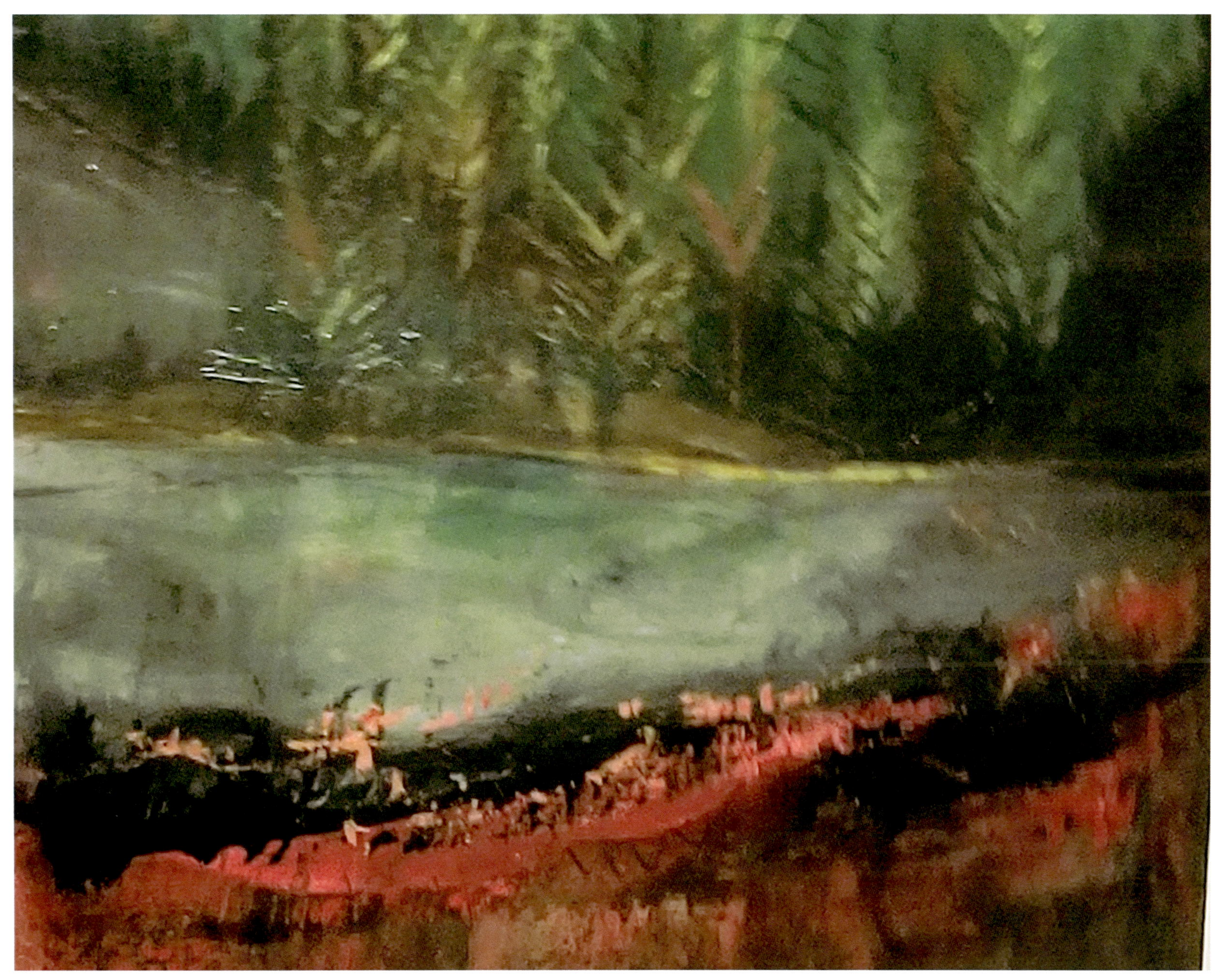

COLLECTOR:
RUBY WHEELER

HIDDEN LAKE (36" X 36")
2015

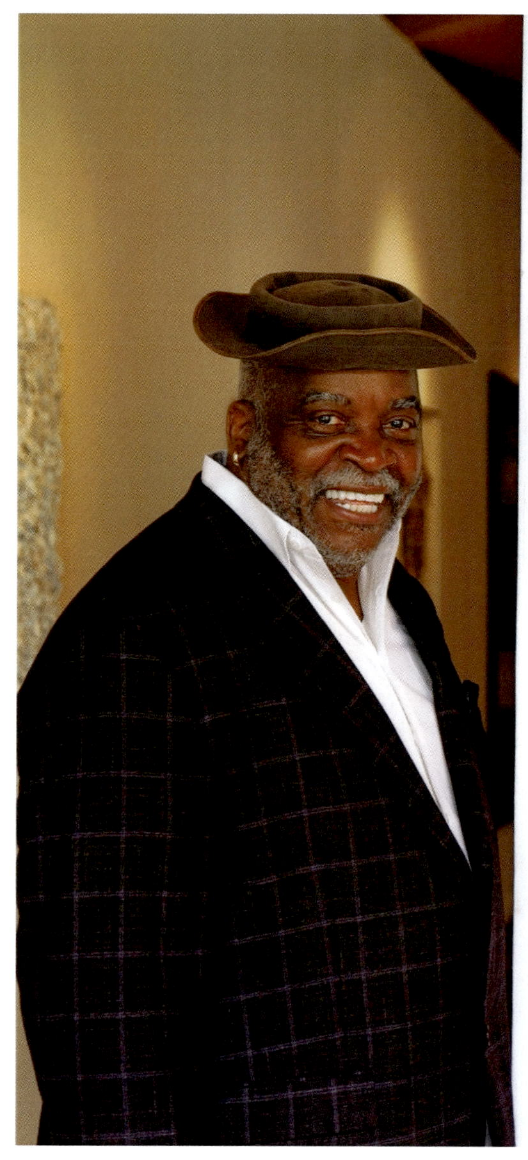

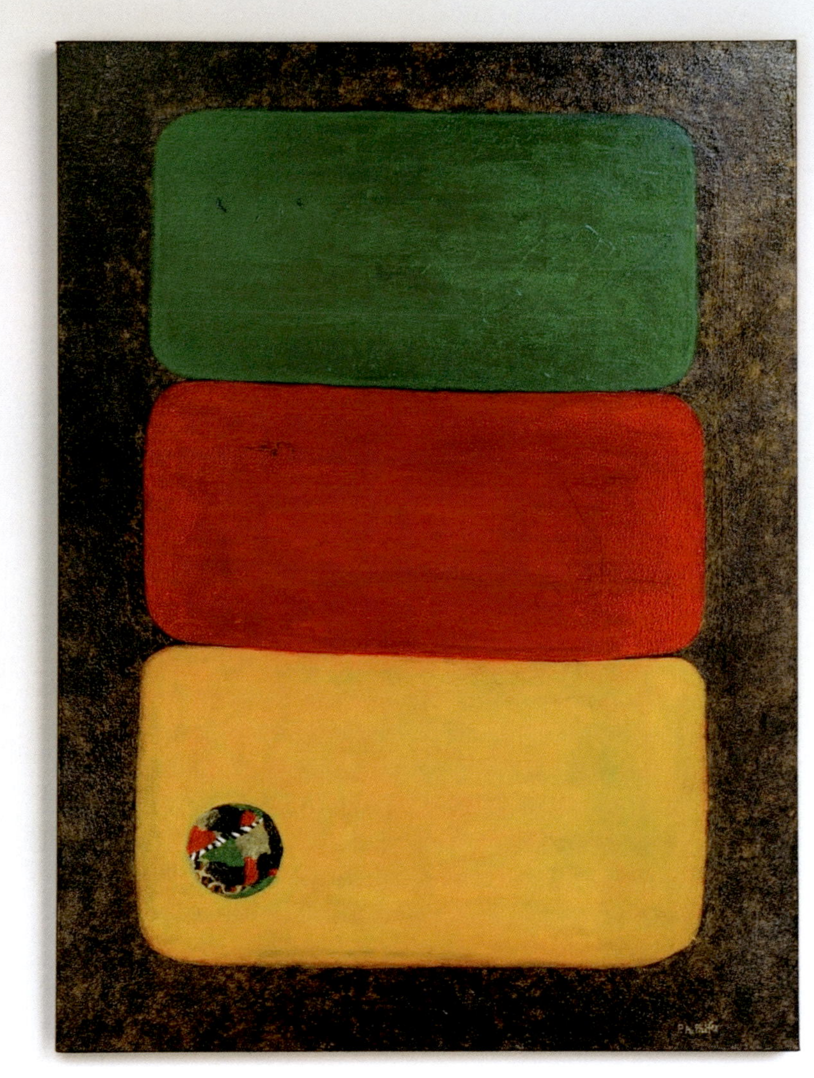

COLLECTOR:
GEORGE N'NAMDI
N'NAMDI CENTER FOR CONTEMPORARY ART

YOU ARE HERE #6 (30" X 40")
2017

I ALWAYS THOUGHT THE ABSTRACTION WAS PROBABLY THE MOST BRILLIANT THING WE COULD DO, BECAUSE THE ABSTRACTION SHOWED OUR AFRICAN-NESS IN THE ART BECAUSE AFRICAN ART IS VERY ABSTRACT.

- GEORGE N'NAMDI

PHOTO BY GARY WASHINGTON

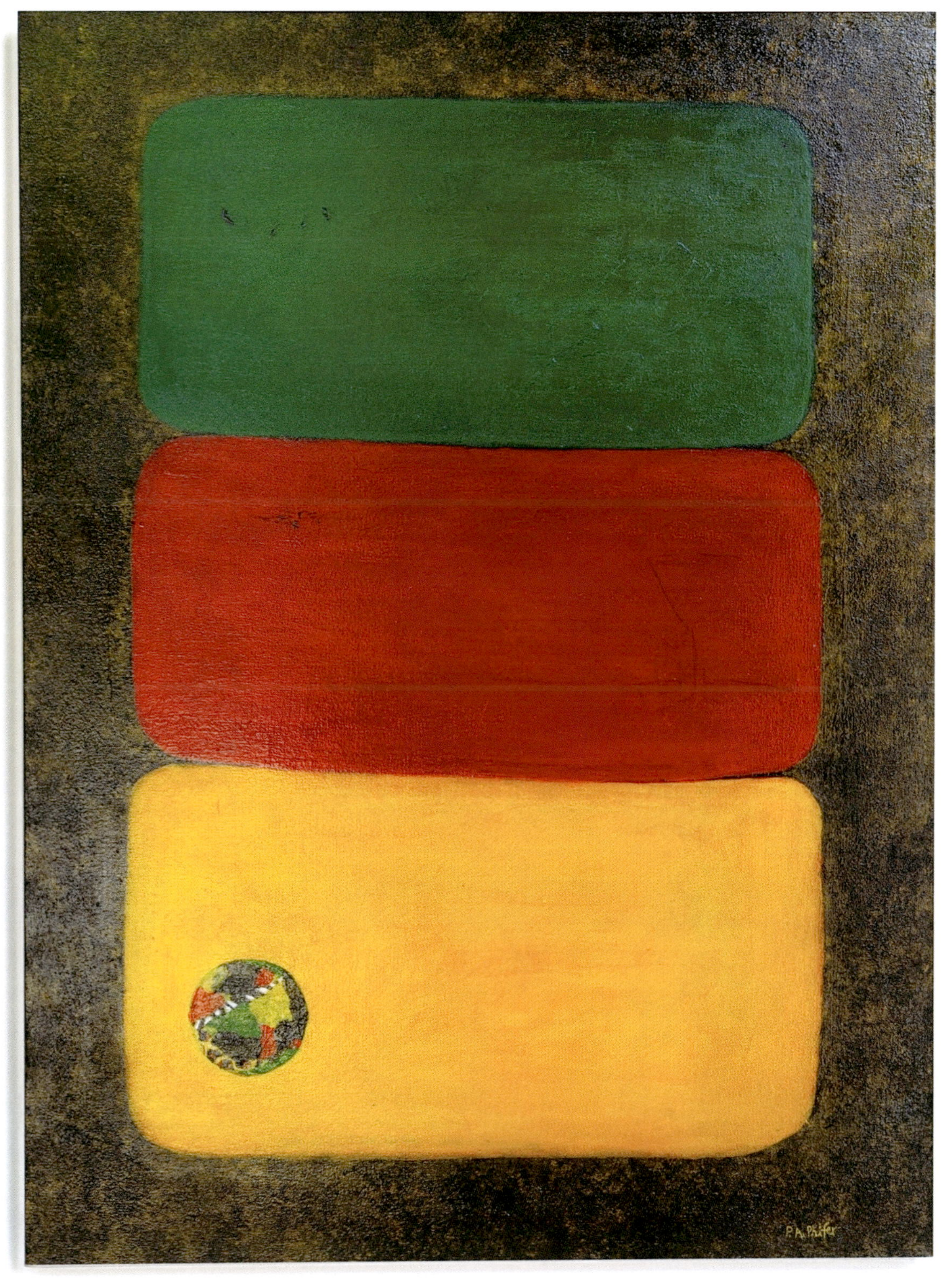

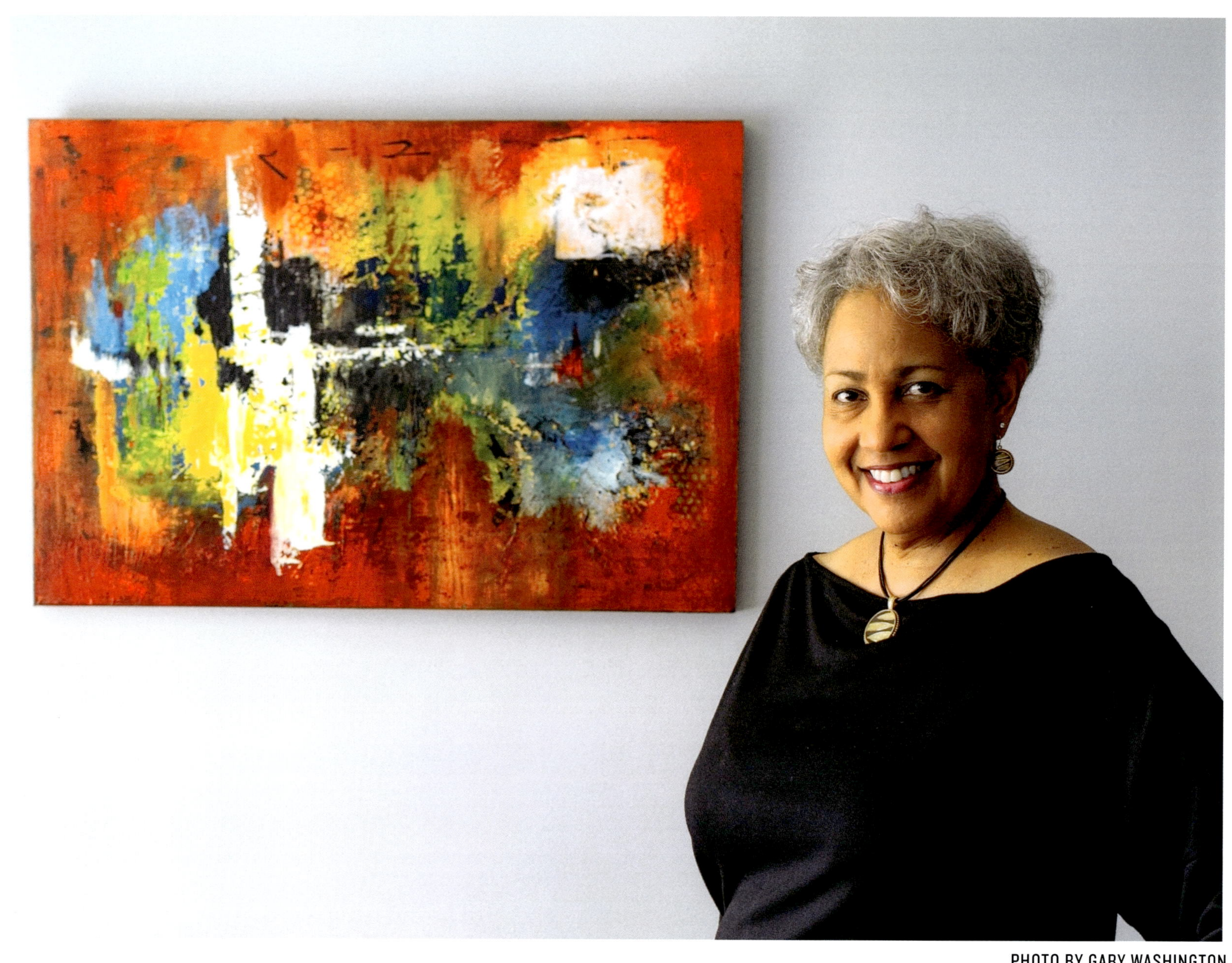

PHOTO BY GARY WASHINGTON

COLLECTOR:
DEBRA DEBOSE

ENIGMATIC REFLECTIONS (24" X 36")
2017

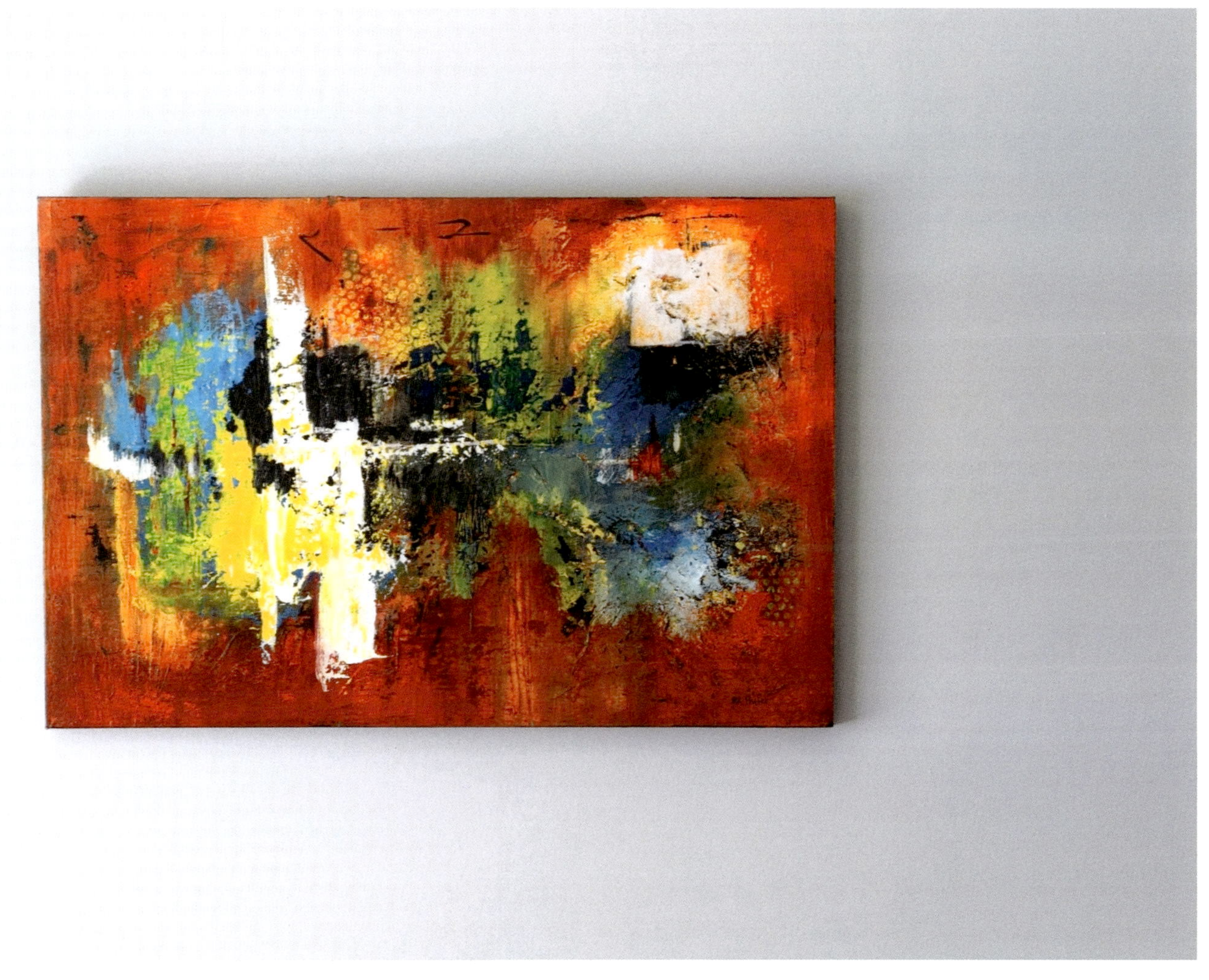

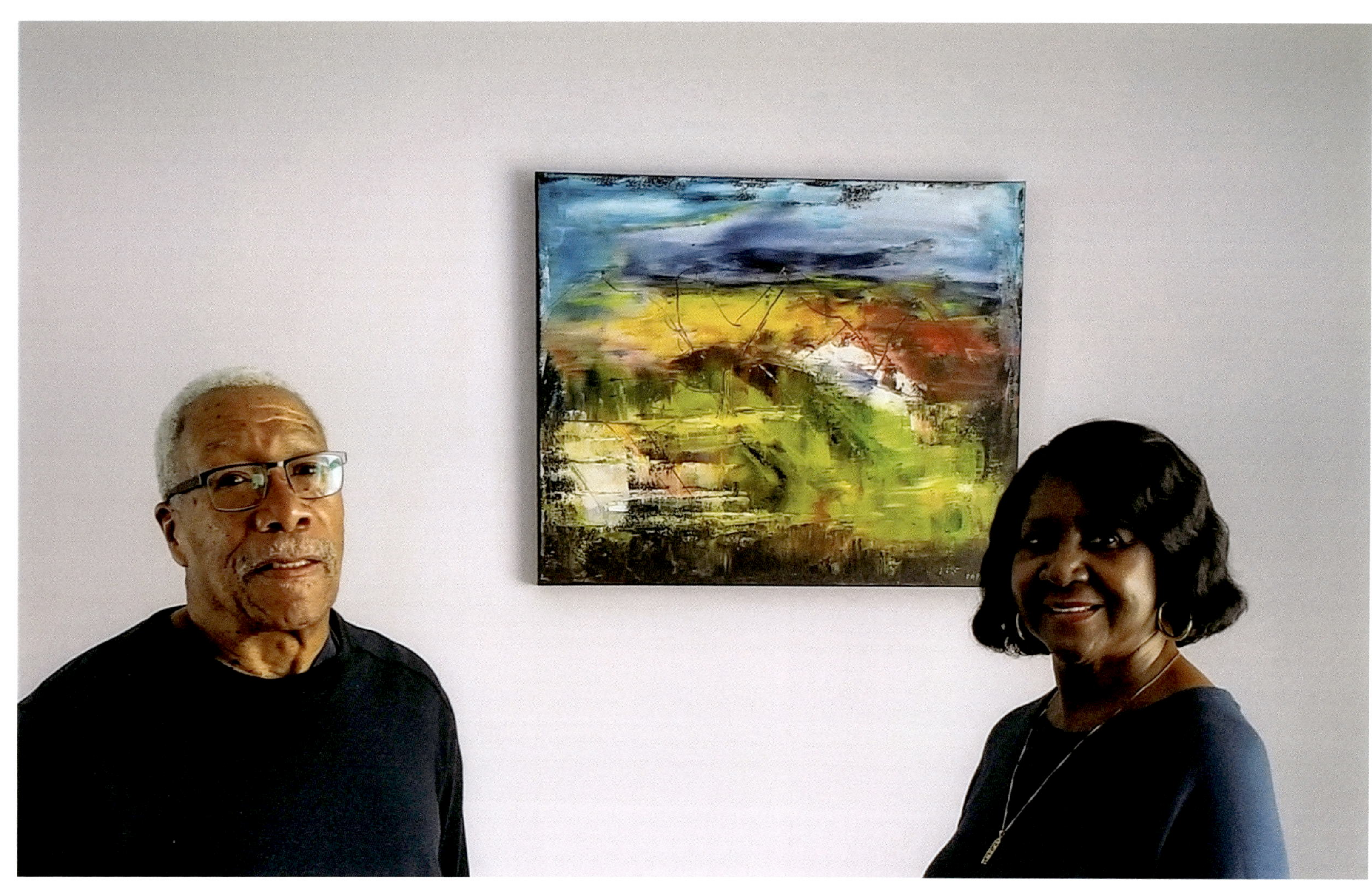

COLLECTOR:
BERNARD + RUTH DUNN-KELLY

PEACE IN THE VALLEY (30" X 24")
2017

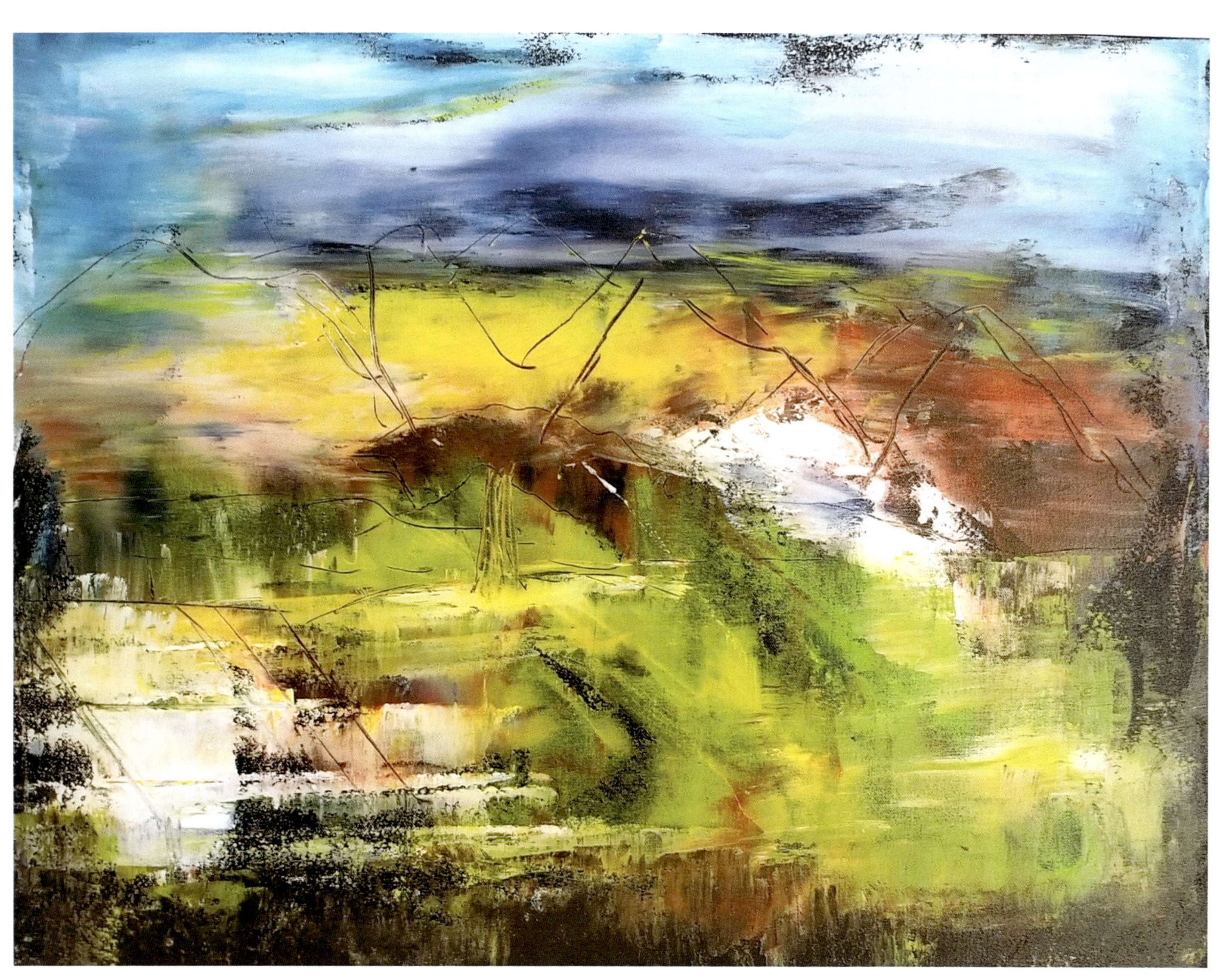

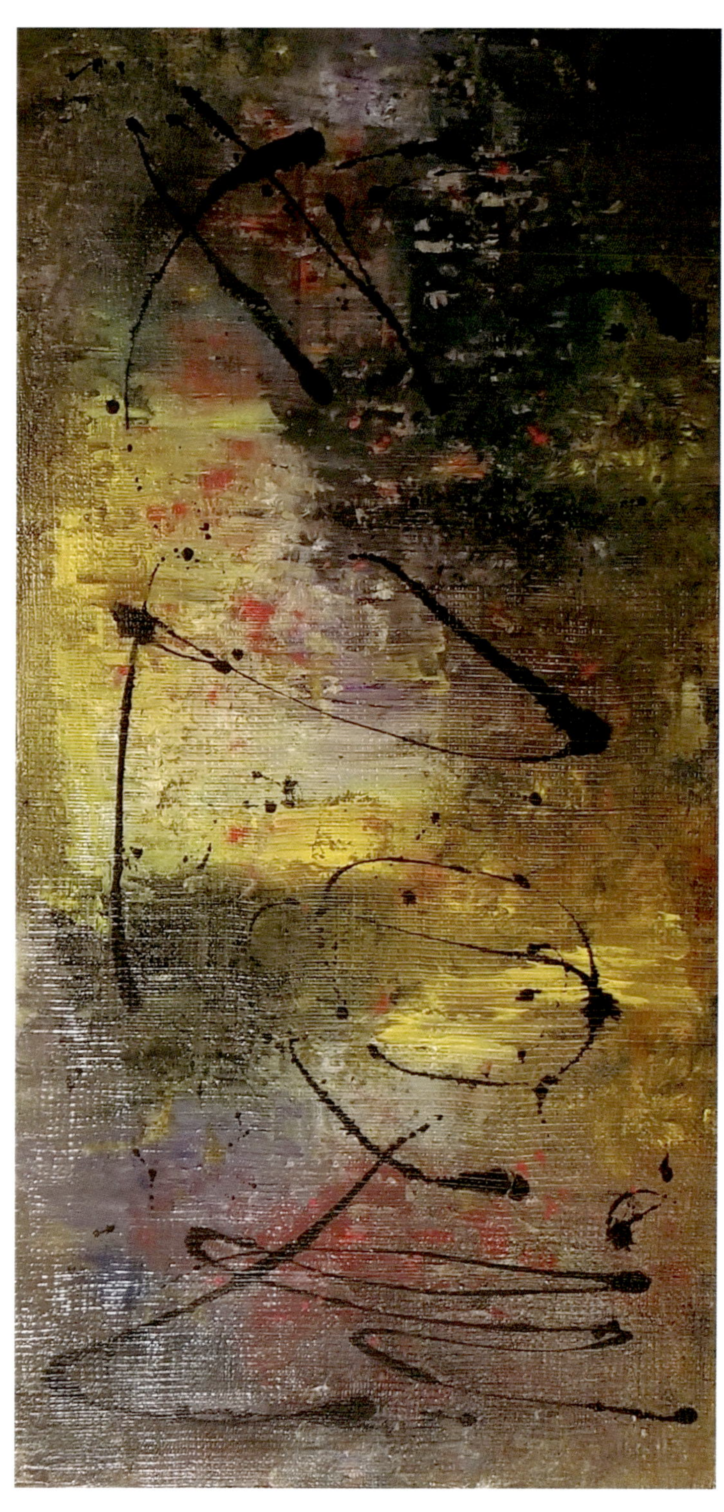

COLLECTOR:
STEPHEN AND
JACQUI LEWIS-KEMP

WELL ORIENTED (48X36)
2017

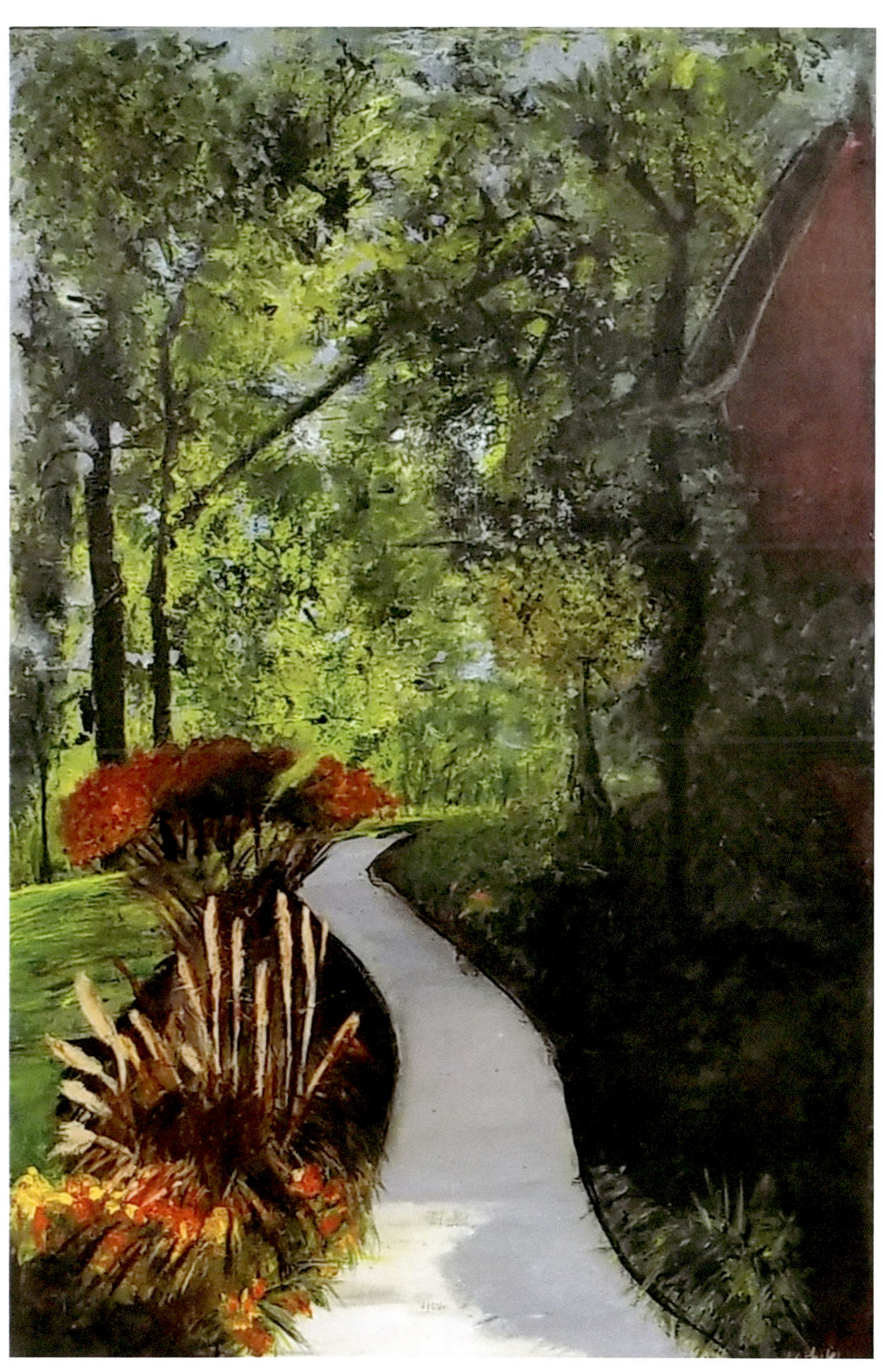

COLLECTOR:
FREDDIE + MARGARET WILSON

WALK WITH ME (24 X 36)
2016

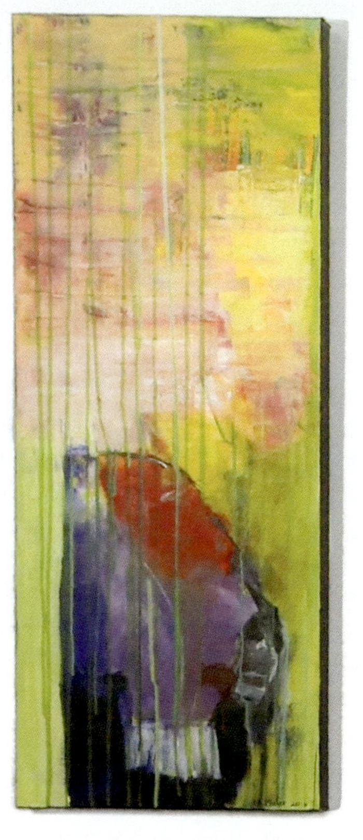

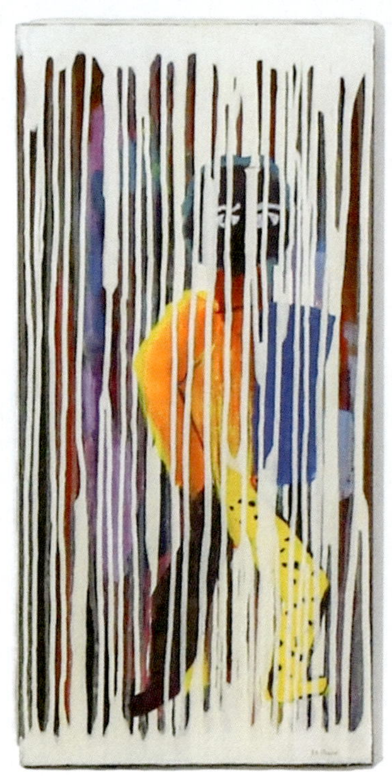

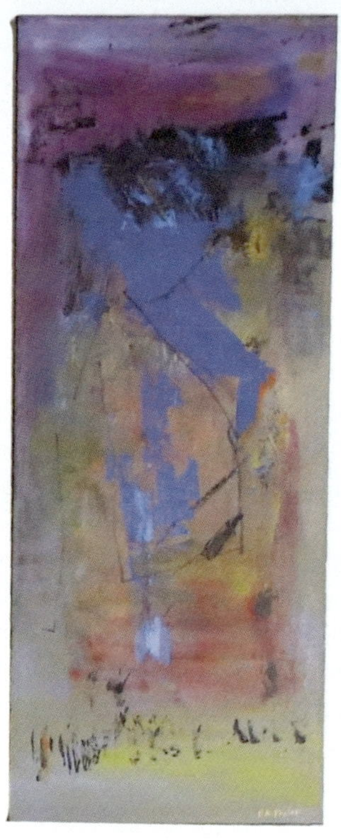

COLLECTOR:
DANNON + BRIGETTE HOLLY

FROM LEFT TO RIGHT:
INEFFABLE (16" X 40" X 1.5")
2017

WHITE WASHED (15" X 30" X 1.5")
2017

PURPLE REIGN (16" X 40" X 1.5")
2017

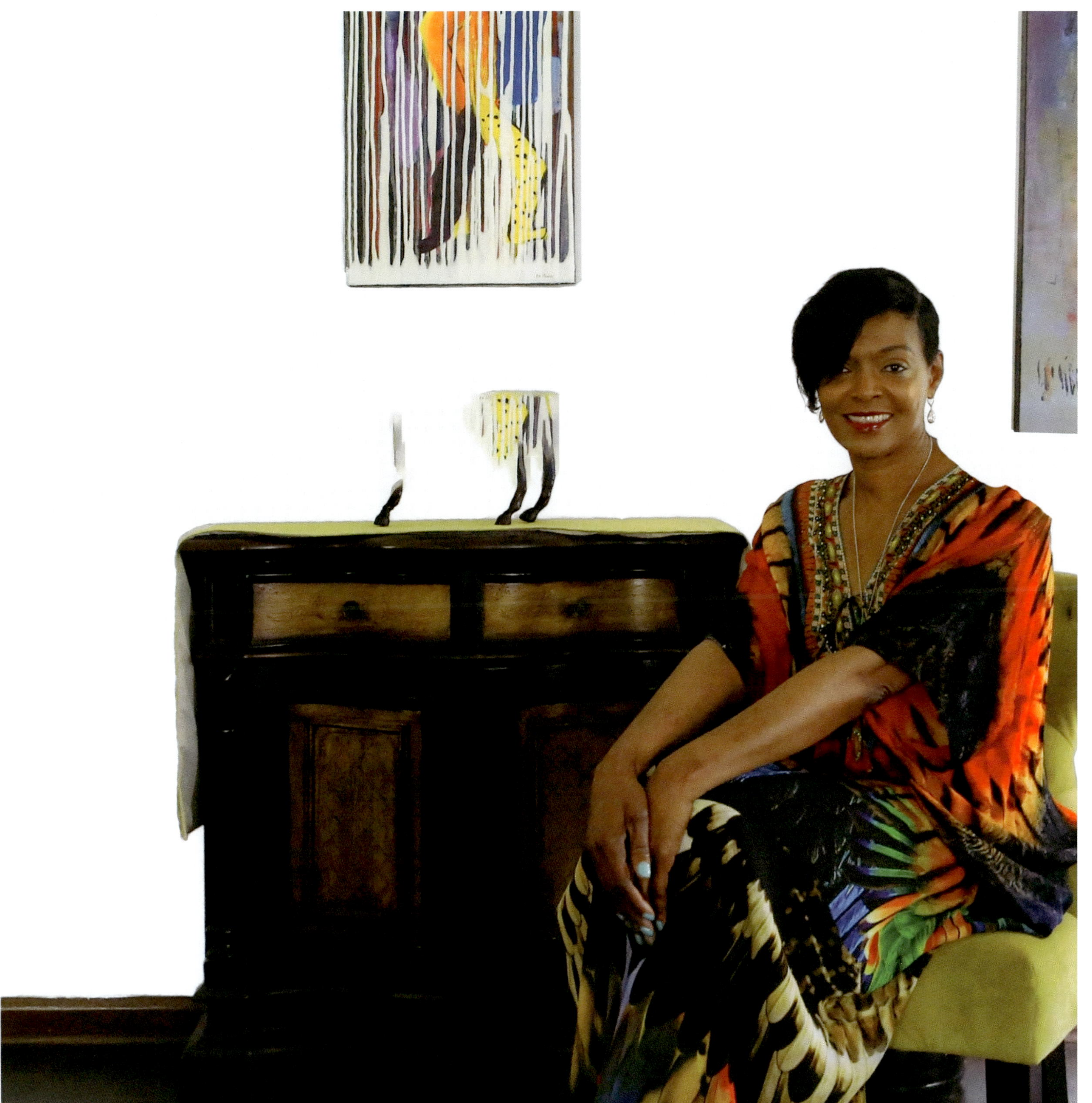

PHOTOS BY GARY WASHINGTON

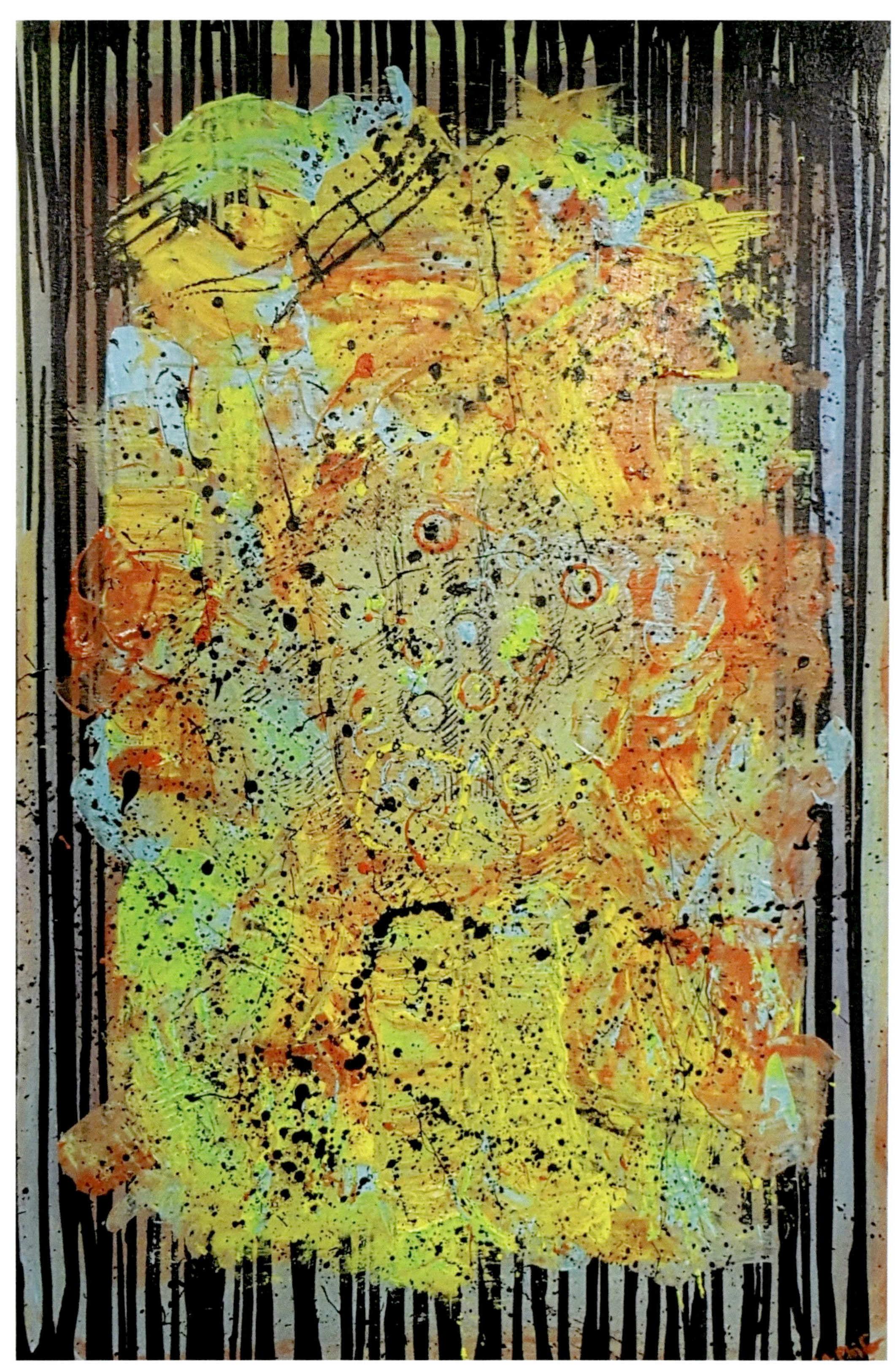

UNBOUND (25X36)
2015

MACK ALIVE
PERMANENT COLLECTION

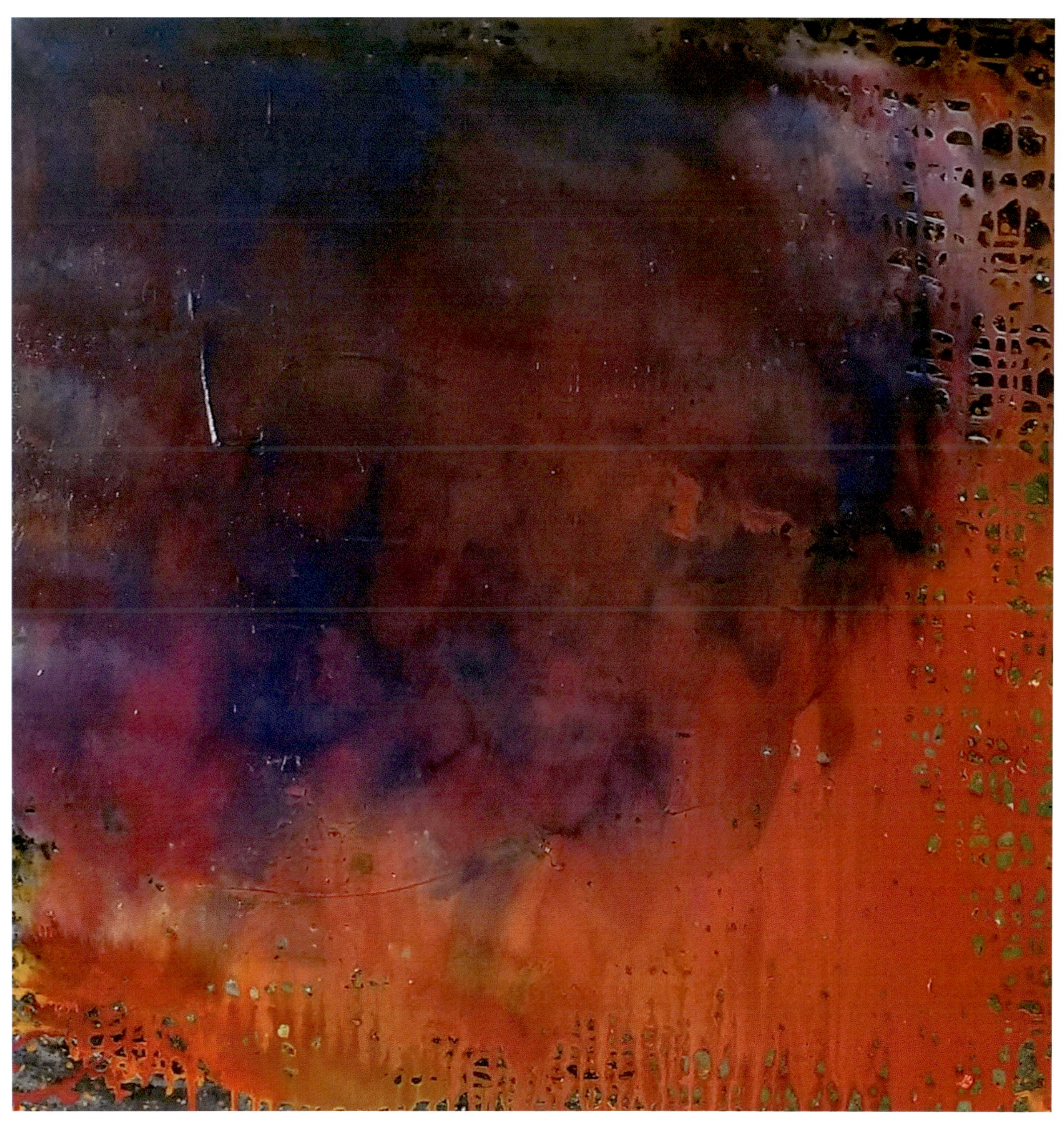

UNTITLED 2019 COLLECTOR: JAMES + JOAN LEMAHIEU FORSTER

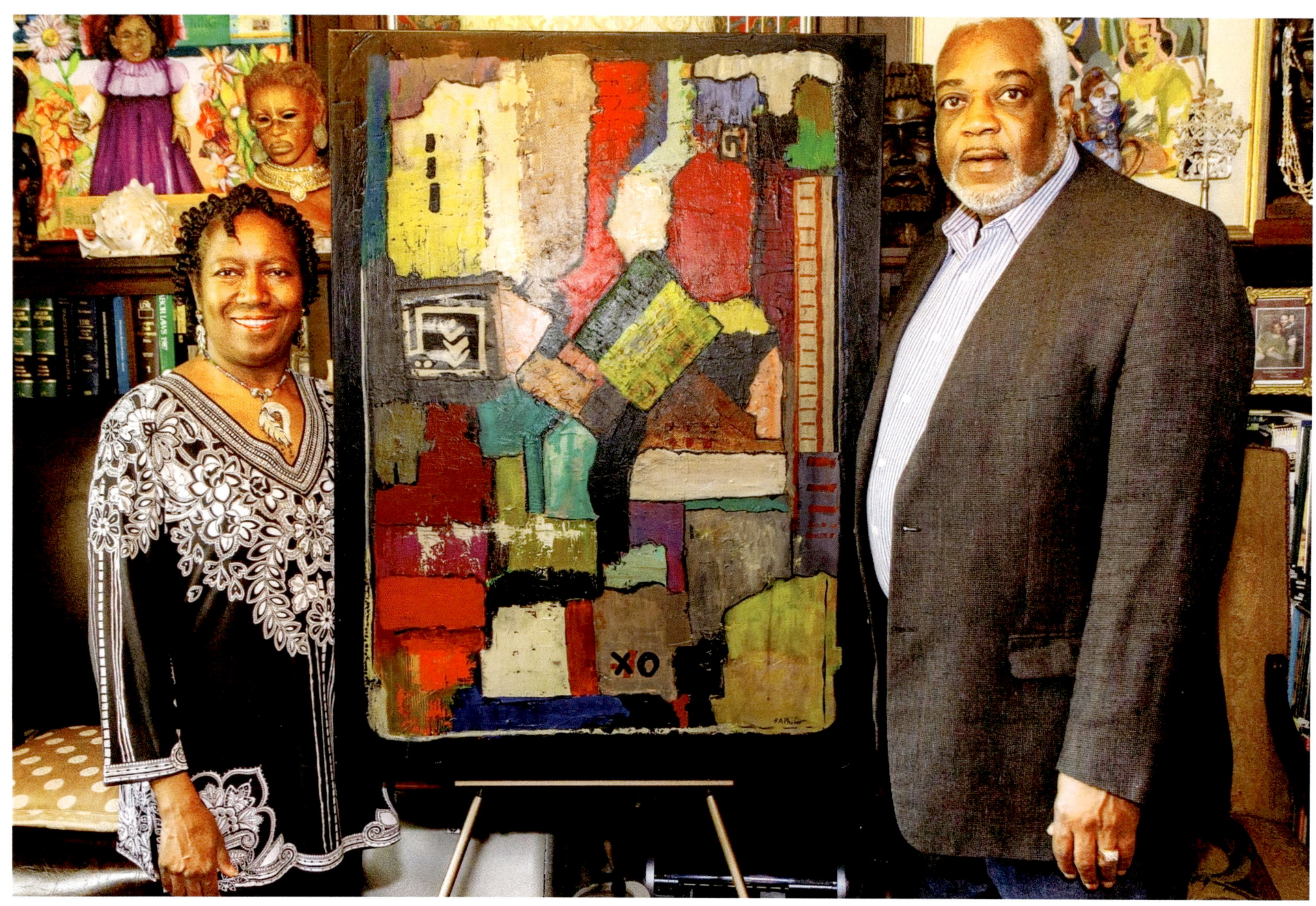

COLLECTOR:
DAVID + LINDA WHITAKER

FOR GILDA, BLOCK BY BLOCK (30" X 40")
2018

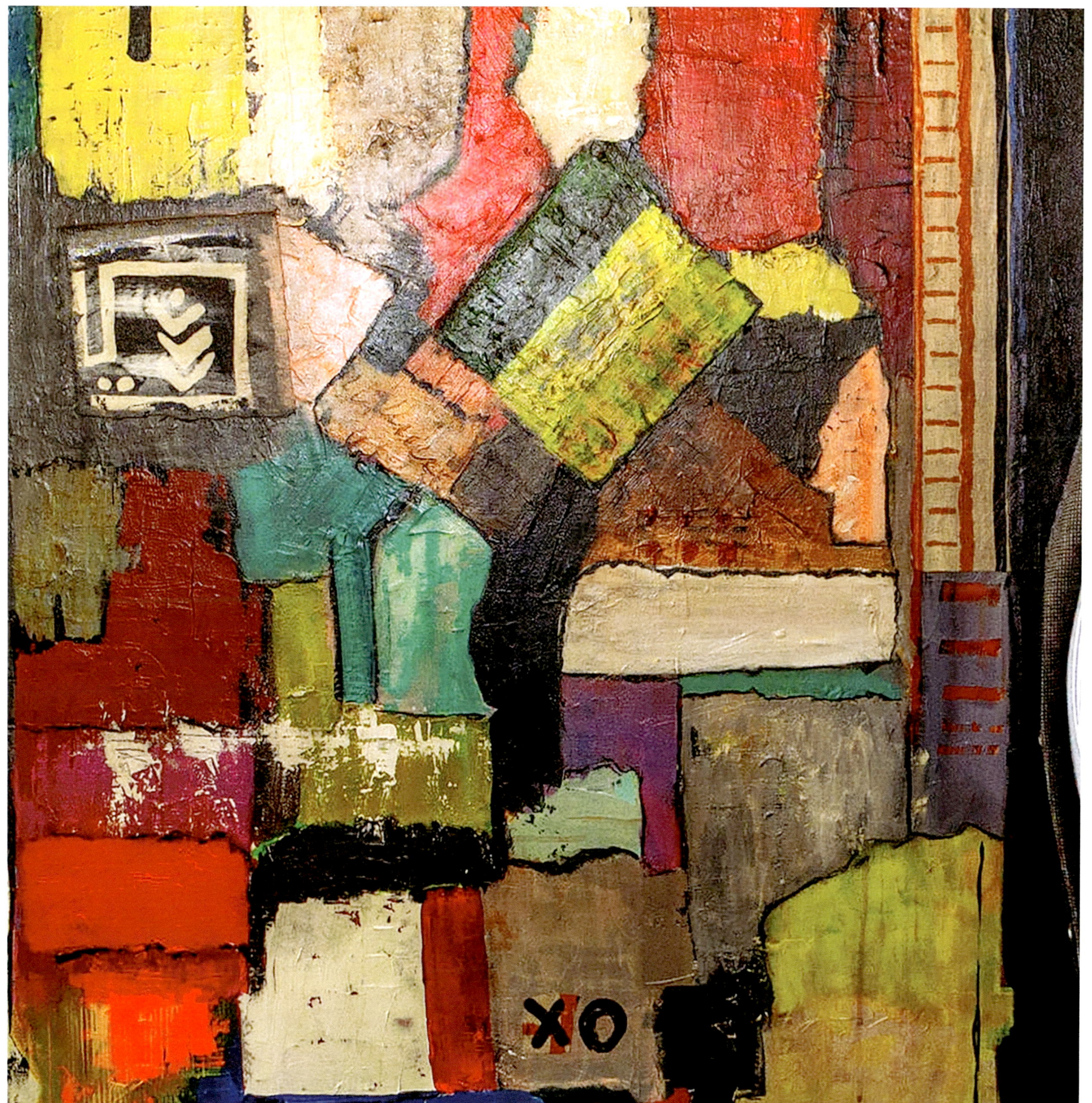
XO

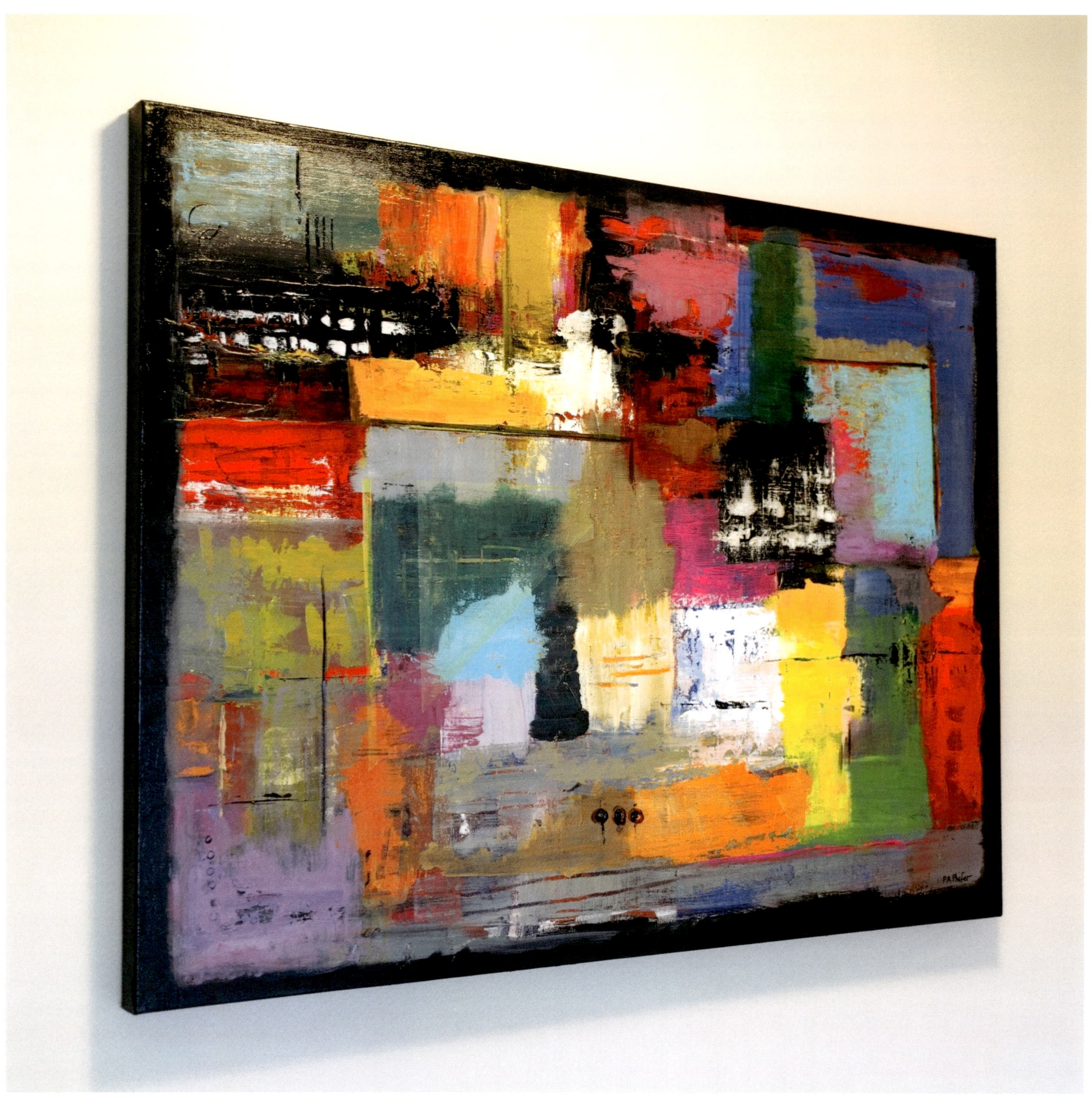

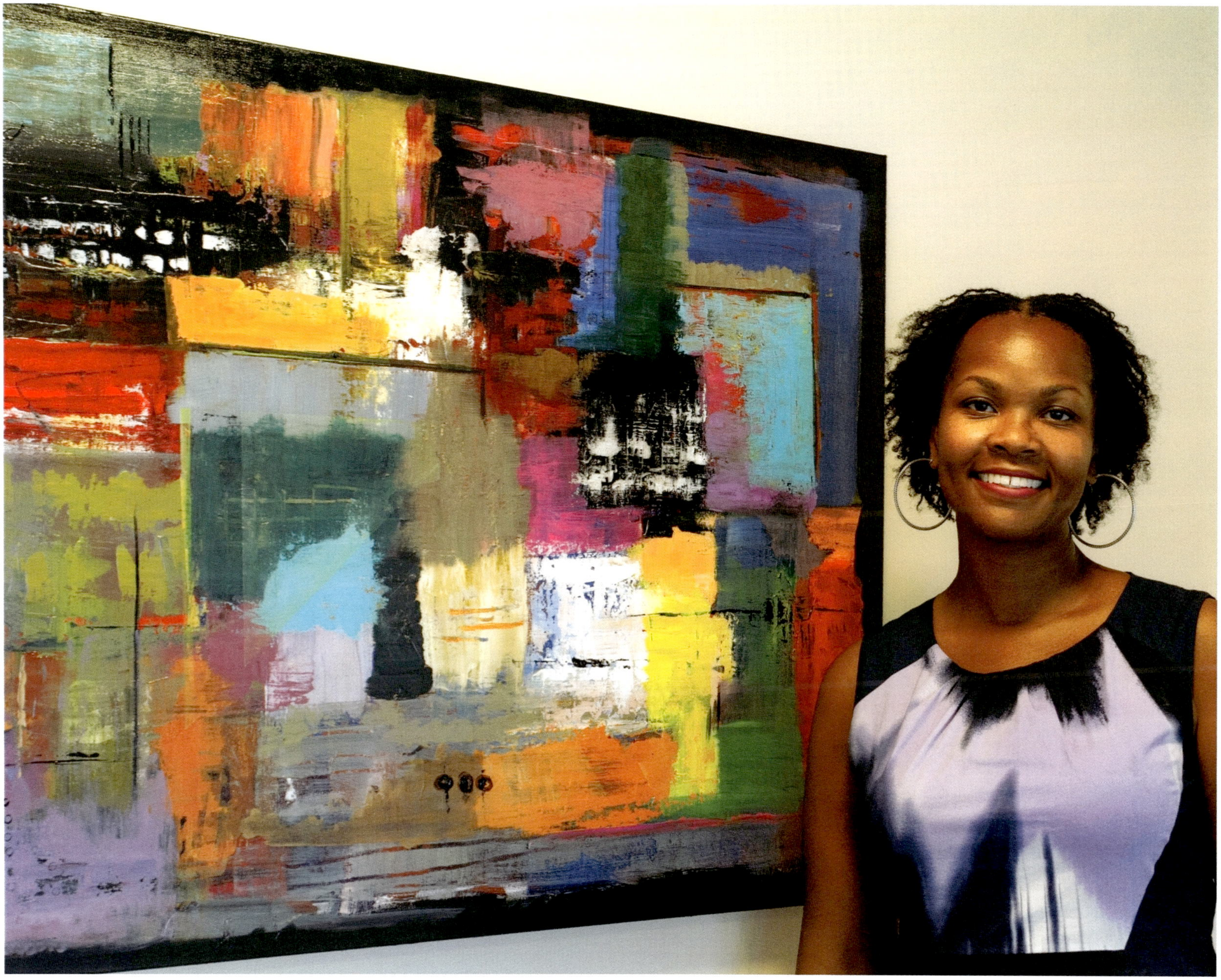

PHOTO BY GARY WASHINGTON

COLLECTOR:
KETURAH JEFFERIES

FOR GILDA #3 (40" X 30")
2018

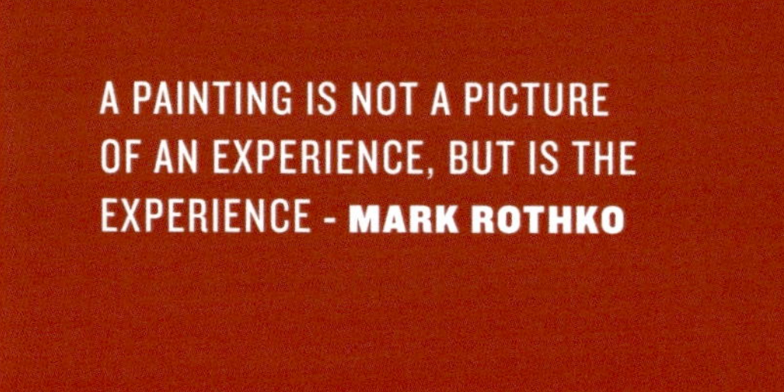

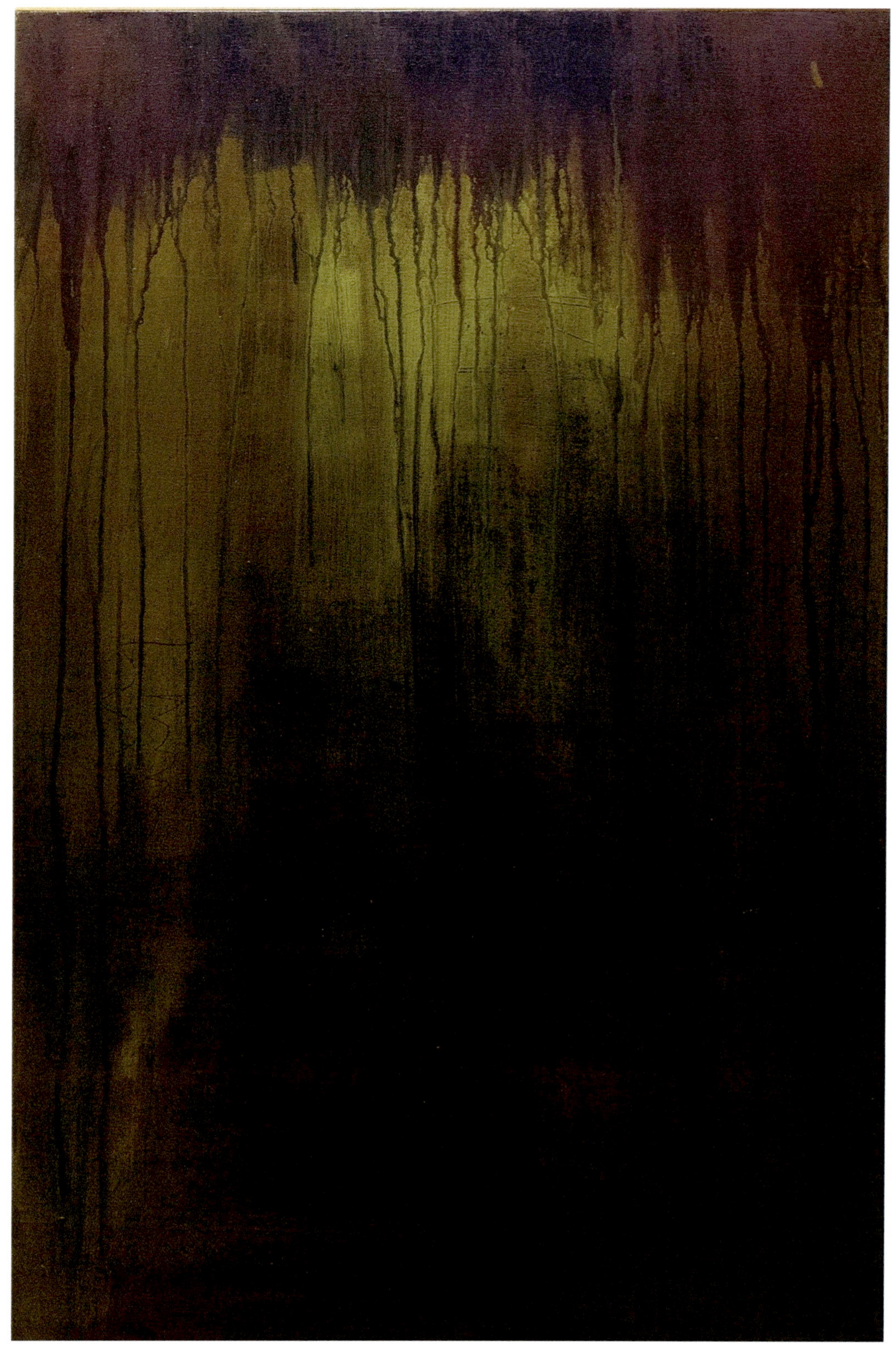

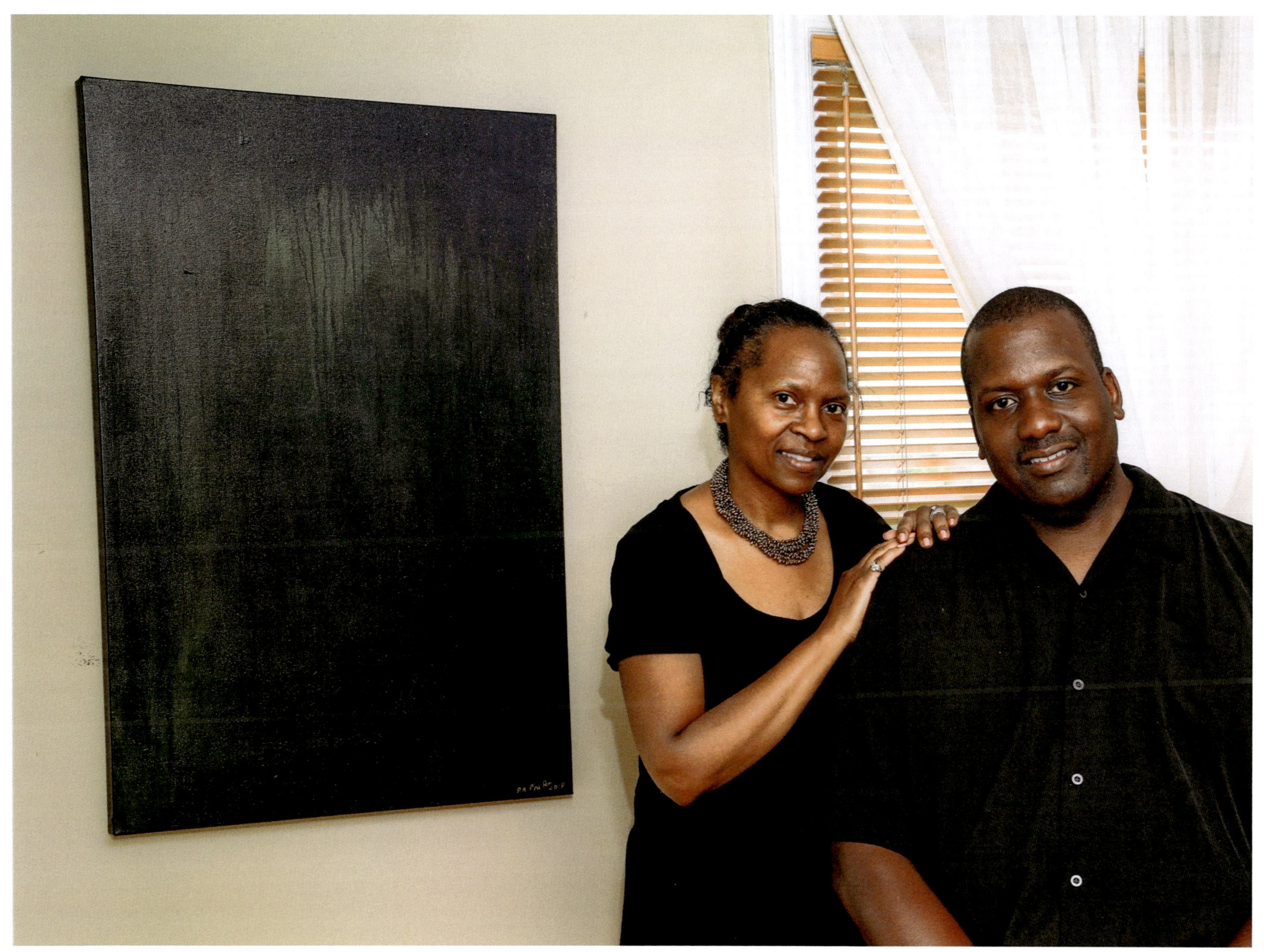

PHOTO BY ROGERS FOSTER

COLLECTOR:
BYRON + TRACY FOSTER

CALM (24" X 36")
2018

NO MATTER WHAT I DO, THERE'S NOT A DAY THAT I'M NOT AN ARTIST.
- ED CLARKE

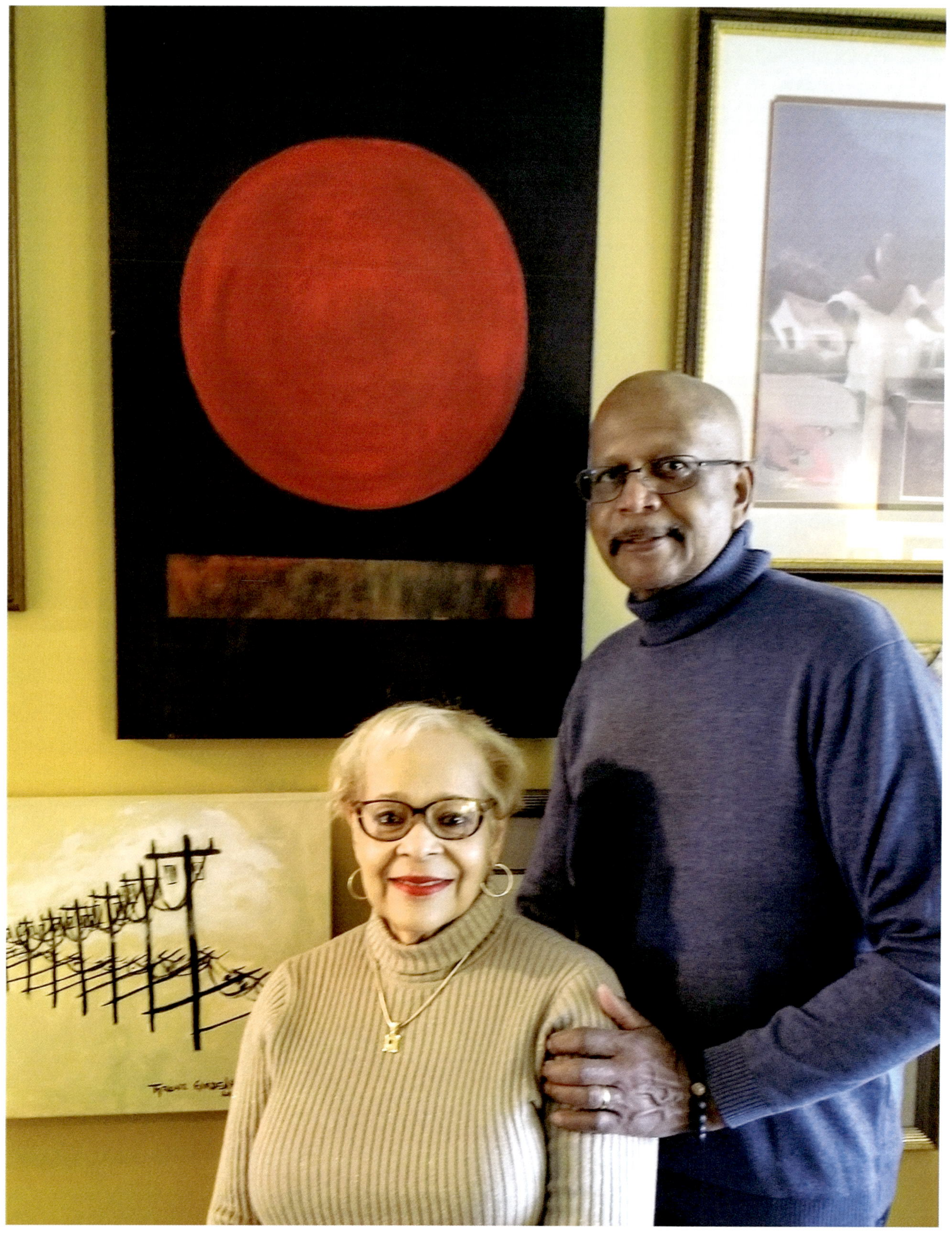

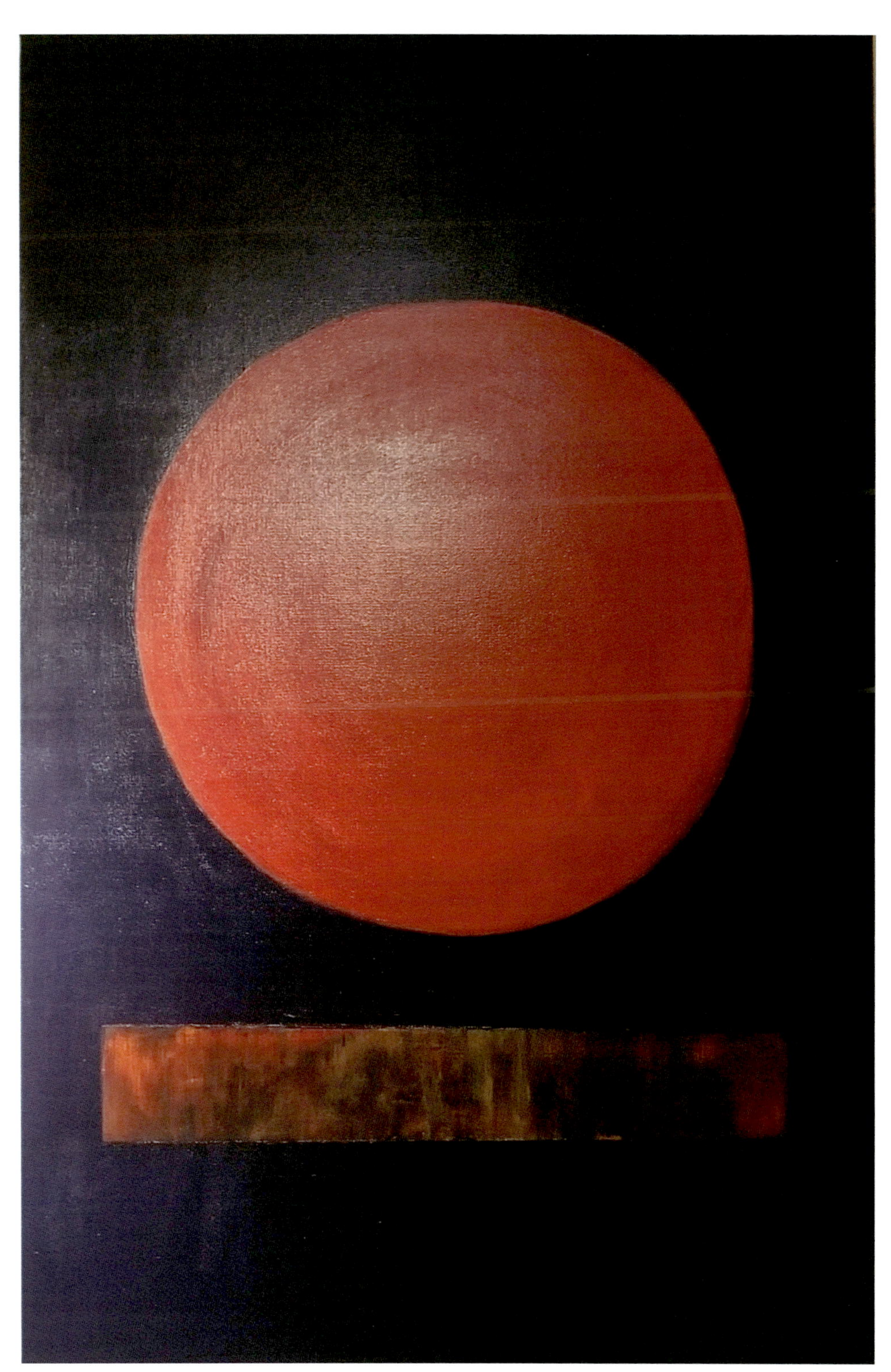

COLLECTOR:
OSCAR + JOAN BRITTON

DOT DASH 2 (24" X 36")
2018

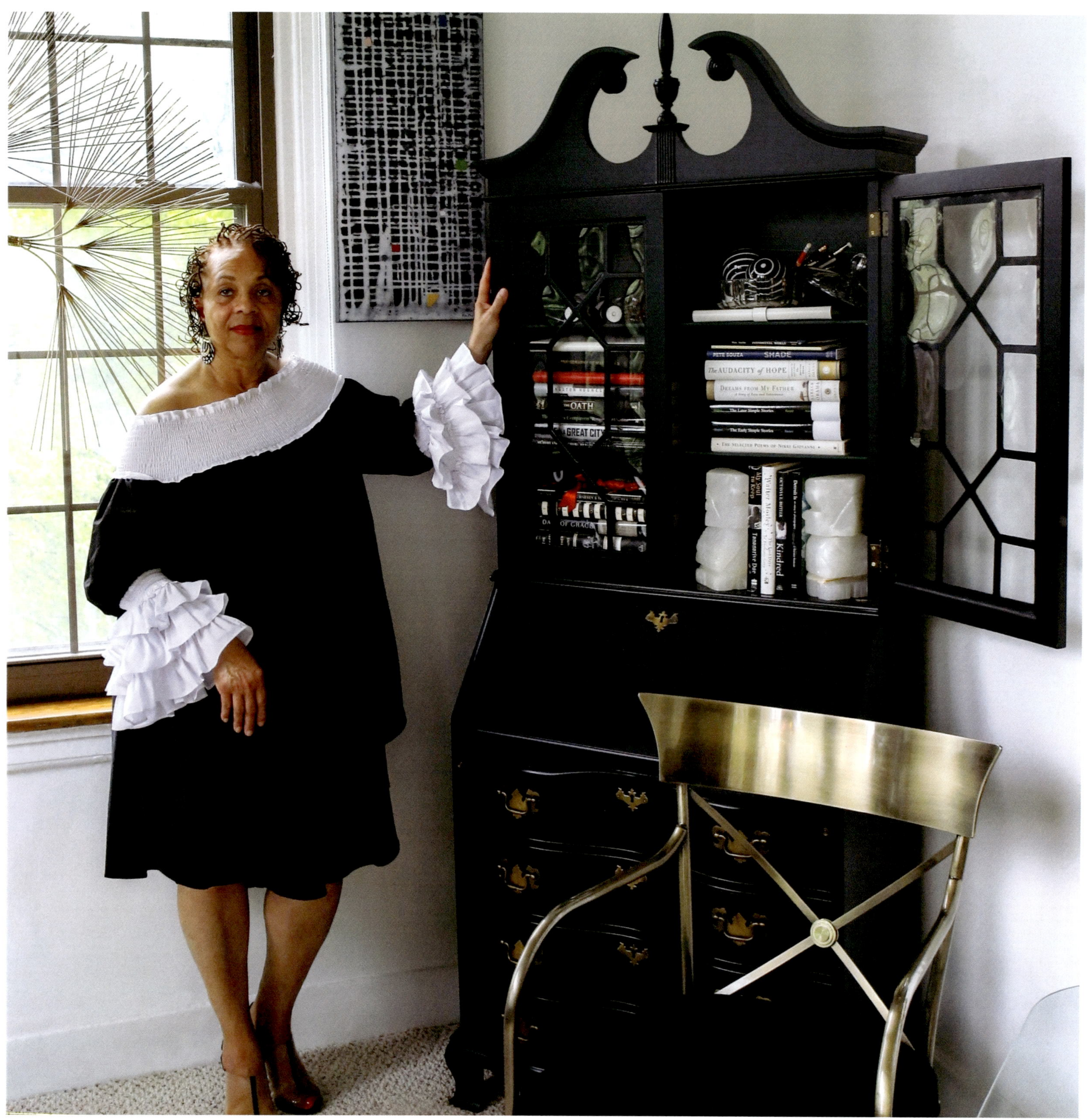
PETE SOUZA SHADE
The AUDACITY of HOPE
DREAMS FROM MY FATHER
THE OATH
GREAT CITY
The Later Simple Stories
The Early Simple Stories
THE SELECTED POEMS OF NIKKI GIOVANNI
Walter Mosley
Tananarive Due
Kindred

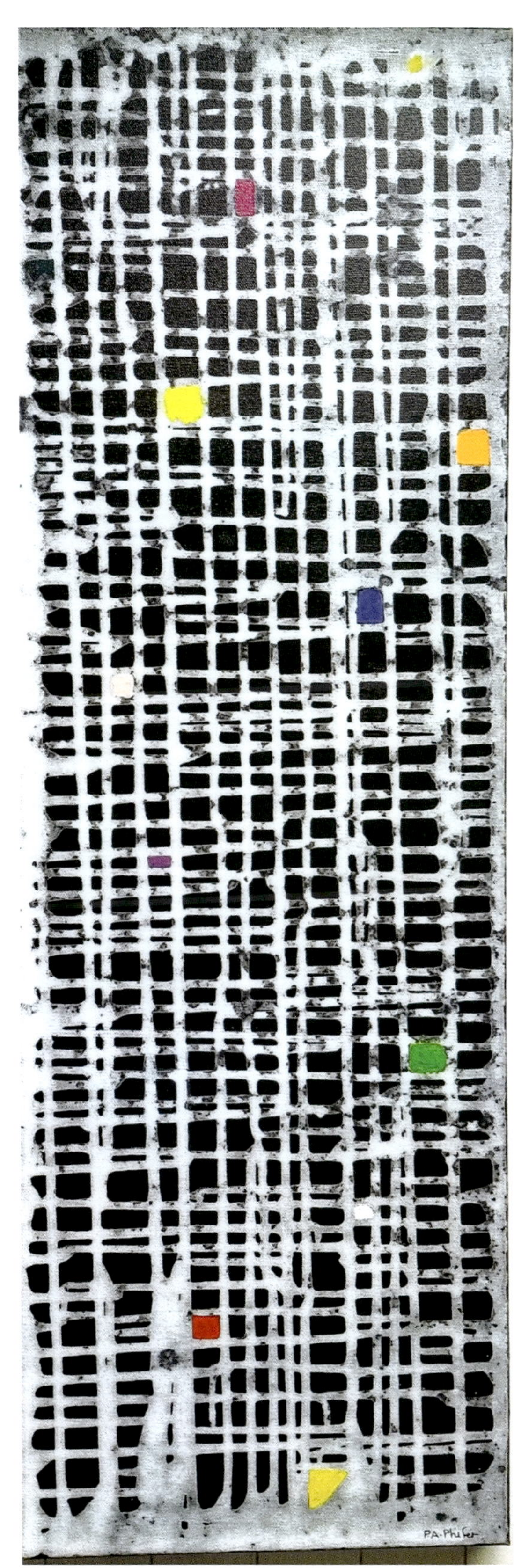

PHOTO BY GARY WASHINGTON

COLLECTOR:
SHARON GAMBLIN

STAY IN YOUR OWN PANE (16" X 48")
2019

THE USE OF COLOR IN MY PAINTINGS IS OF PARAMOUNT IMPORTANCE TO ME. THROUGH COLOR I HAVE SOUGHT TO CONCENTRATE ON BEAUTY AND HAPPINESS, RATHER THAN ON MAN'S INHUMANITY TO MAN. - **ALMA THOMAS**

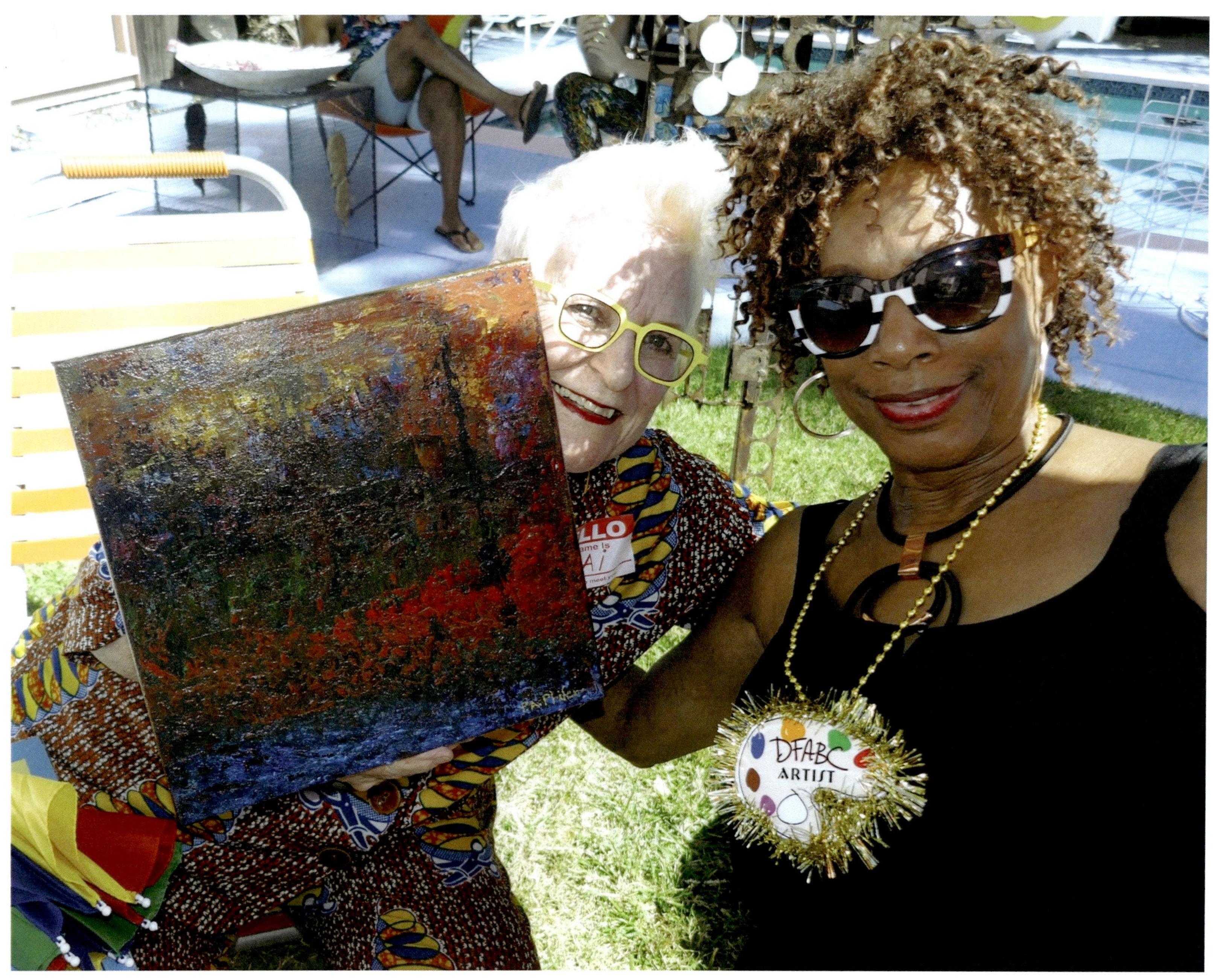

COLLECTOR:
GAI GHERARDI
(LOS ANGELES)

UNTITLED (12" X 12")
2018

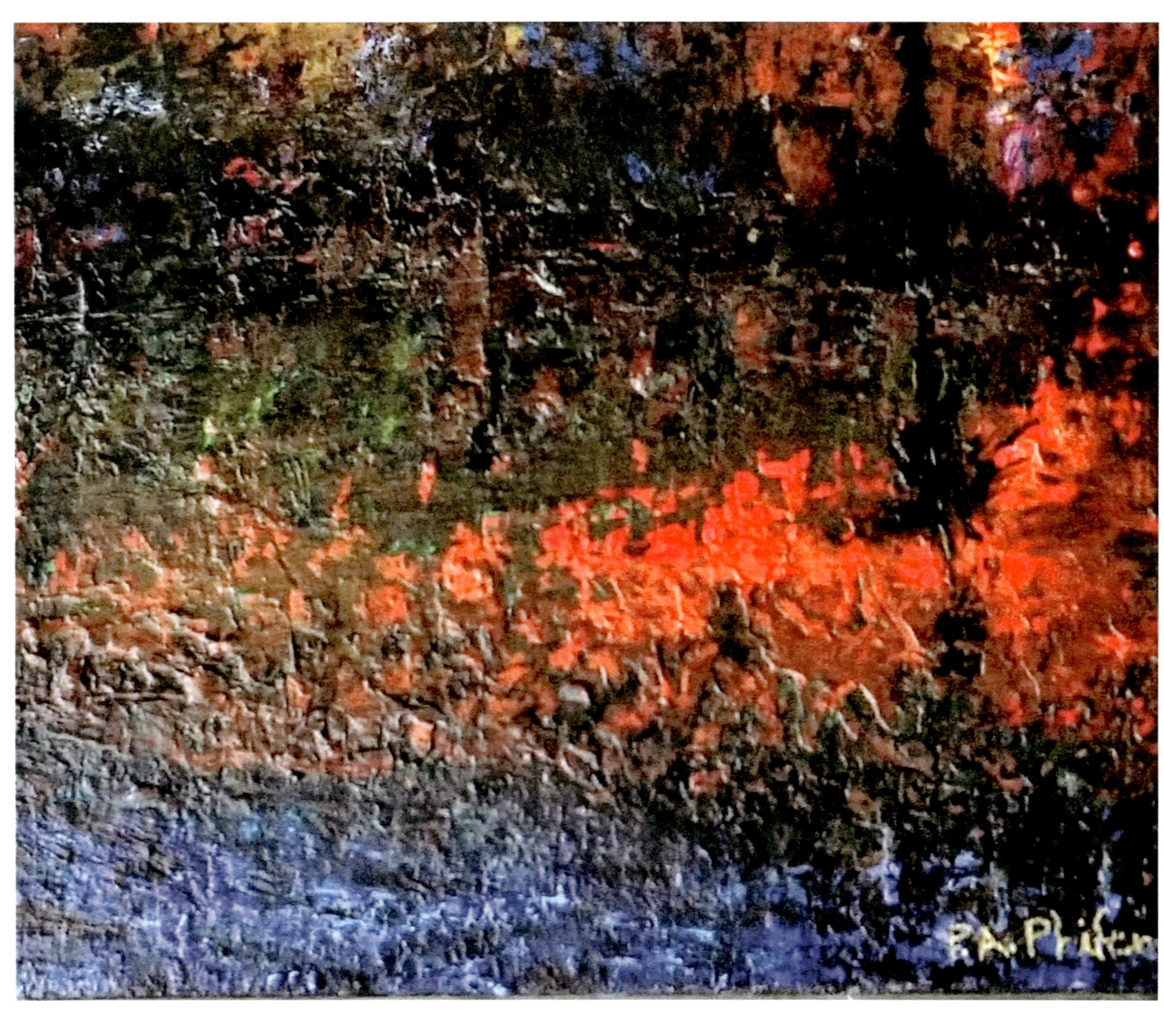

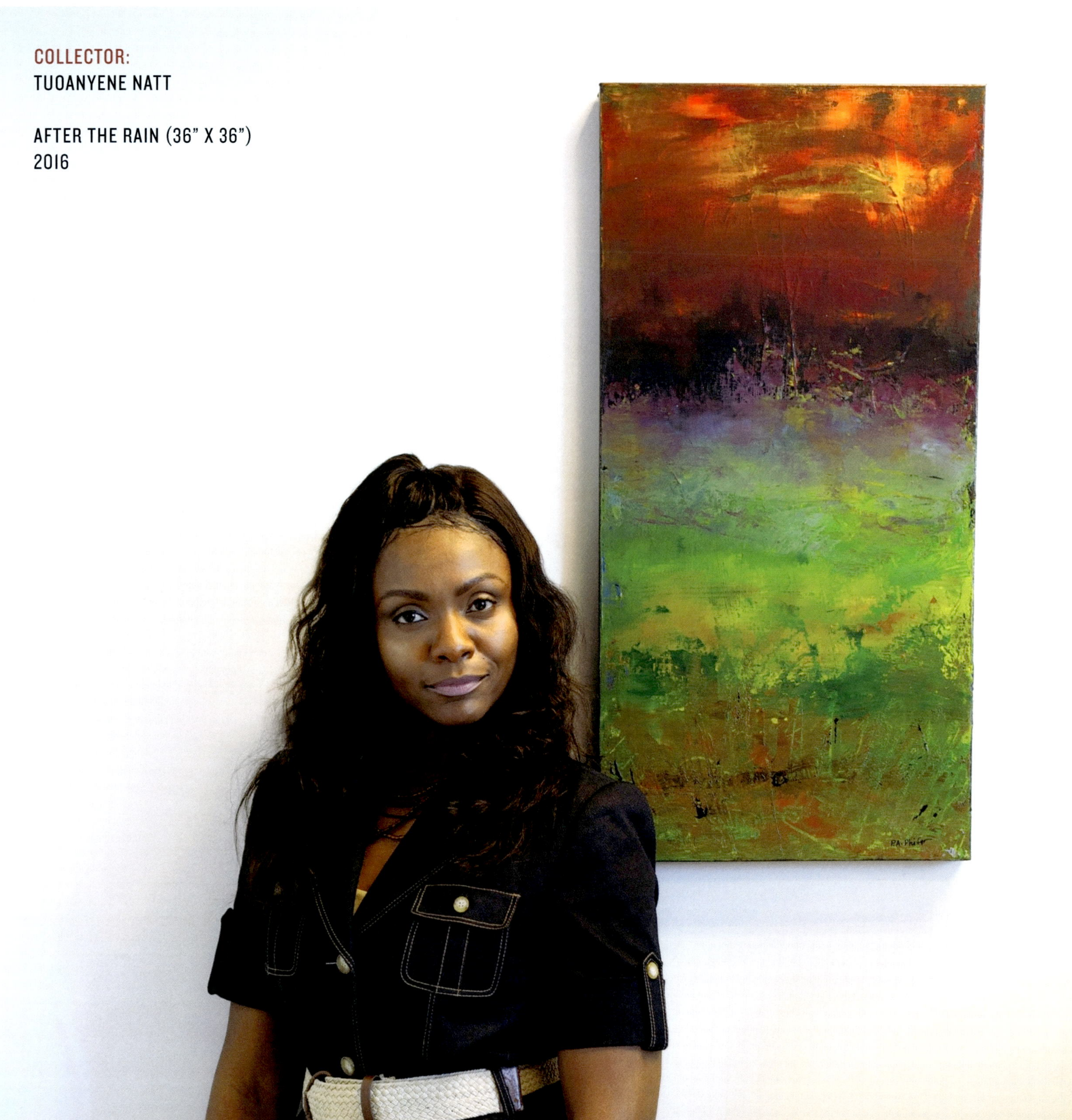

COLLECTOR:
TUOANYENE NATT

AFTER THE RAIN (36" X 36")
2016

PHOTO BY GARY WASHINGTON

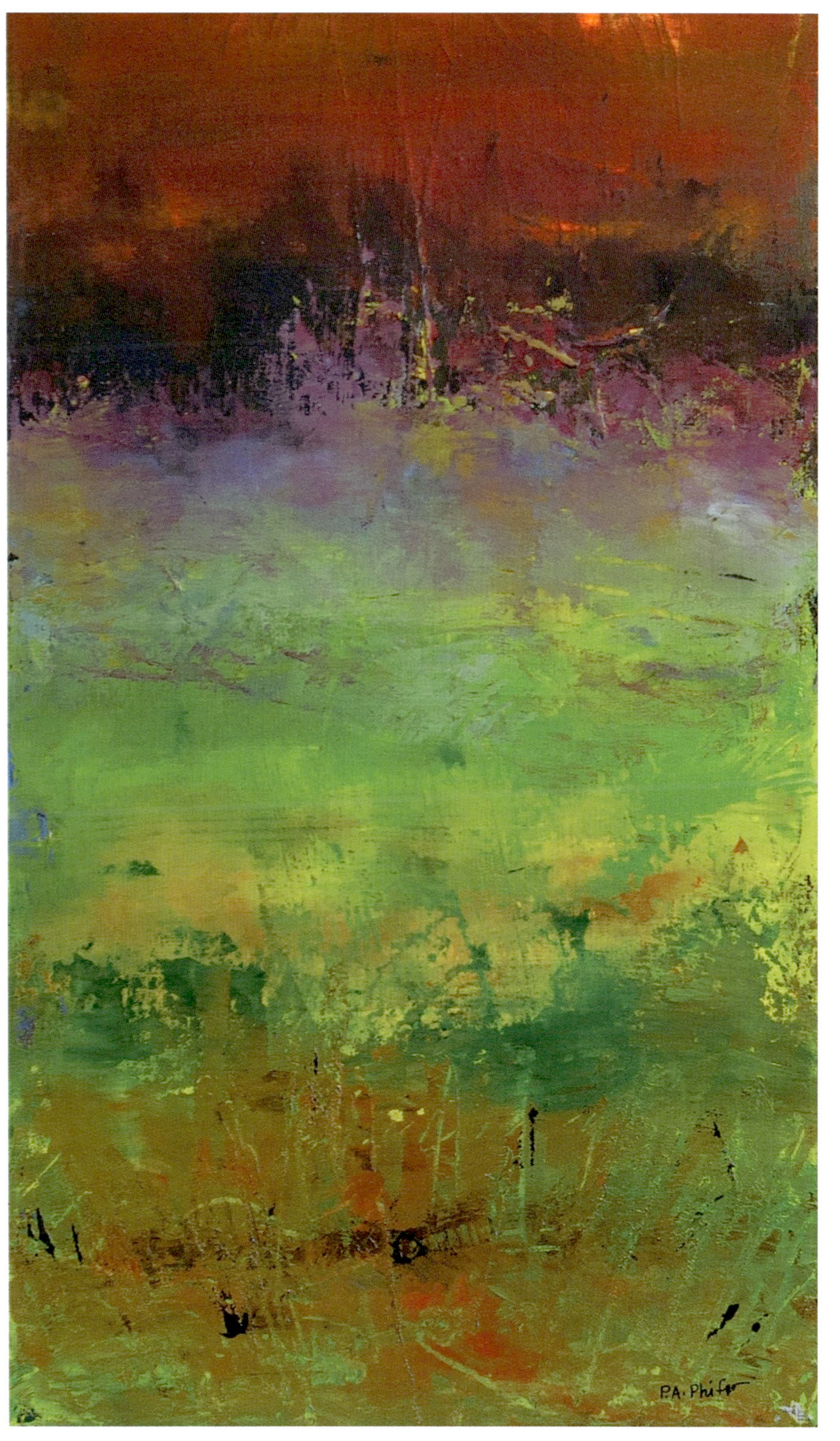
P.A. Phifer

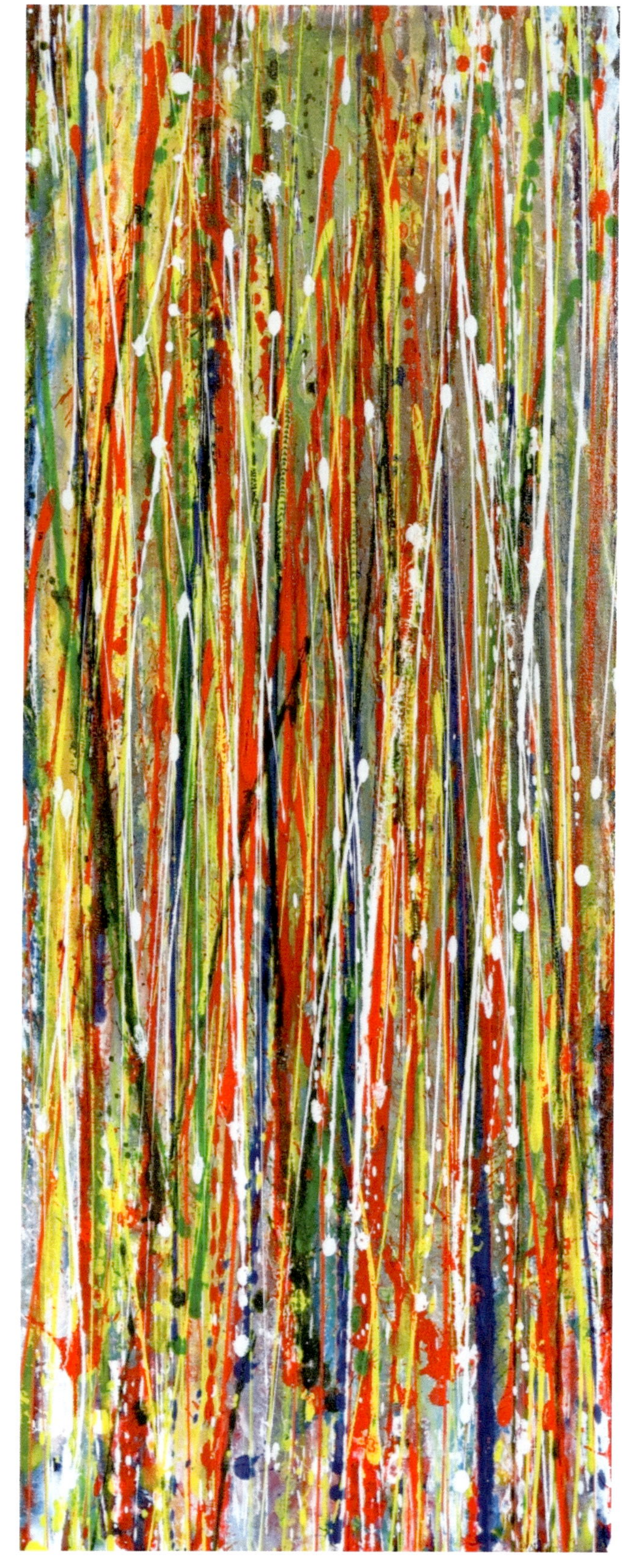

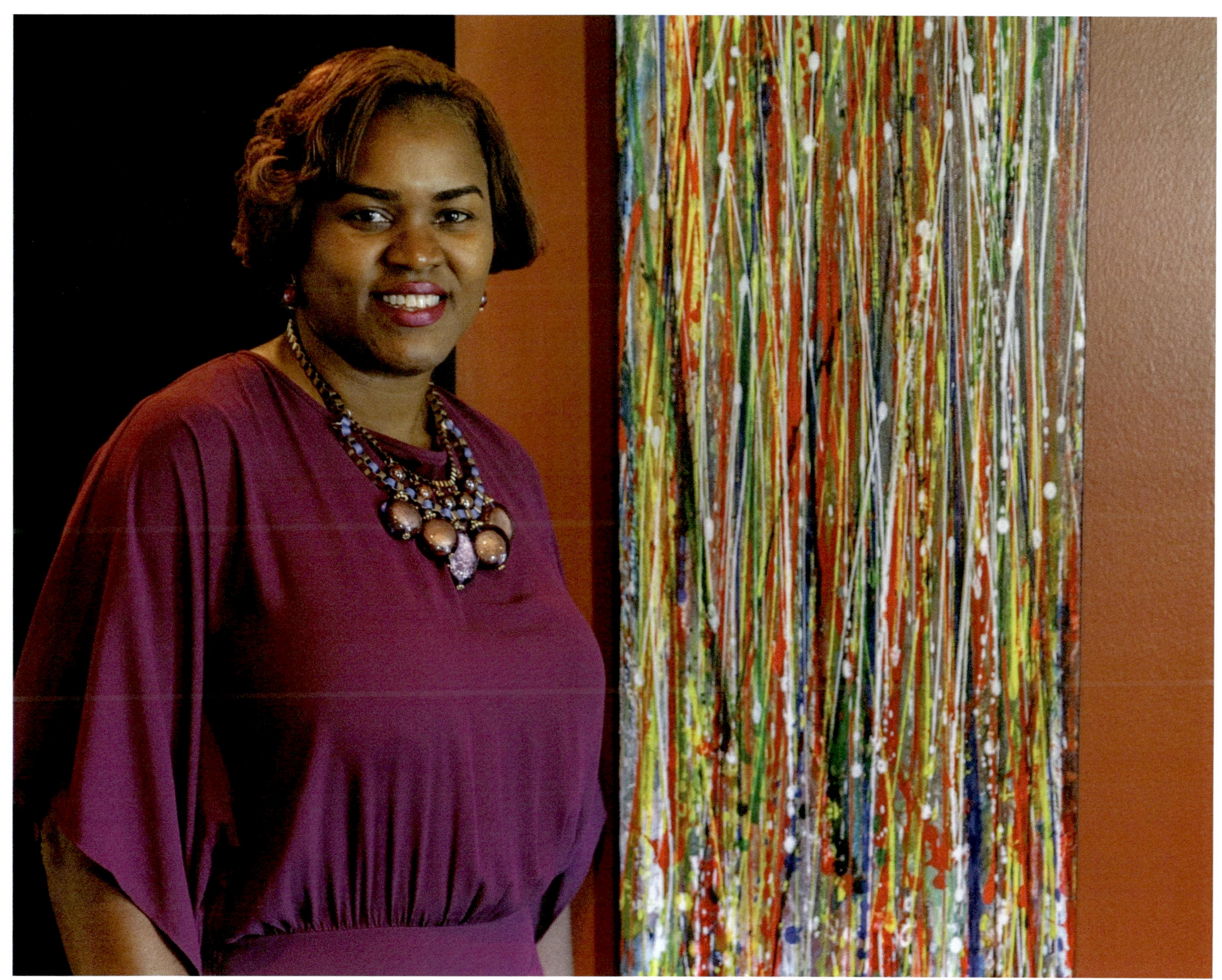

COLLECTOR:
EUCLIDES +
YOLANDA DURFIELD

COLOR MY WORLD
(16" X 40")
2018

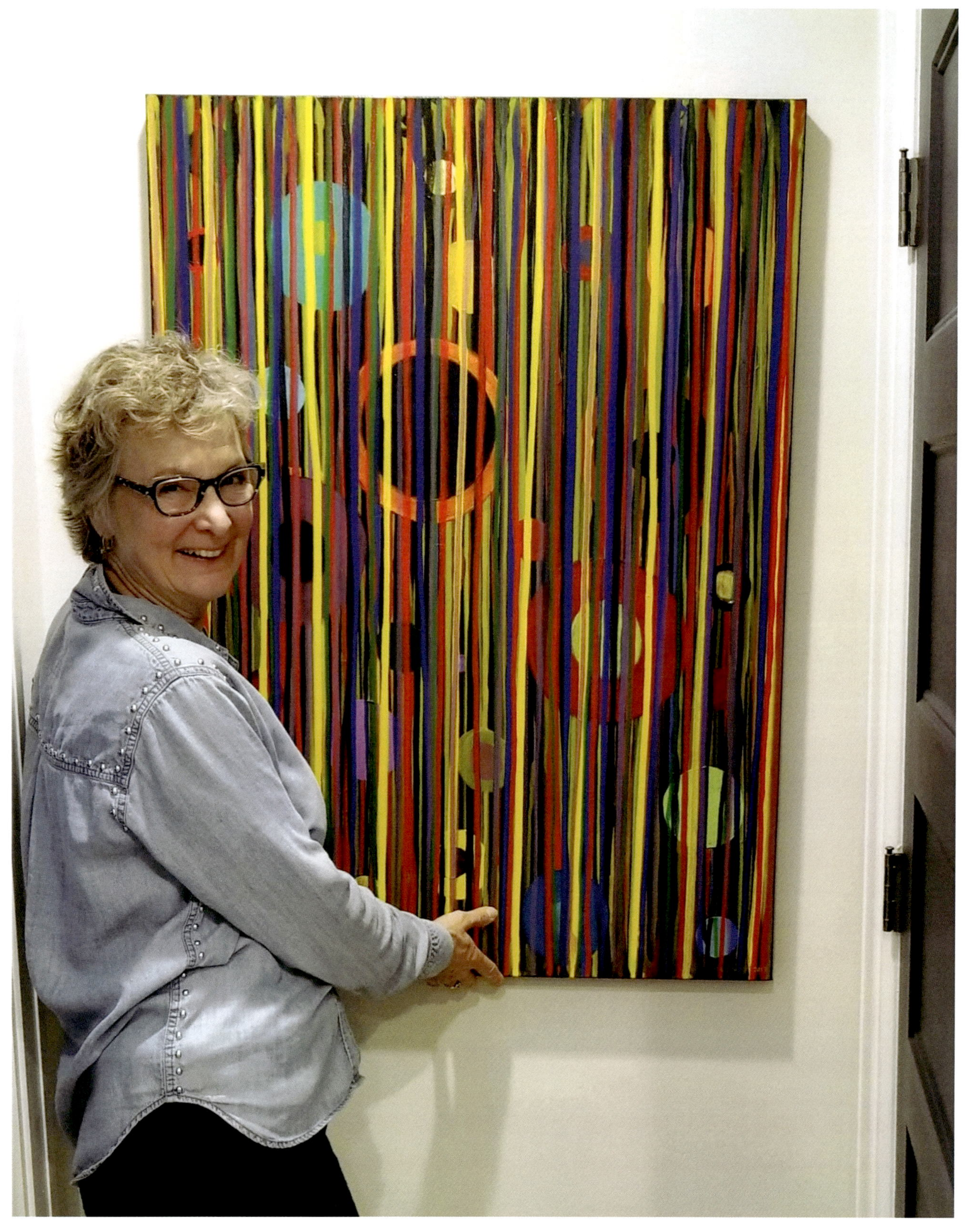

COLLECTOR:
JAMES + JOAN
LEMAHIEU FORSTER

CIRCLES OF LOVE
AND FRIENDSHIP
(30X40)
2018

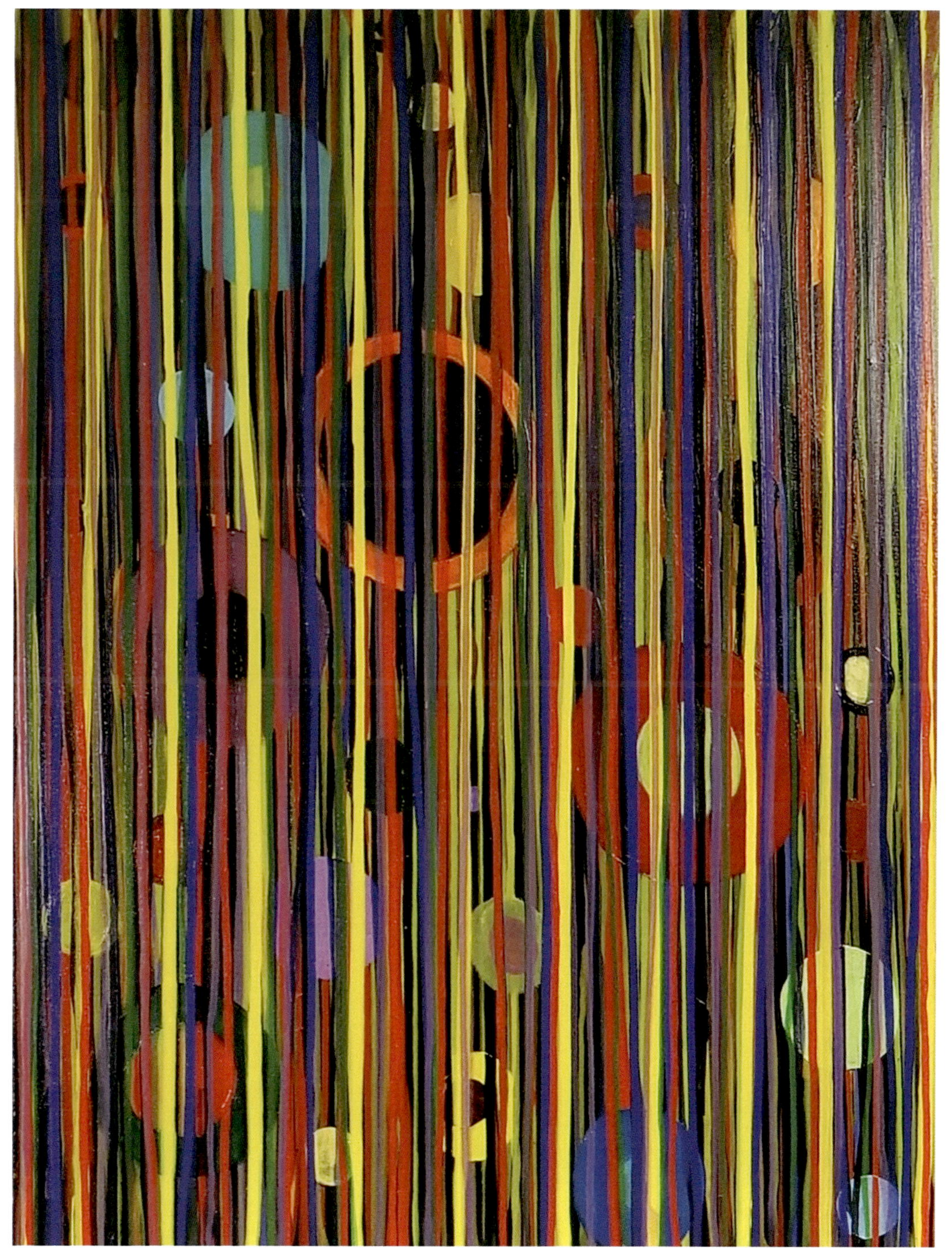

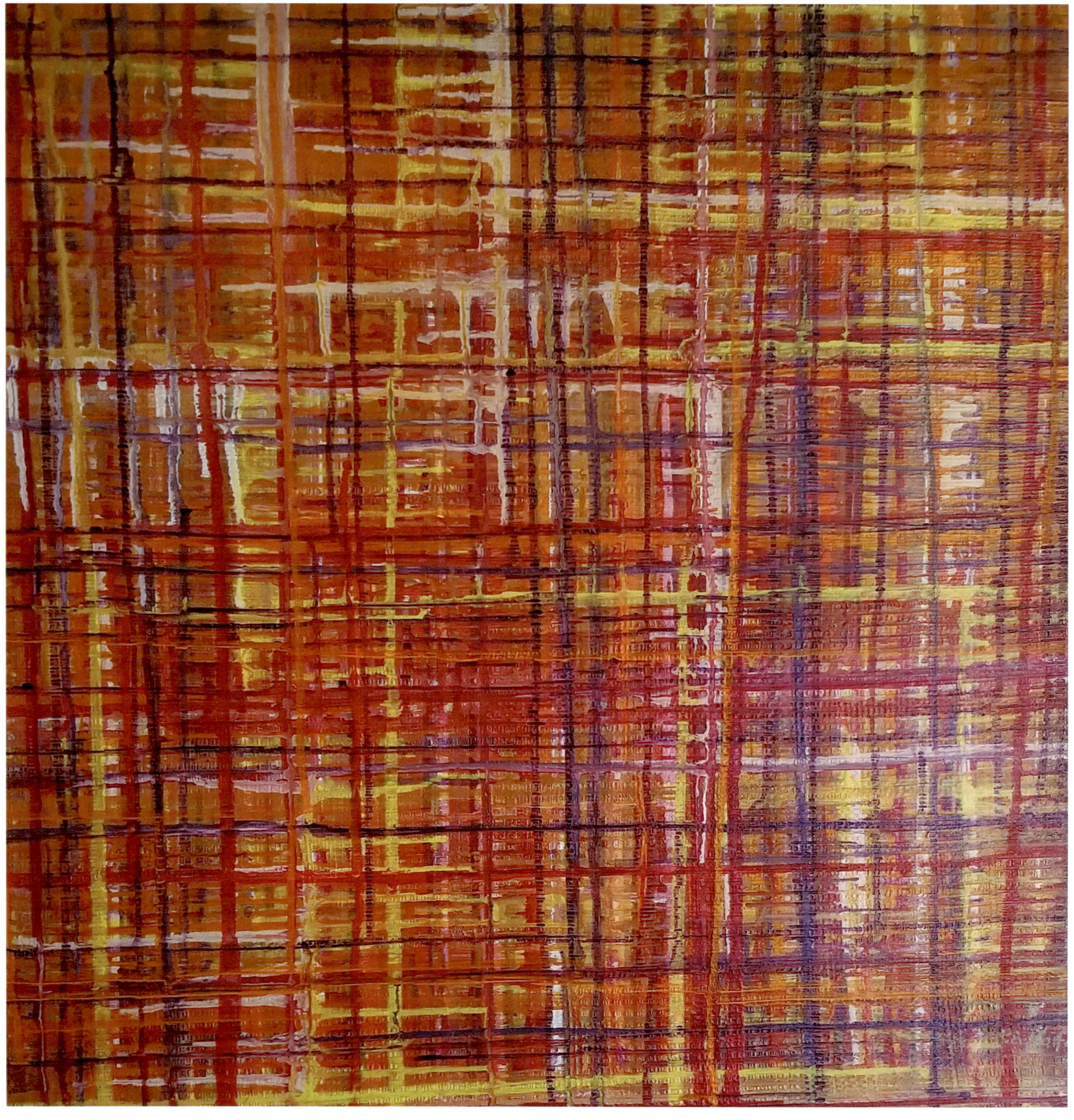

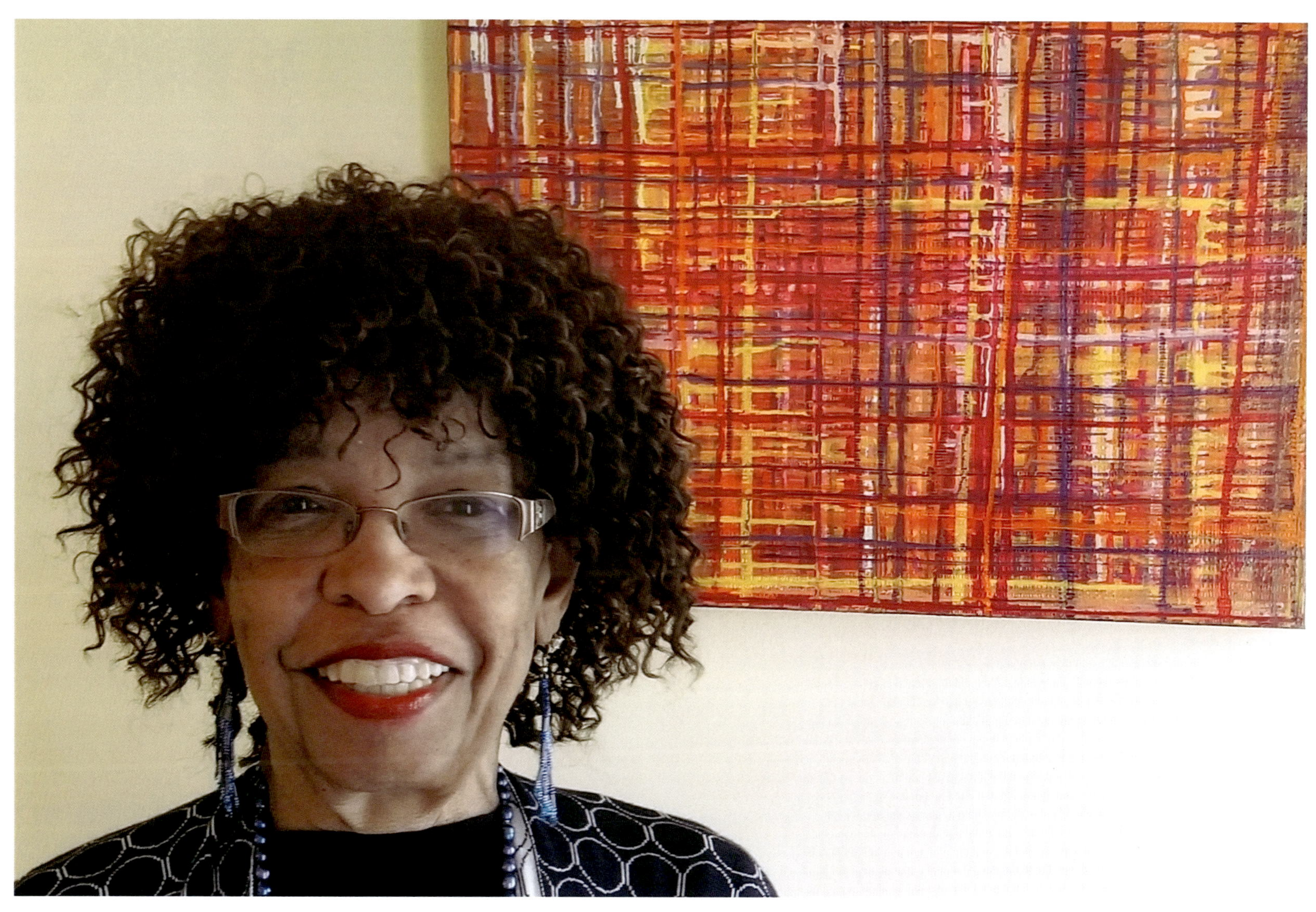

COLLECTOR:
PATRICIA BAKER

INTEMPERATE (24X24)
2016

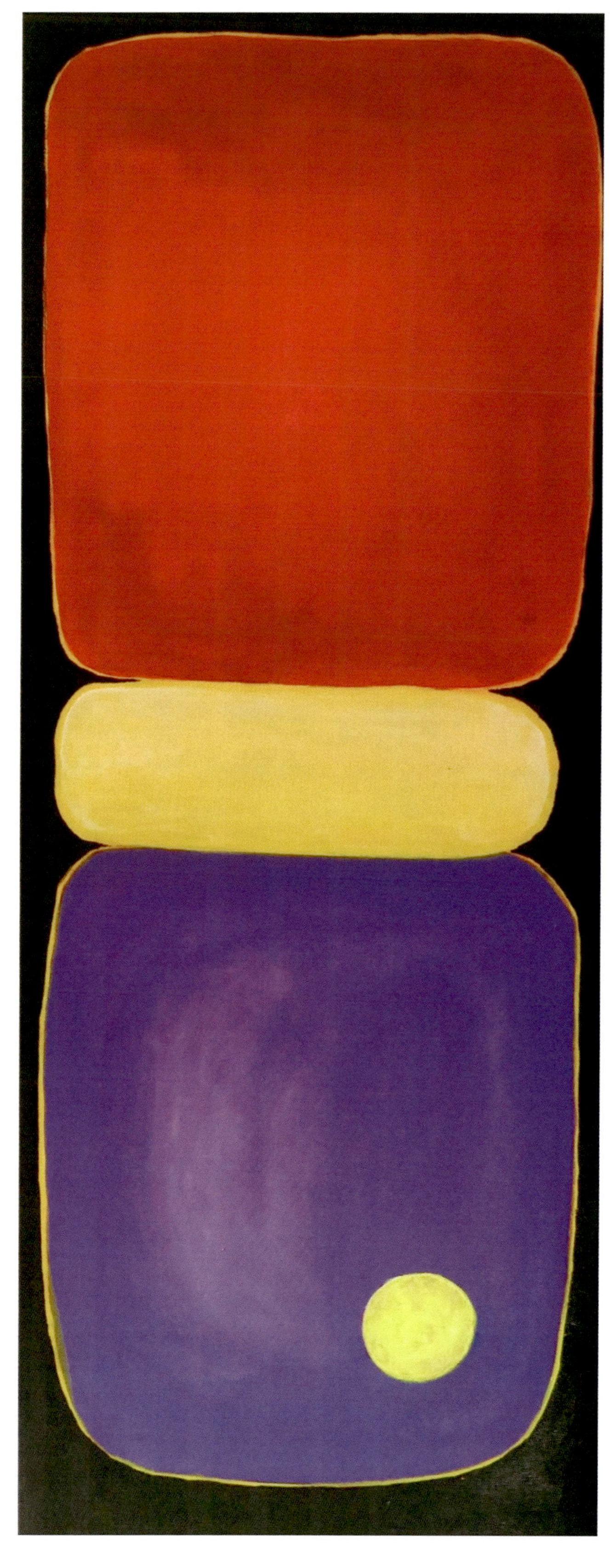

COLLECTOR:
CHARLENE URESY

YOU ARE HERE #4 (16X40)
2016

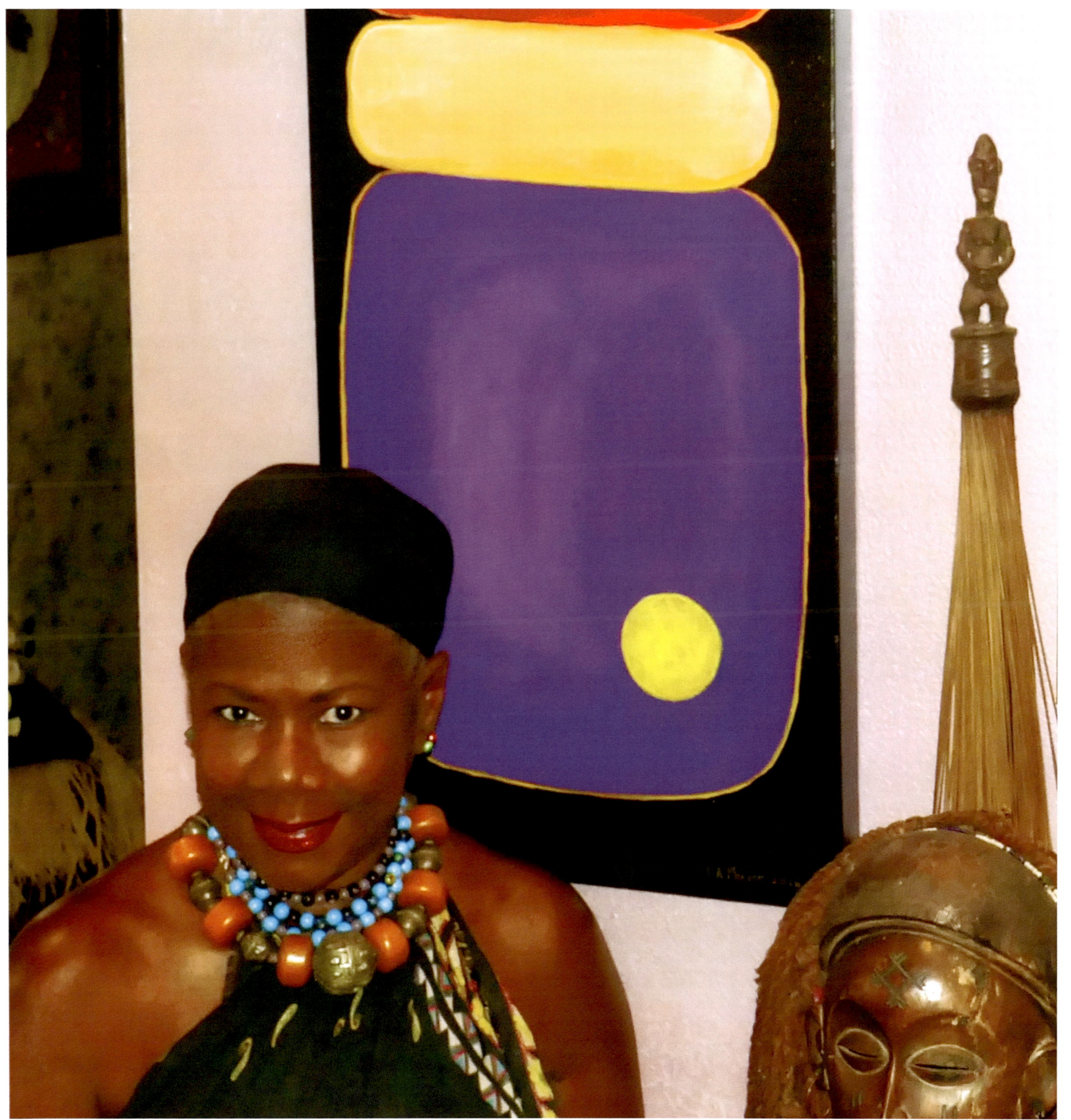

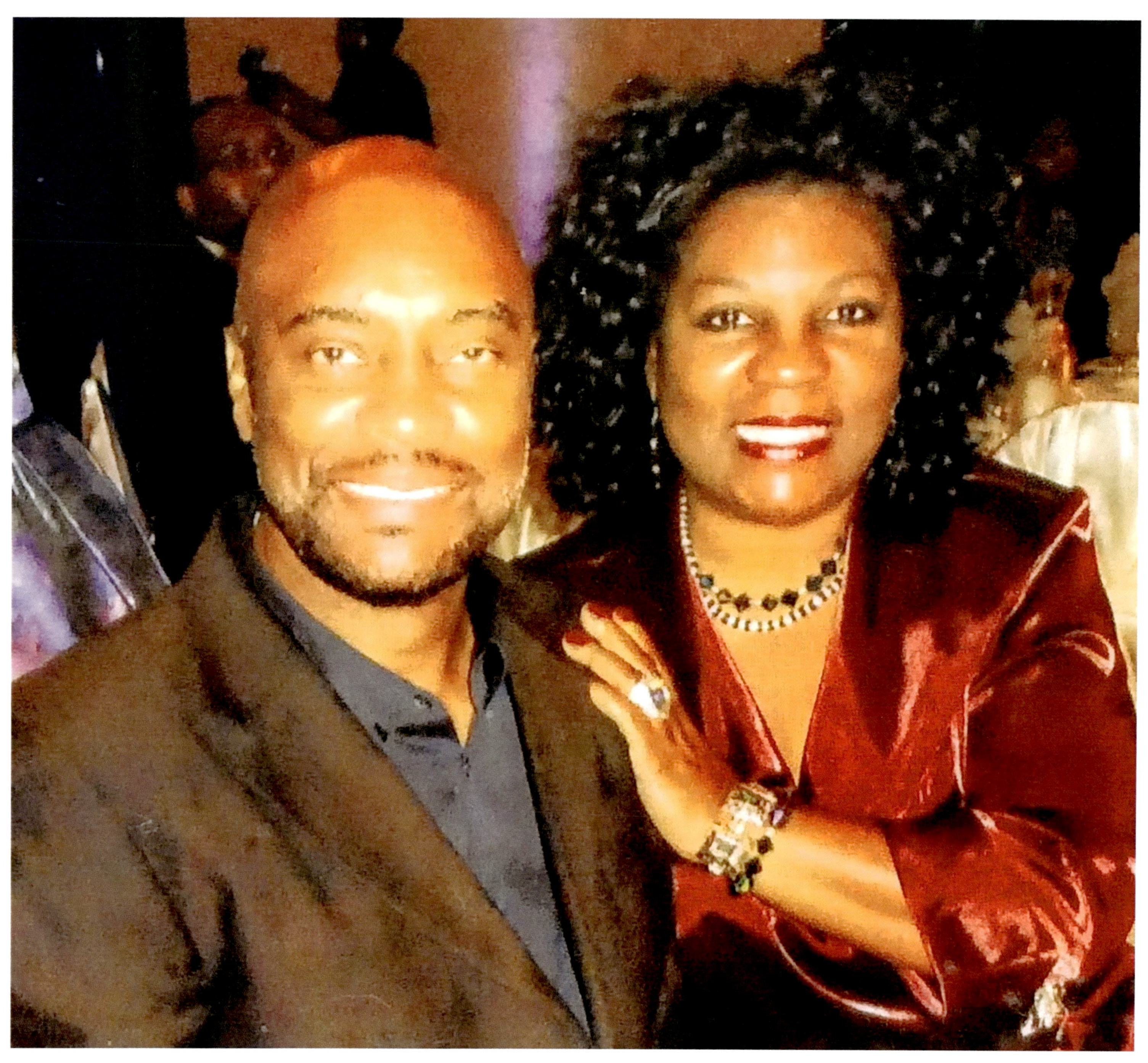

COLLECTOR:
ALFRED + ROSEMARY SUMMERS
GARDEN TRELLIS (11" X 14")
2019

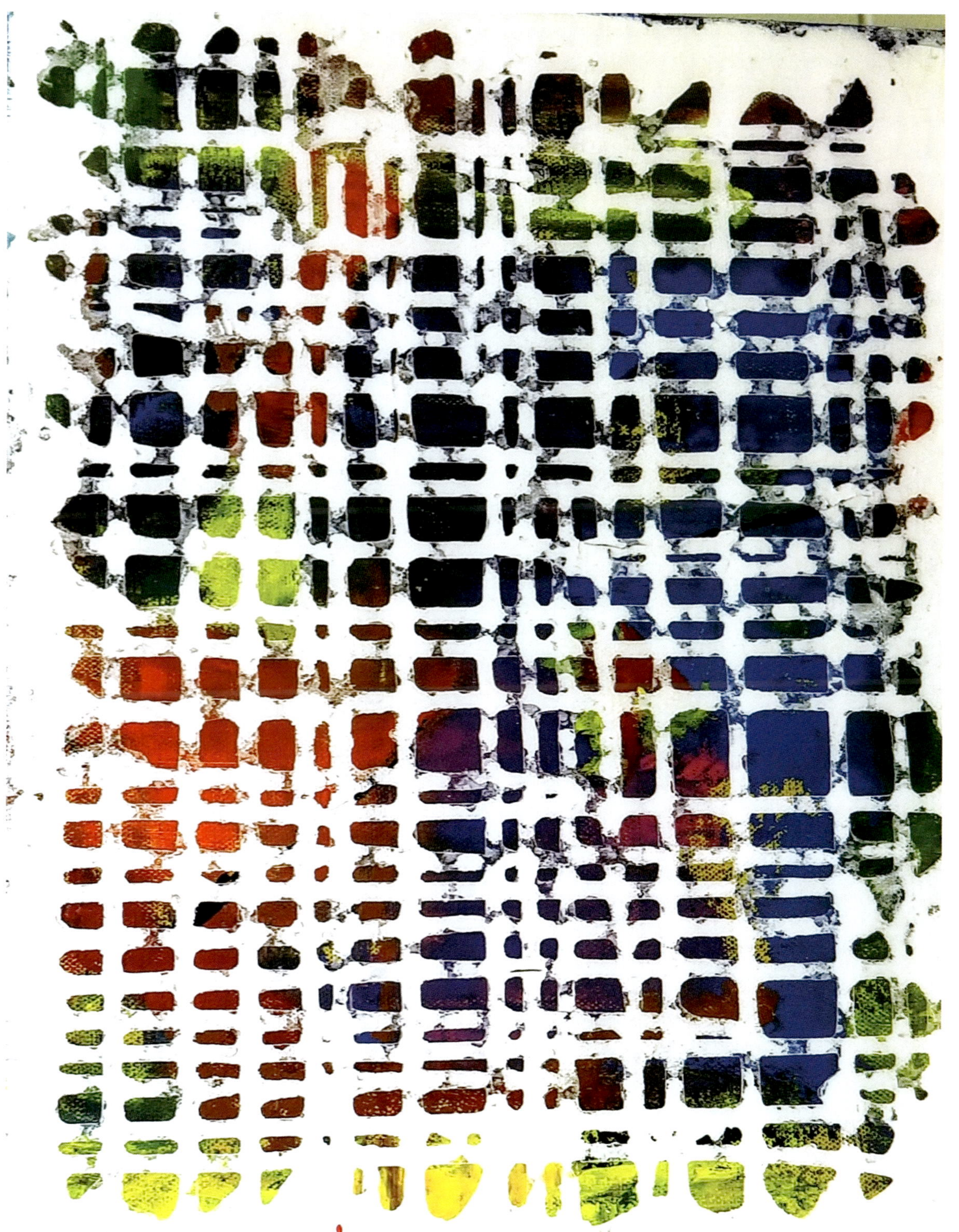

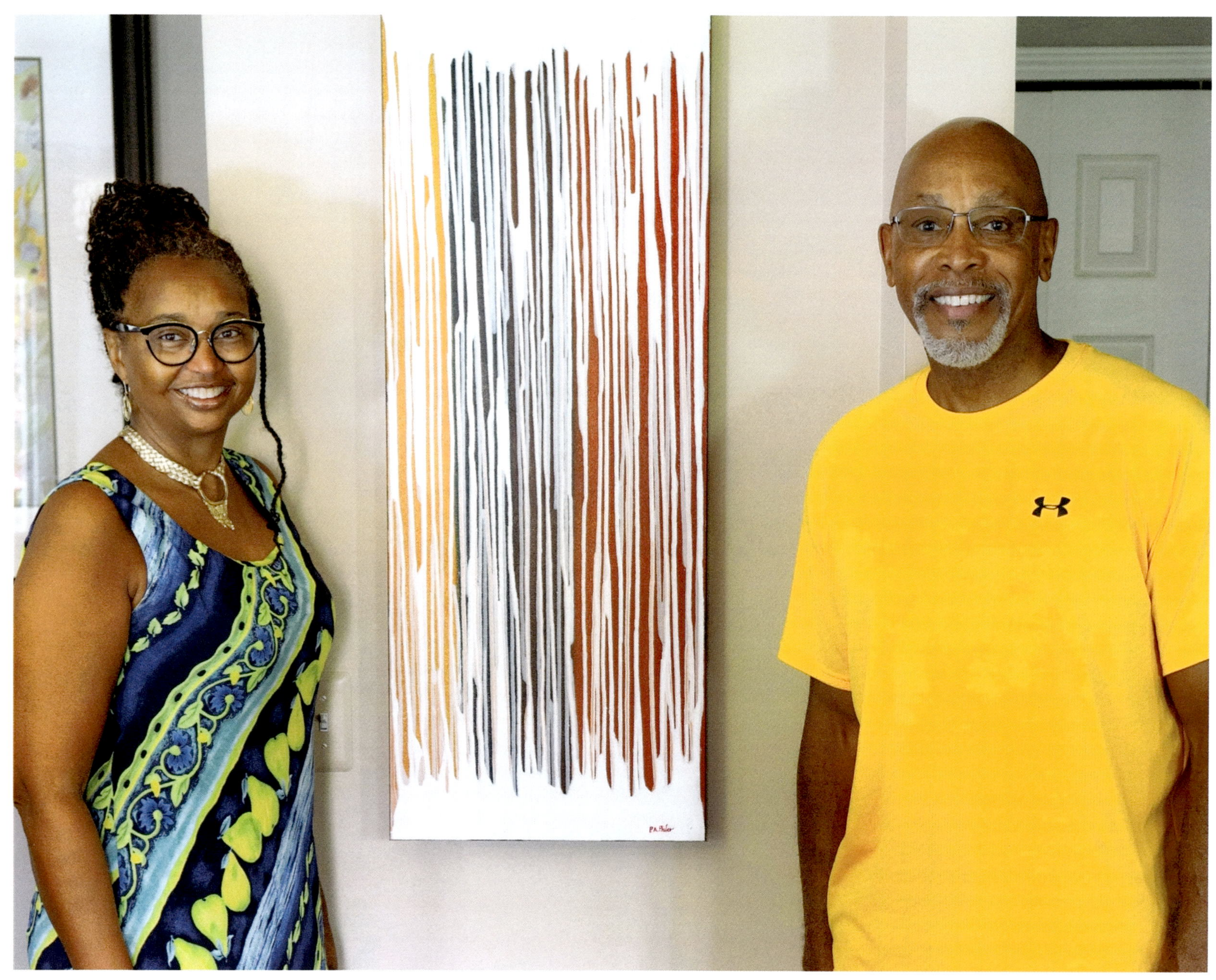

PHOTO BY GARY WASHINGTON

COLLECTOR:
ROBERT + BEVERLY ALLEN

SYNCOPATED #10 (16" X 40")
2018

TO ME ART IS AN ADVENTURE INTO AN UNKNOWN WORLD, WHICH CAN BE EXPLORED ONLY BY THOSE WILLING TO TAKE THE RISK. - **MARK ROTHKO**

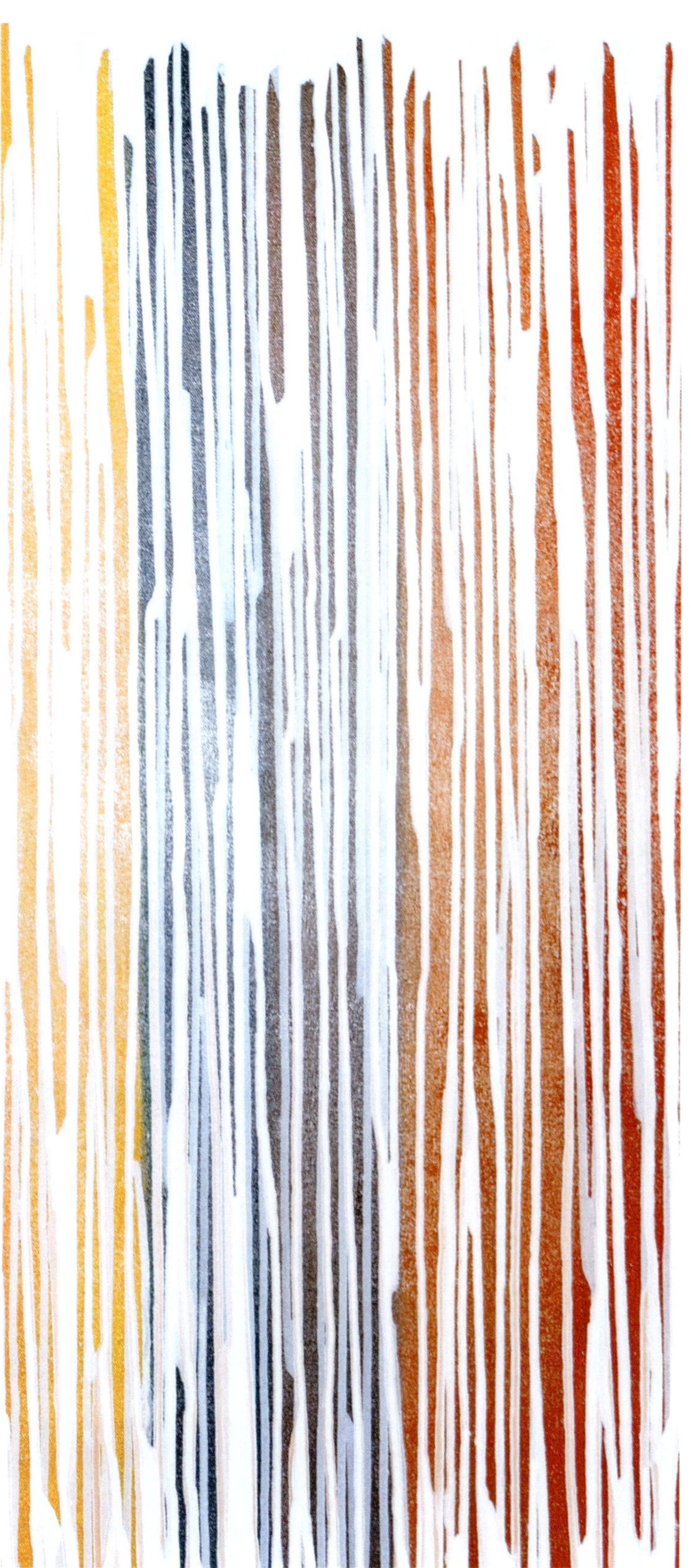

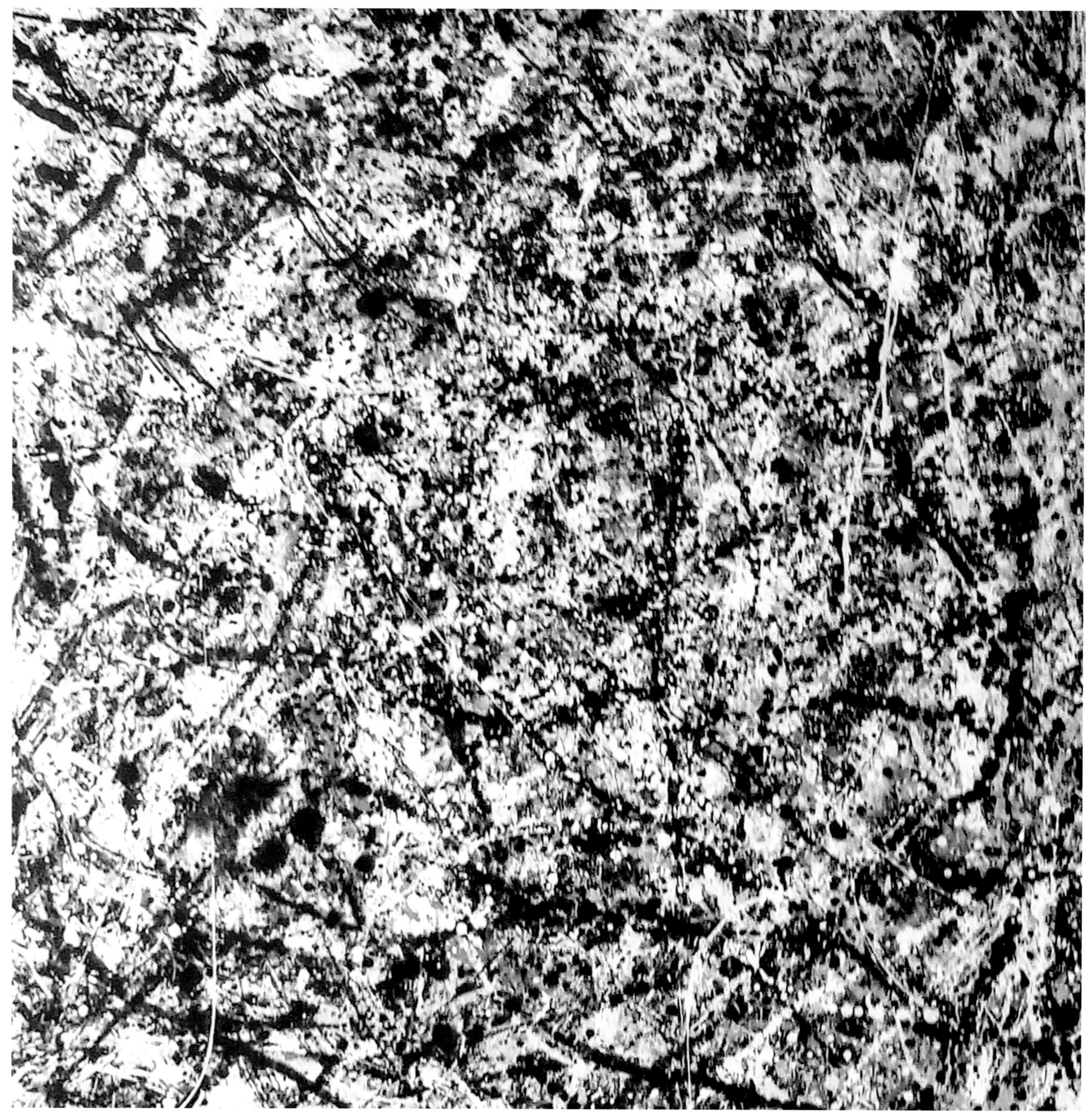

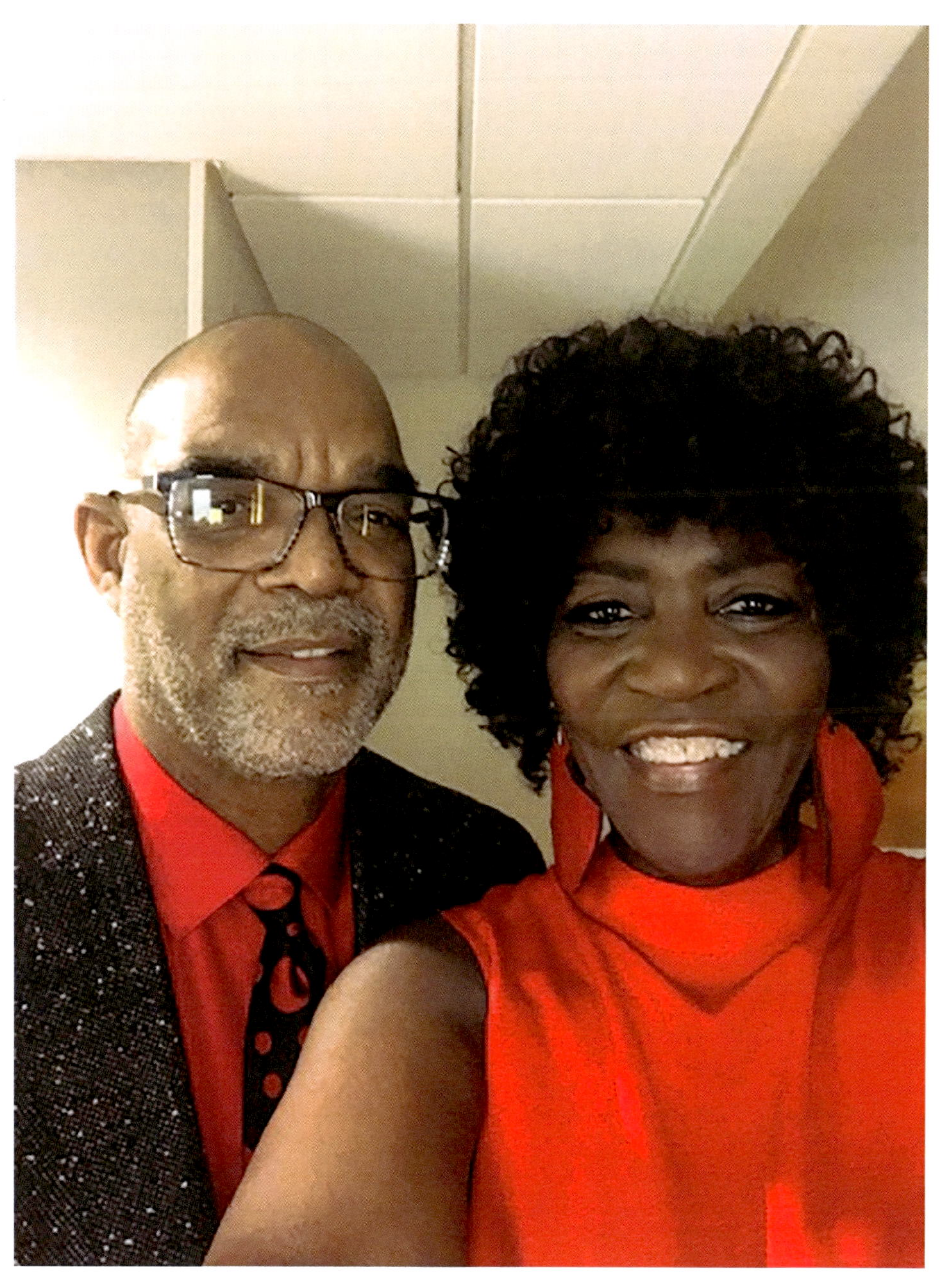

COLLECTOR:
WYATT + ELEANOR HARRIS

UNITY (36" X 36")
2017

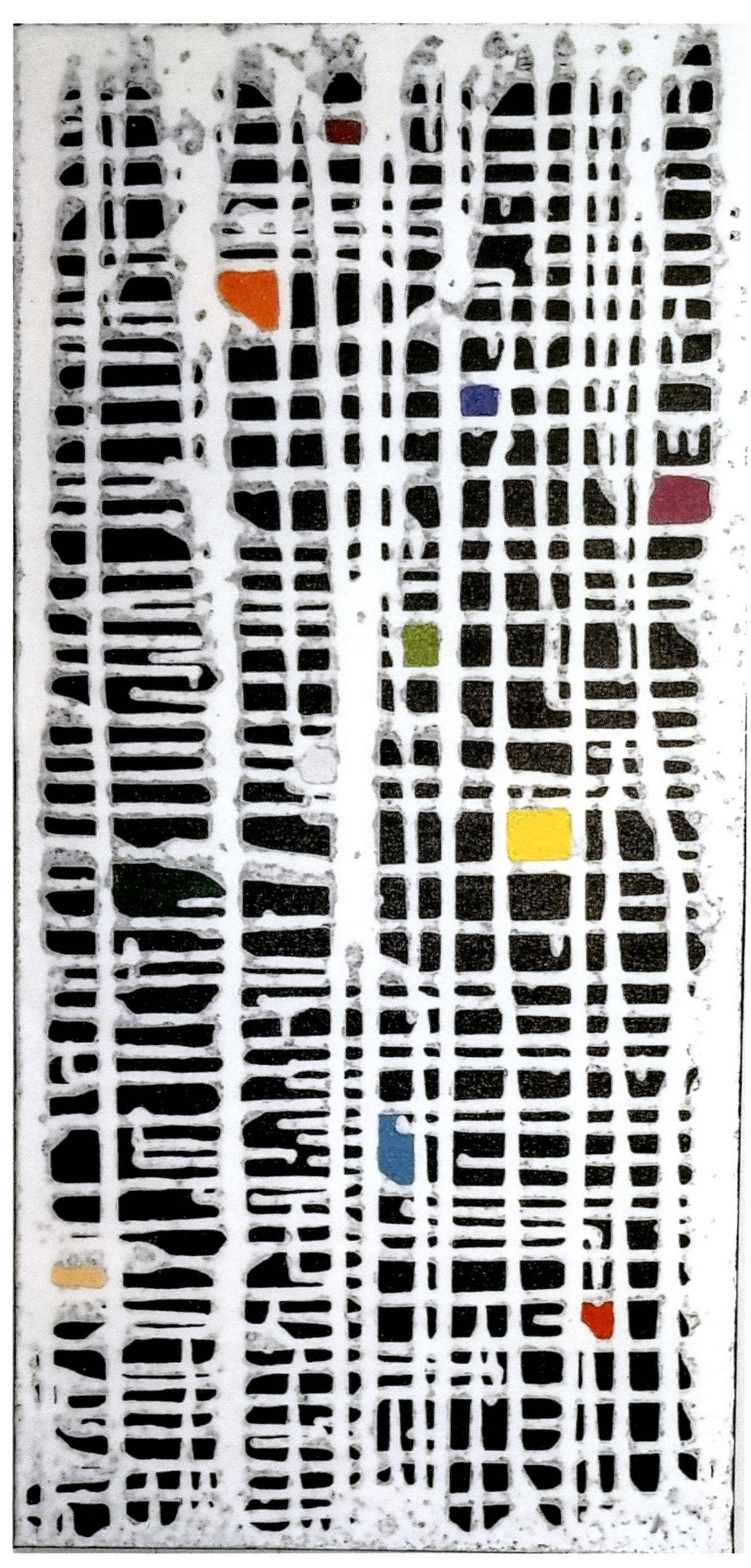

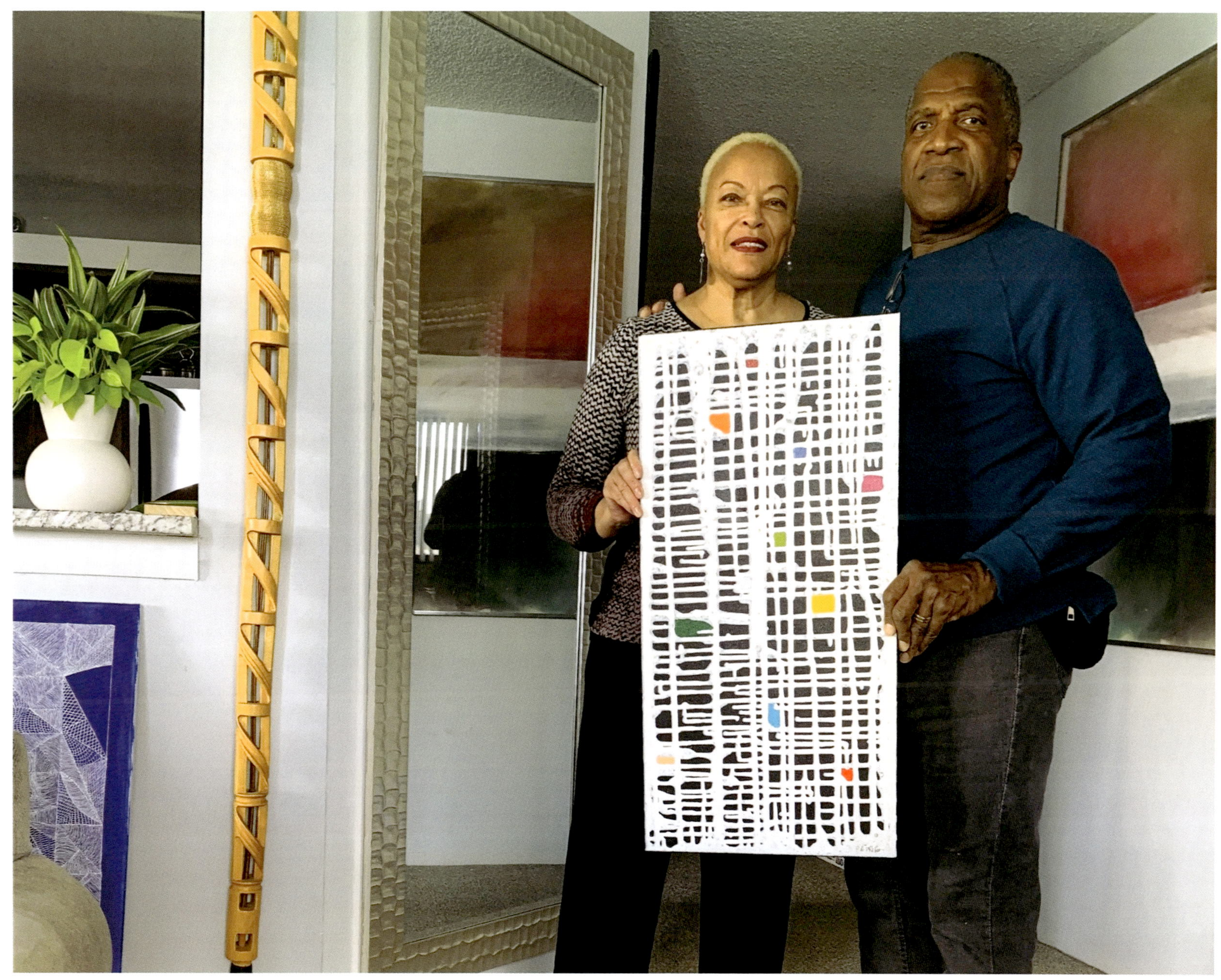

COLLECTOR:
PAUL + DAPHNE MEANS CURTIS

STAY IN YOUR OWN PANE #4 (15 X 30)
2019

I ROTATE THE CANVAS, SO I CAN SEE WHERE THERE IS IMBALANCE. I TAKE IF OFF THE WALL AND WORK ON THE FLOOR,FLINGING PAINT TO CREATE LINES AND MOVEMENT - **MICHAEL GROSS**

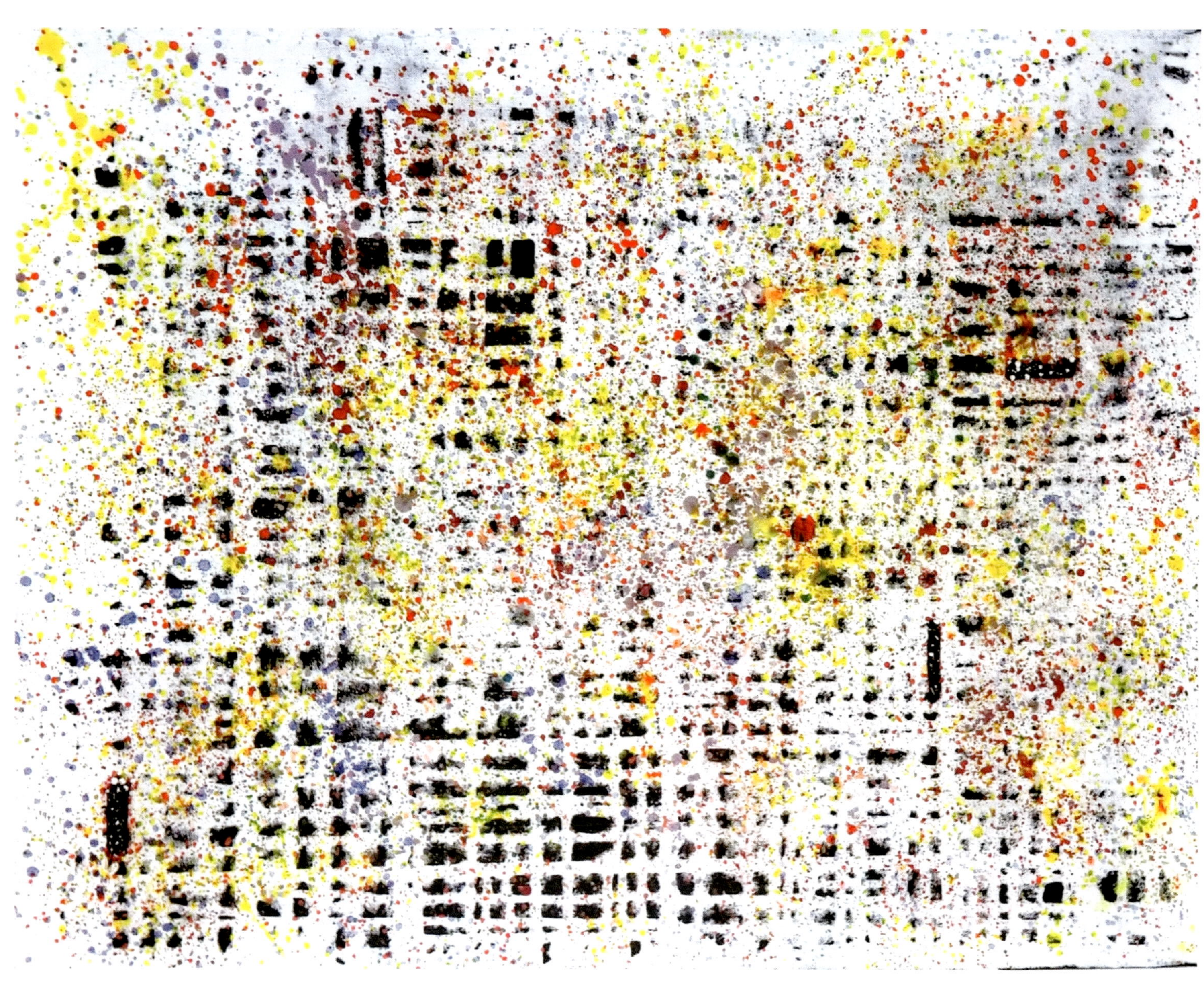

DIASPORIC POLLINATION (36 X 24)
2019
PROMOTIONAL PAINTING FOR
CHARLES H. WRIGHT MUSEUM
VISION OF DETROIT EXHIBIT 2020

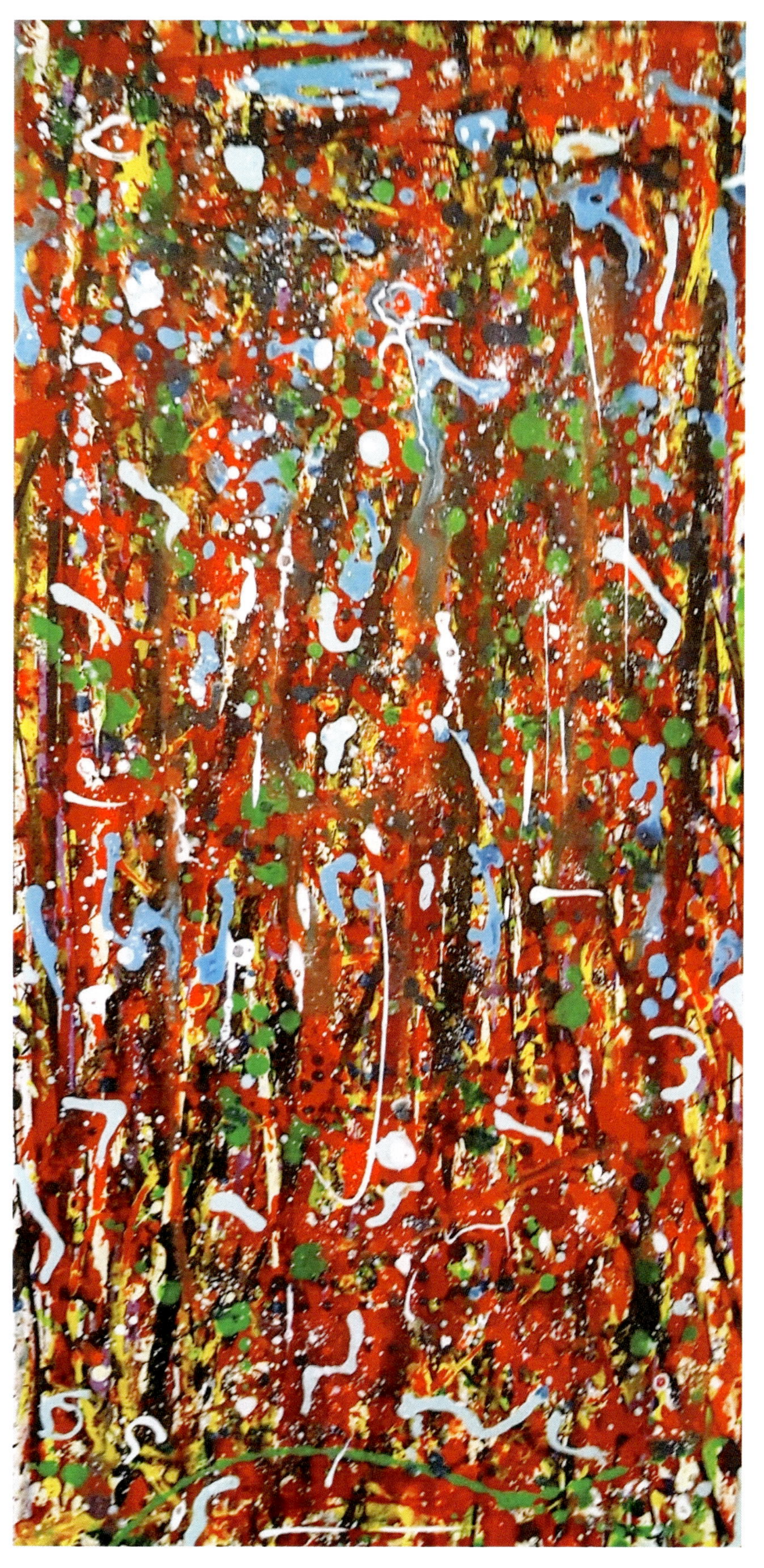

COLLECTOR:
JUDGE DEBORAH GERALDINE
BLEDSOE FORD WATSON

DREAMIN' (15X30)
2017

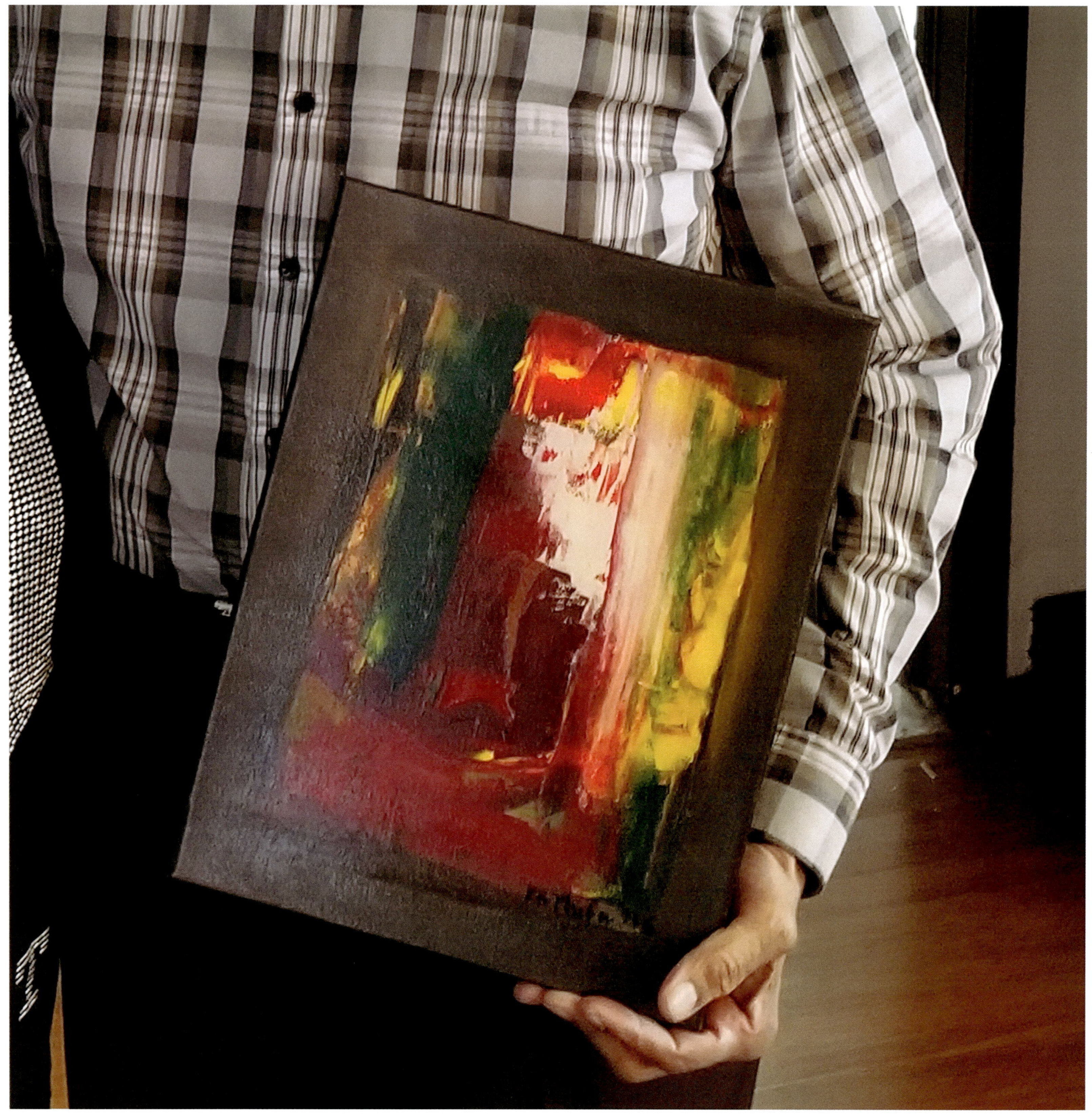

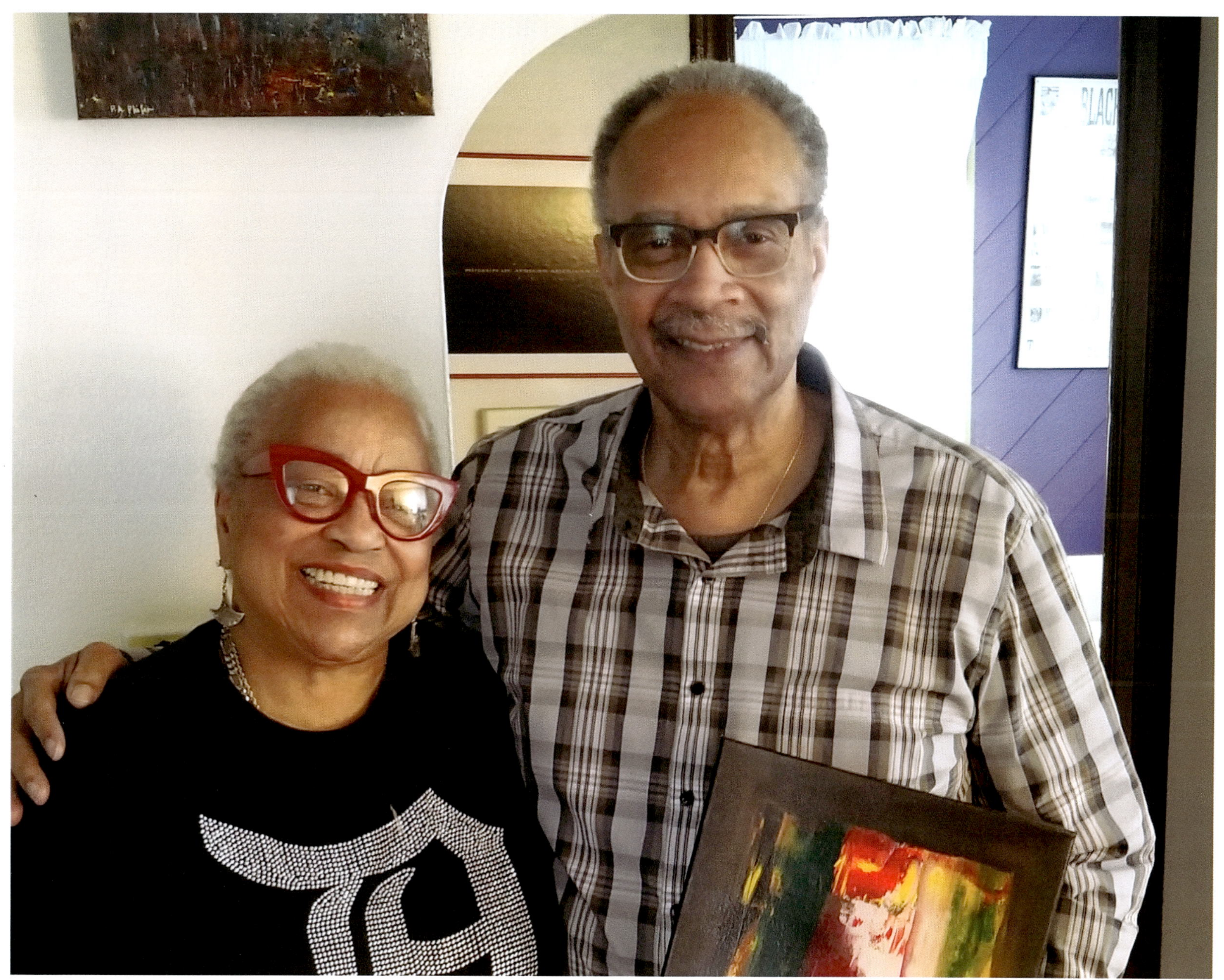

COLLECTOR:
PATRICK + MARGARET TUCKER

UNTITLED (11" X 14")
2018

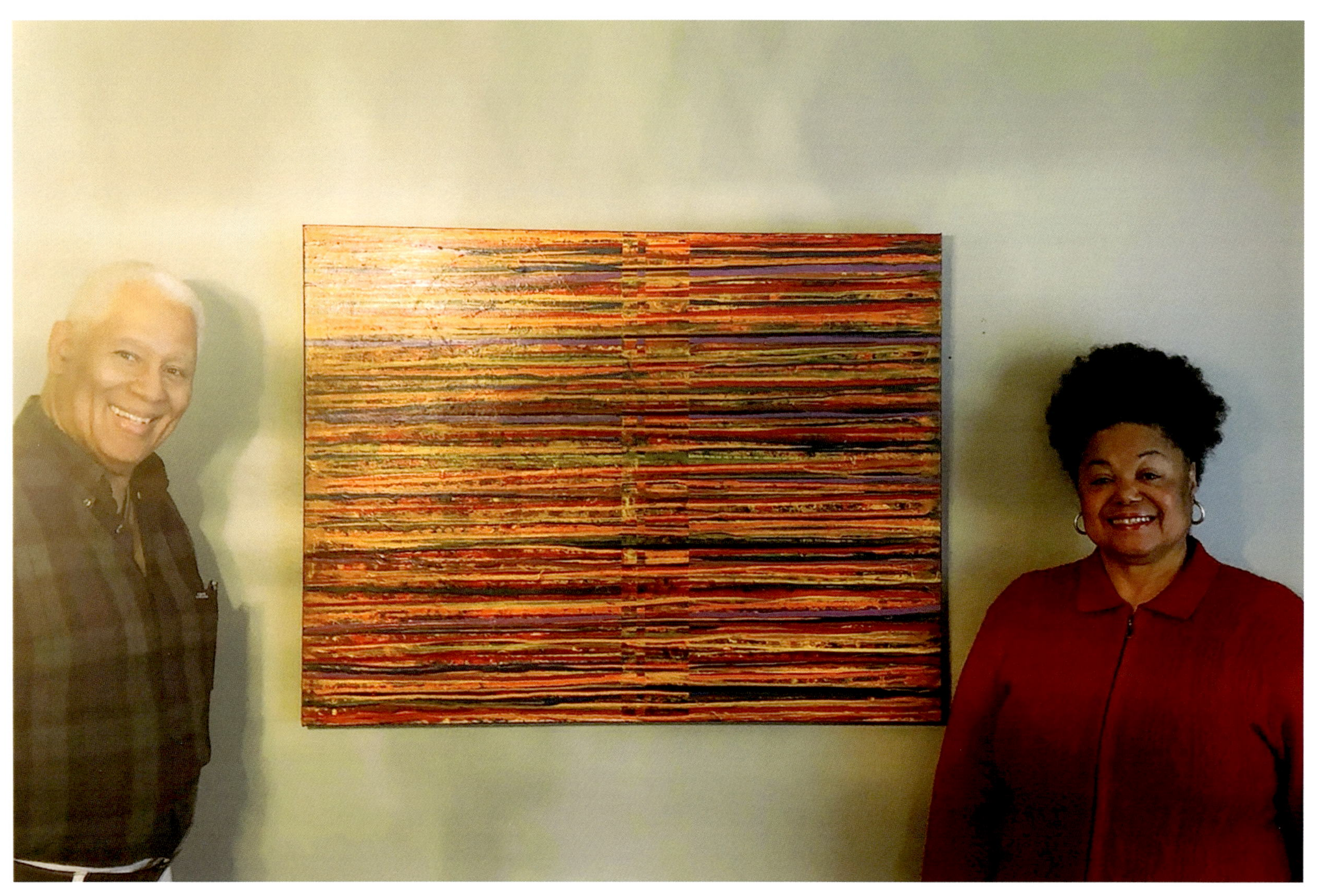

COLLECTOR:
HELENA + DEXTER MAYS

STRIATED (30 X 40)
2019

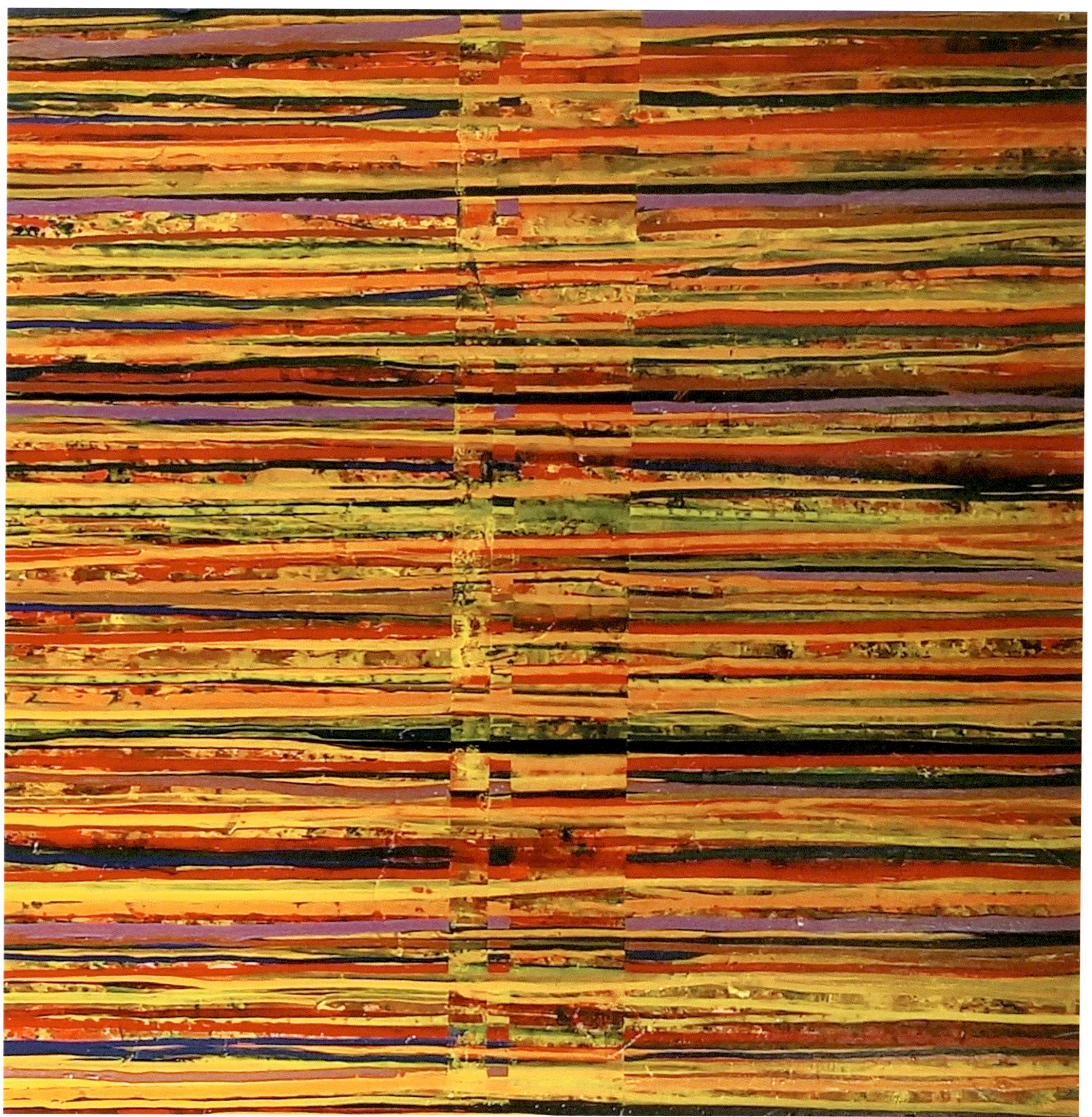

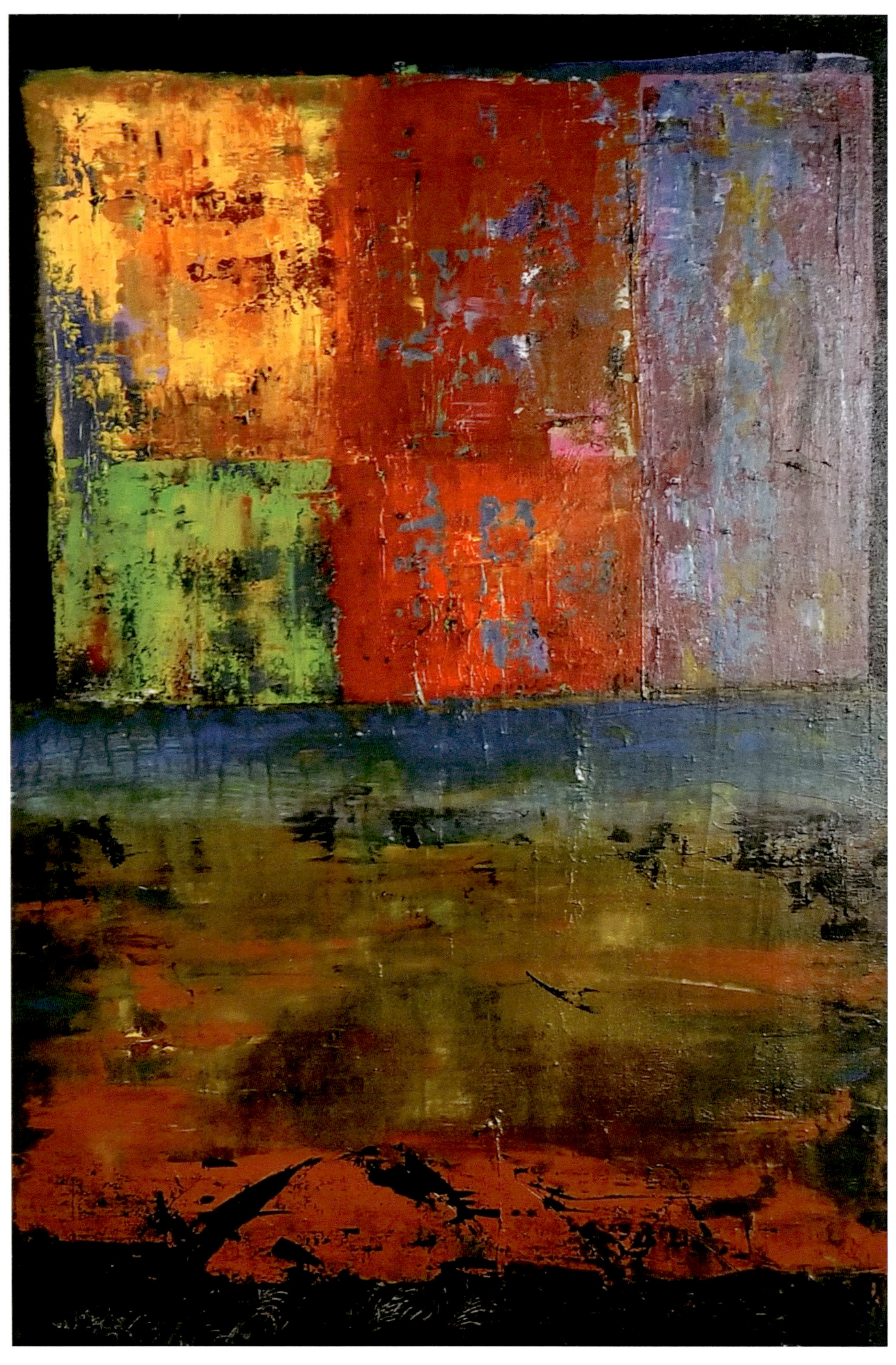

LEFT:
COLLECTOR :
DORIS WITHERSPOON

UNTITLED (24" X 36")
2018

RIGHT:
COLLECTOR:
SHARON GAMBLIN

CIRCLES OF LOVE AND
CIRCLES OF FRIENDSHIP

(36" X 36")
2017

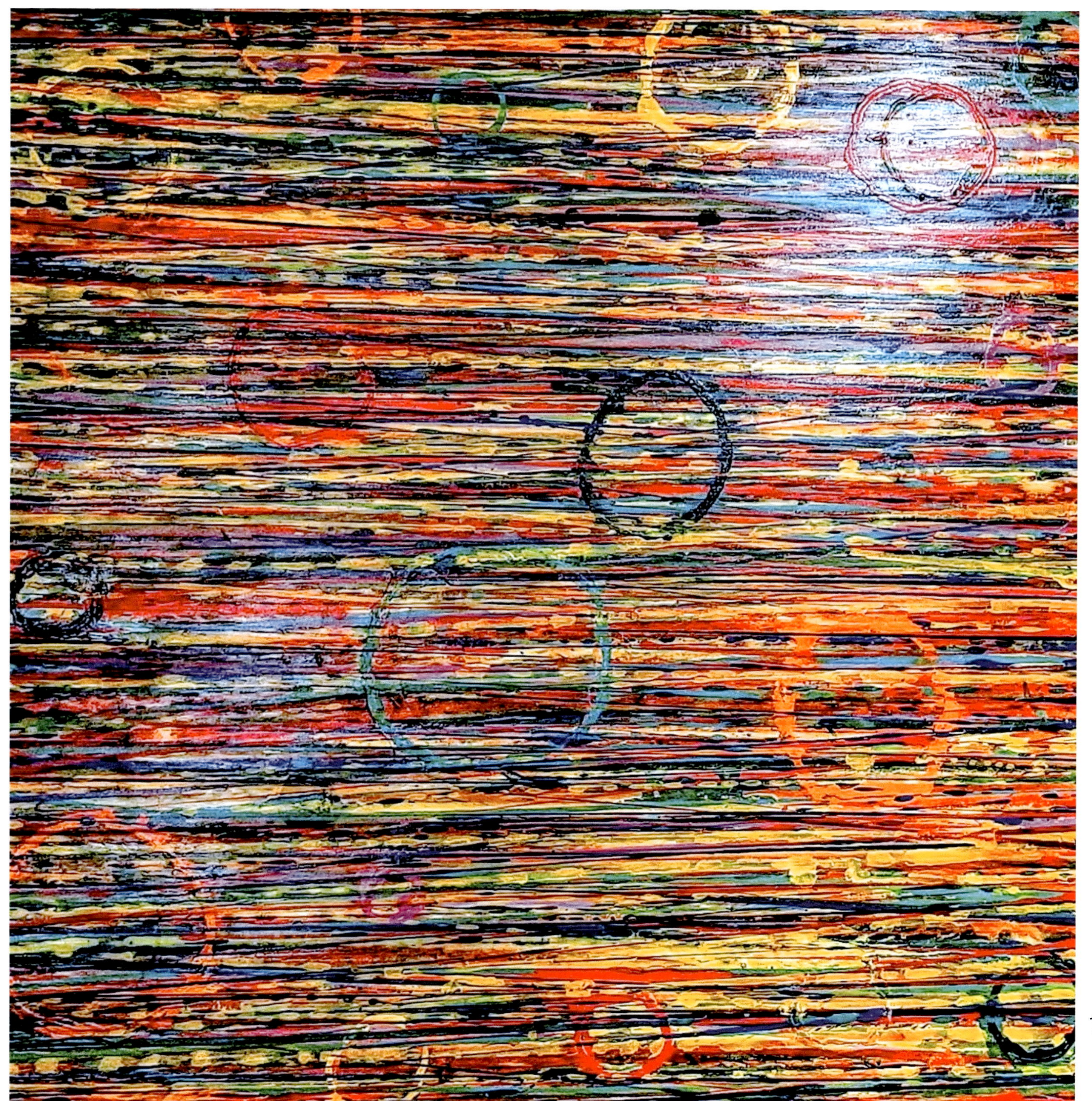

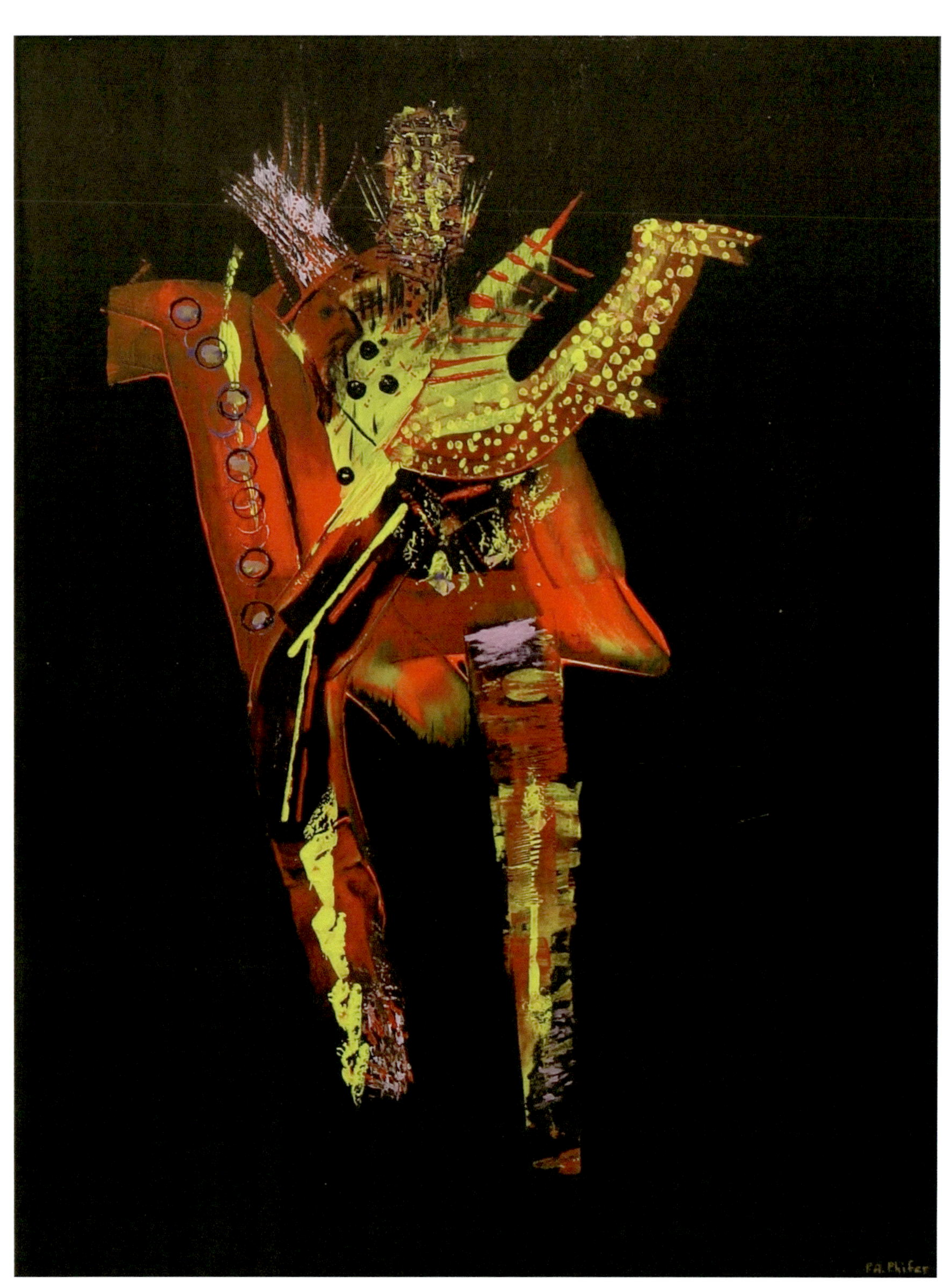

COLLECTOR:
JAMES DOZIER

TRIBAL (33X43)
2015

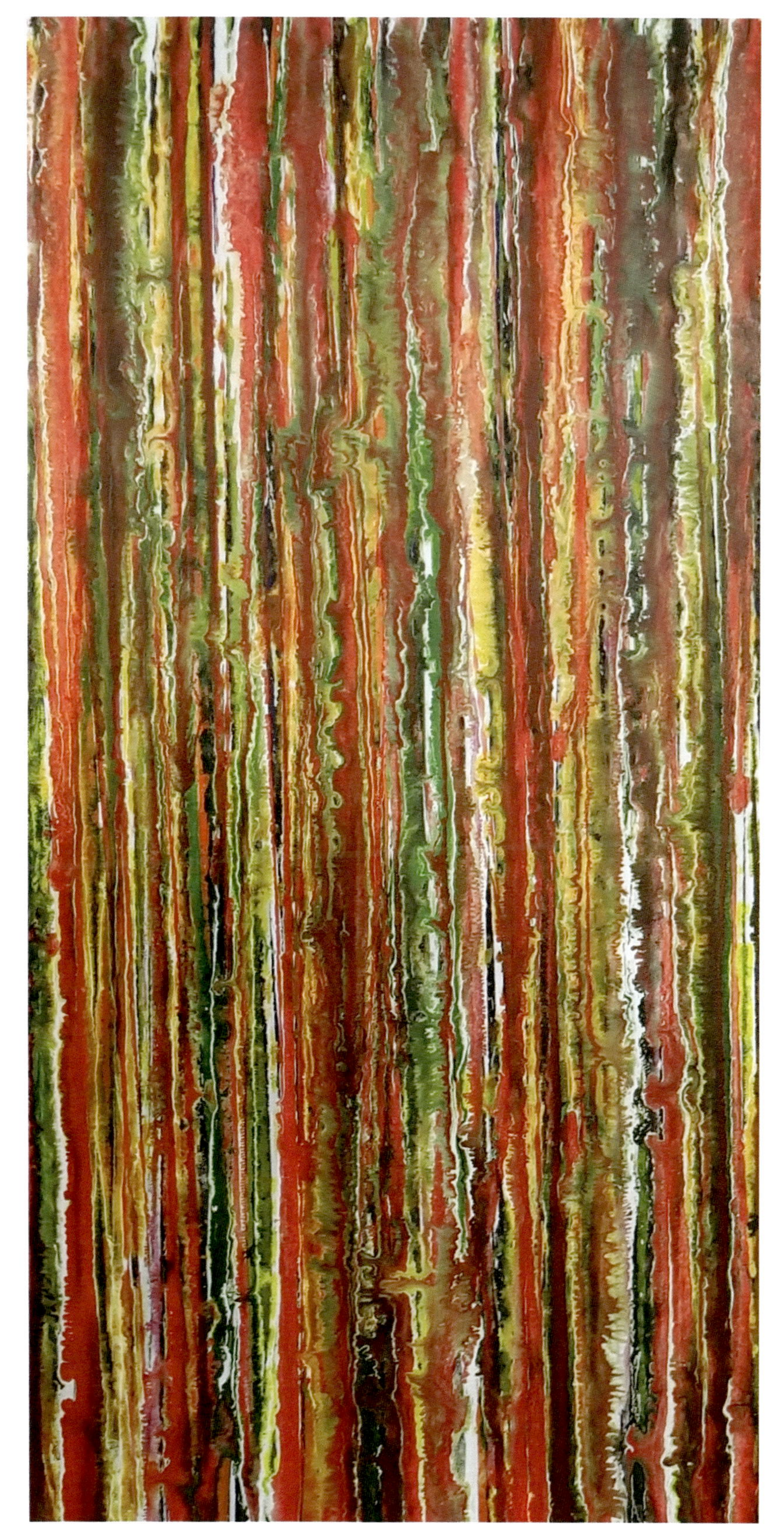

COLLECTOR:
WALTER + HARRIET WATKINS

UNTITLED (15" X 30")
2019

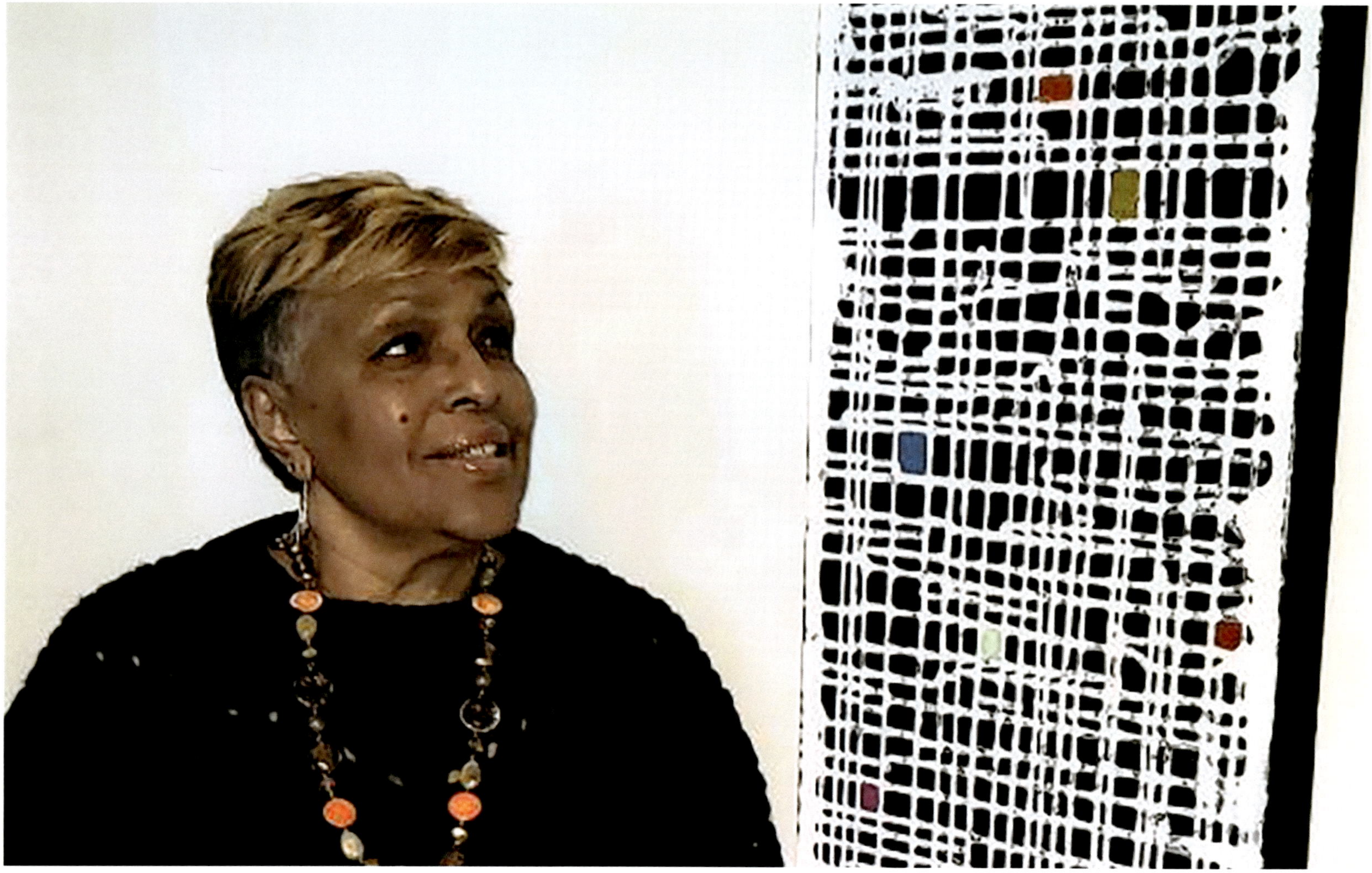

COLLECTOR:
SHARRON MERRITT

STAY IN YOUR OWN PANE #3 (15" X 30")
2019

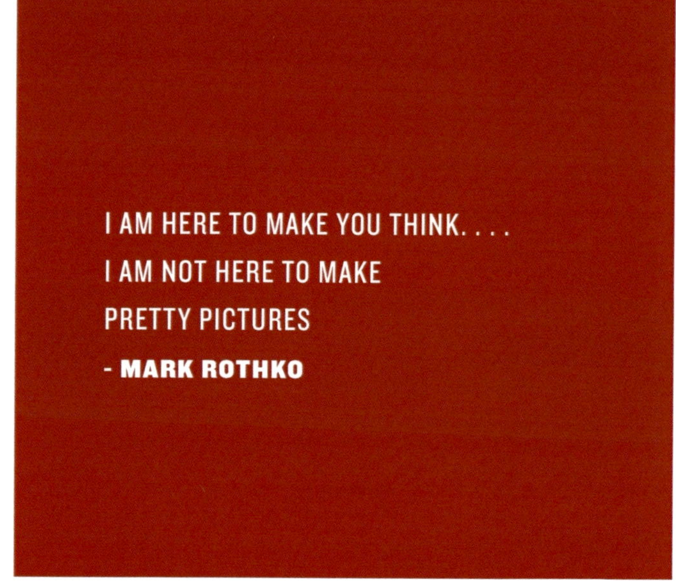

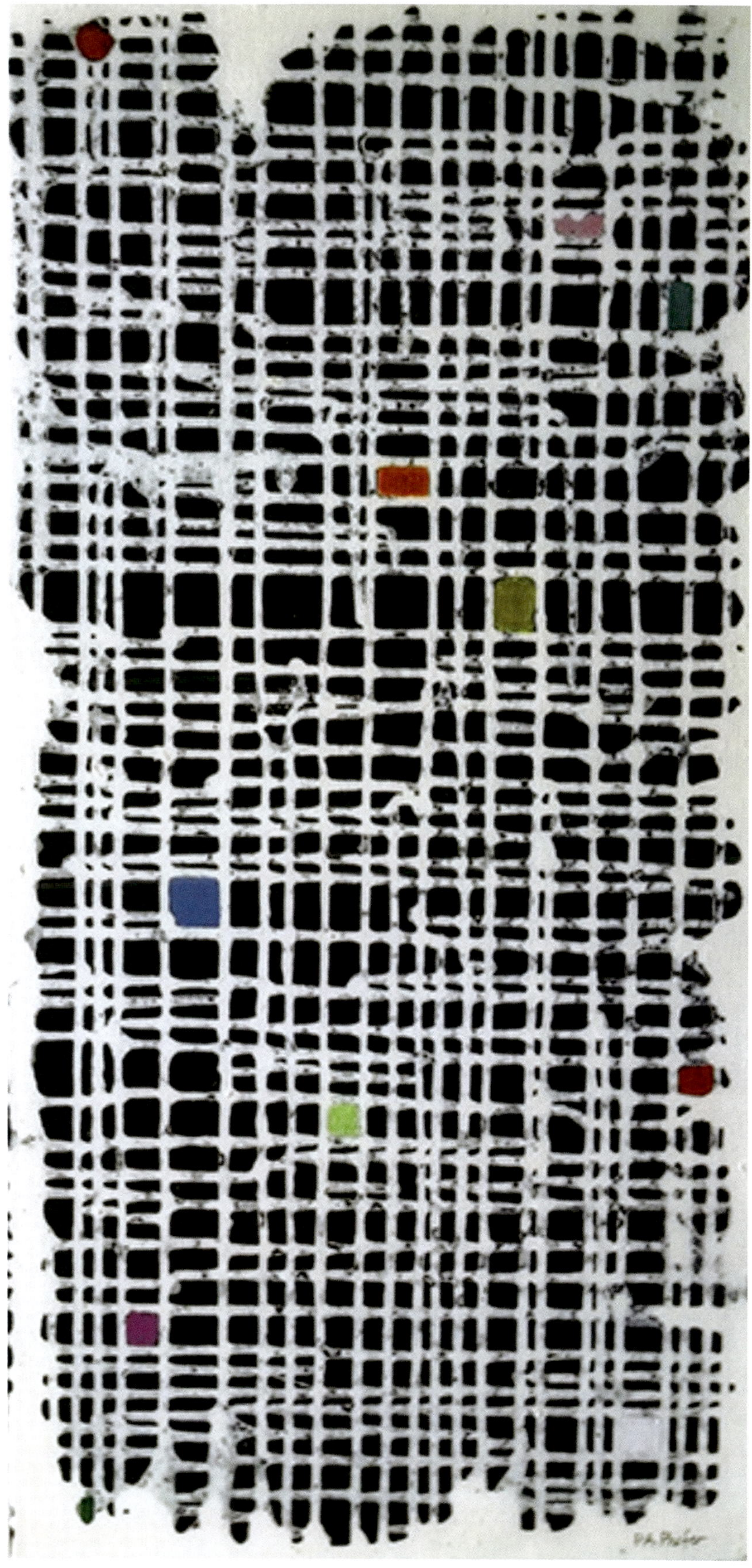

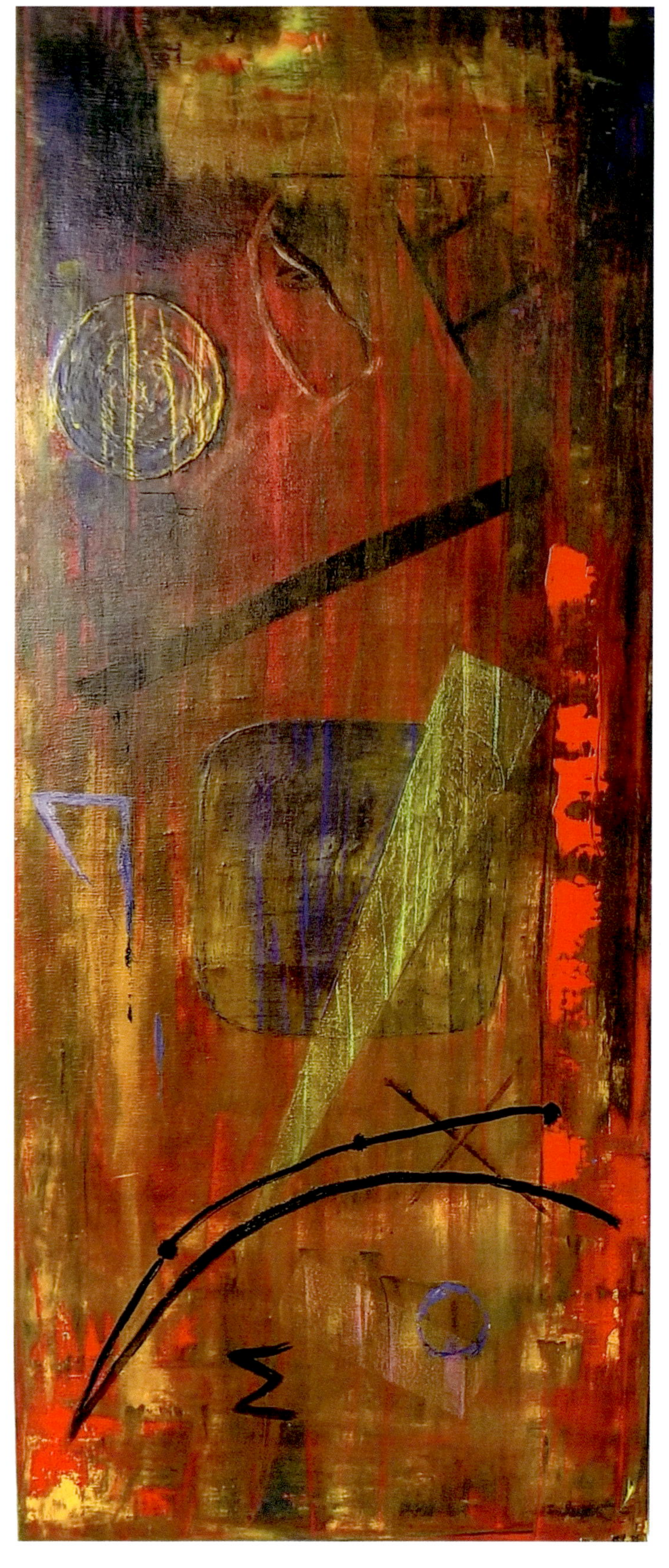

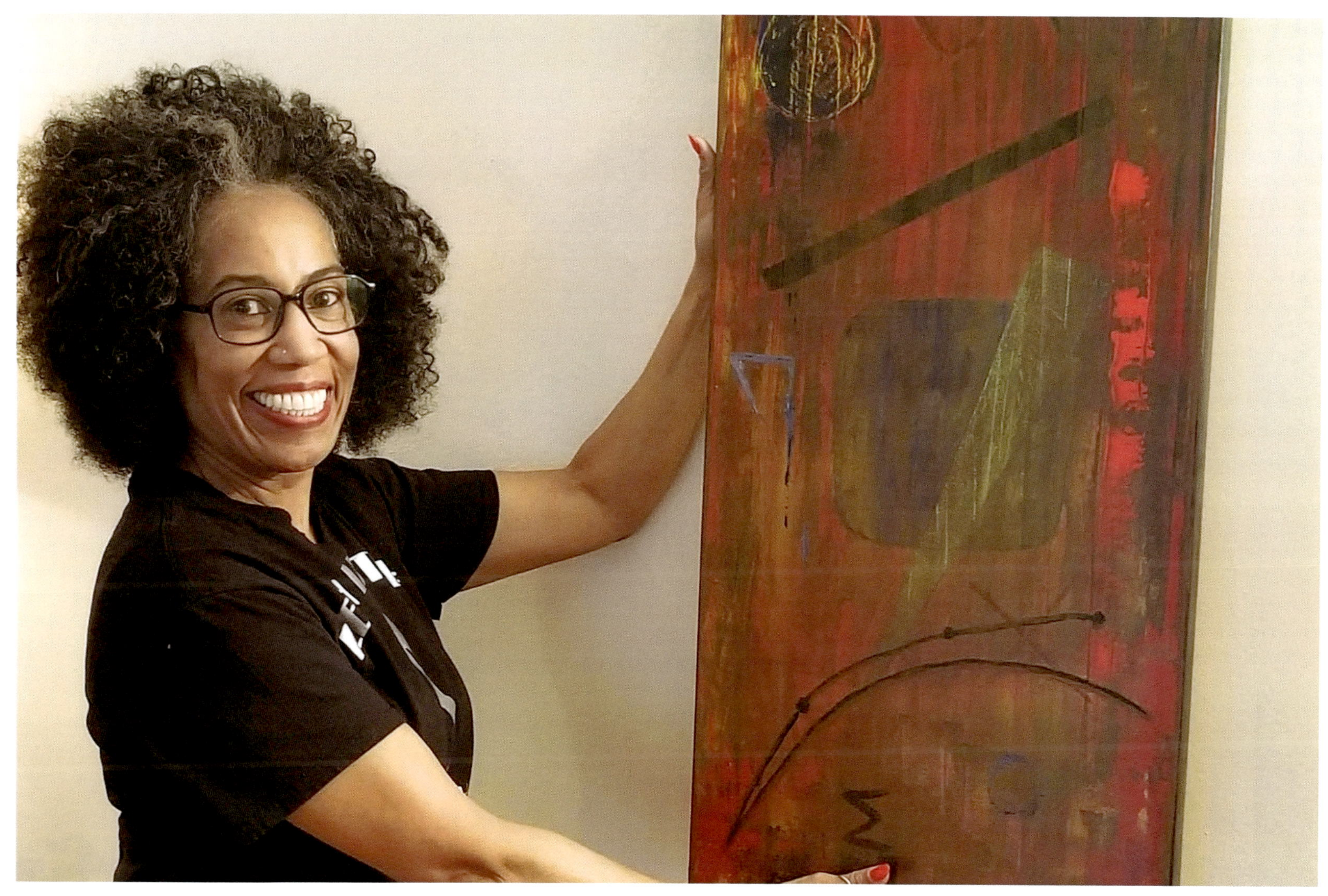

COLLECTOR:
JACQUELINE + ULYSSES BURDELL

HIDDEN FIGURES (16 X 40)
2019

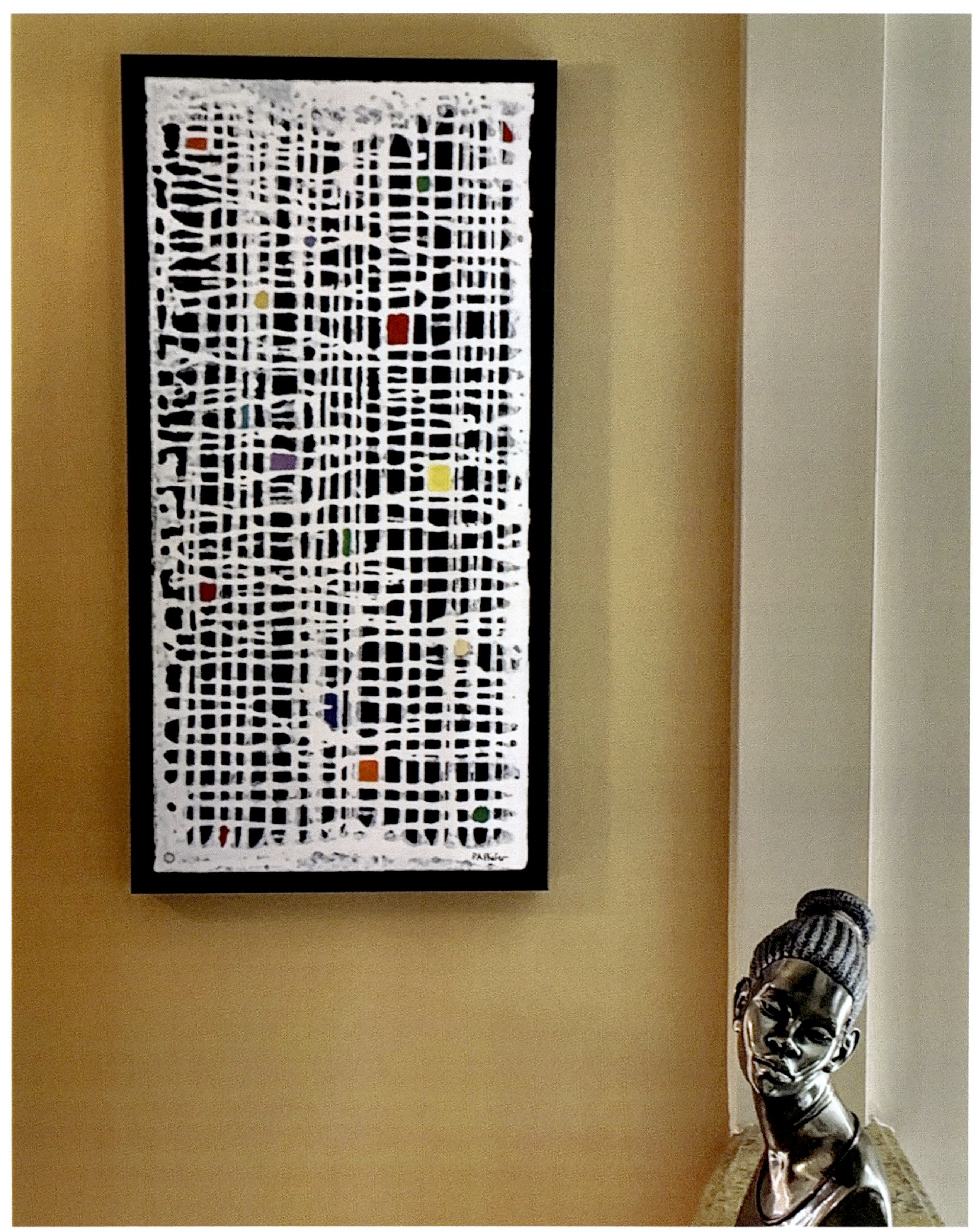

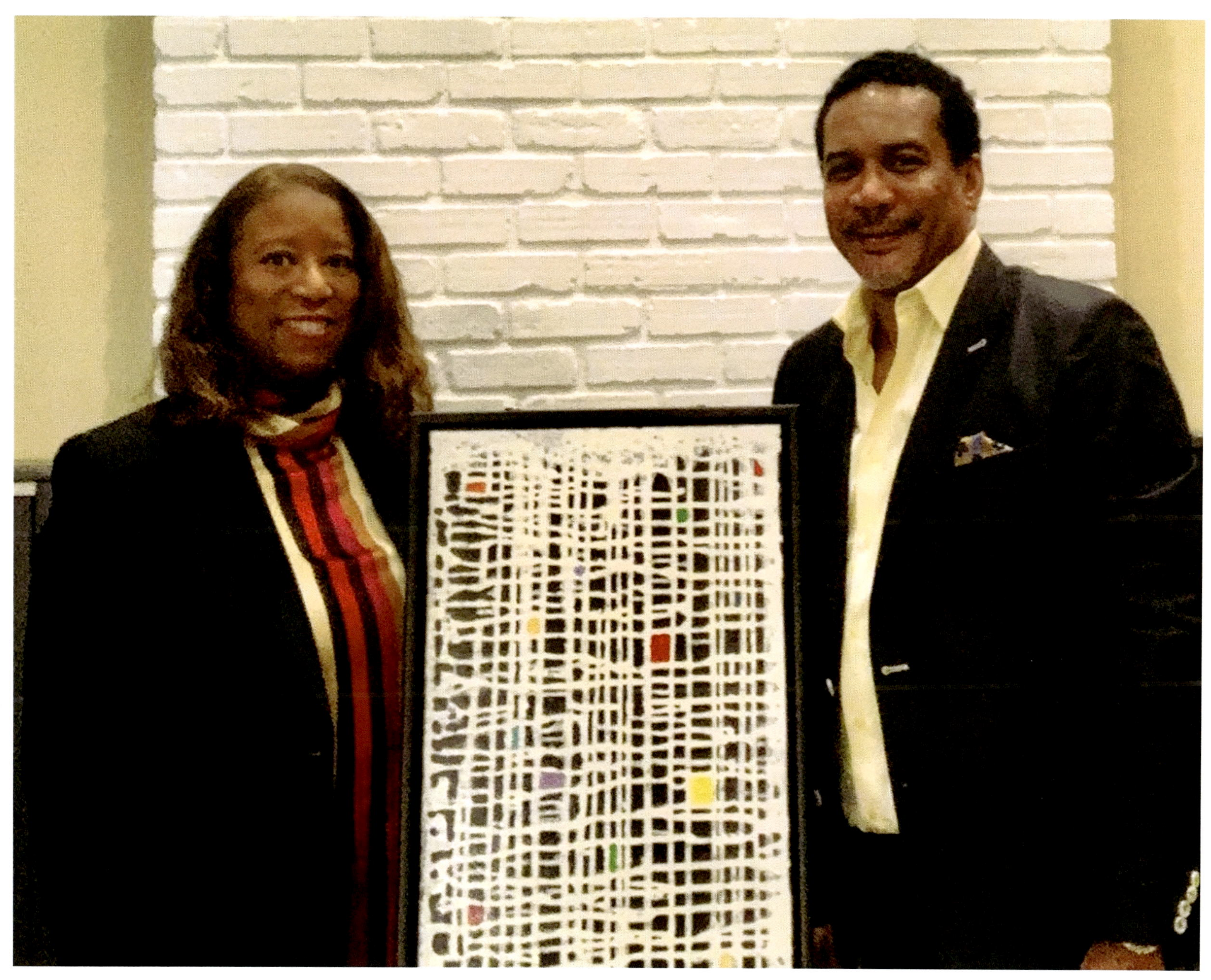

COLLECTOR:
IAN + TARANJI GRANT

STAY IN YOUR OWN PANE #9
2019

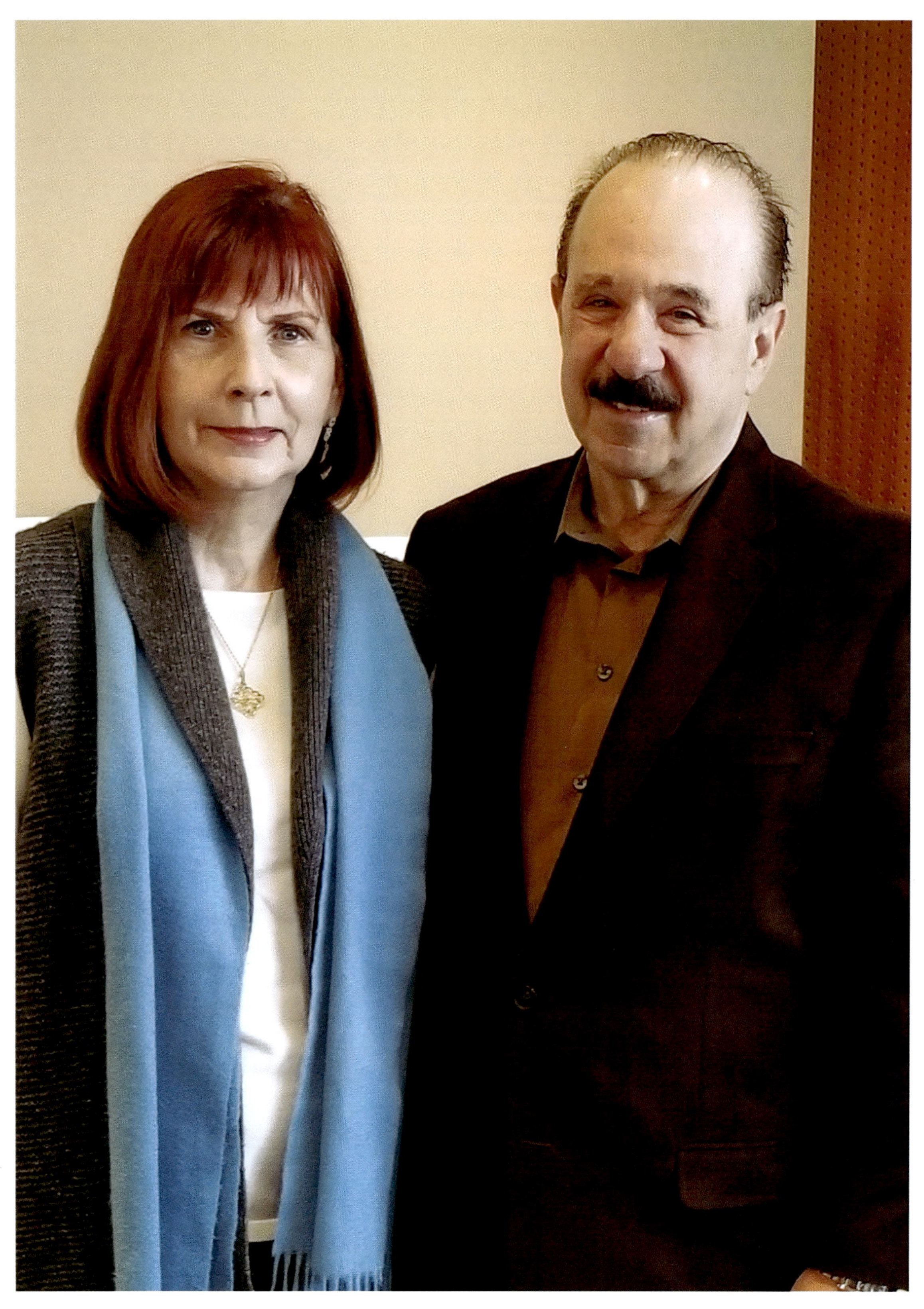

COLLECTOR:
ED AND KAREN OGUL

DIVERSITY (36X36)
2019

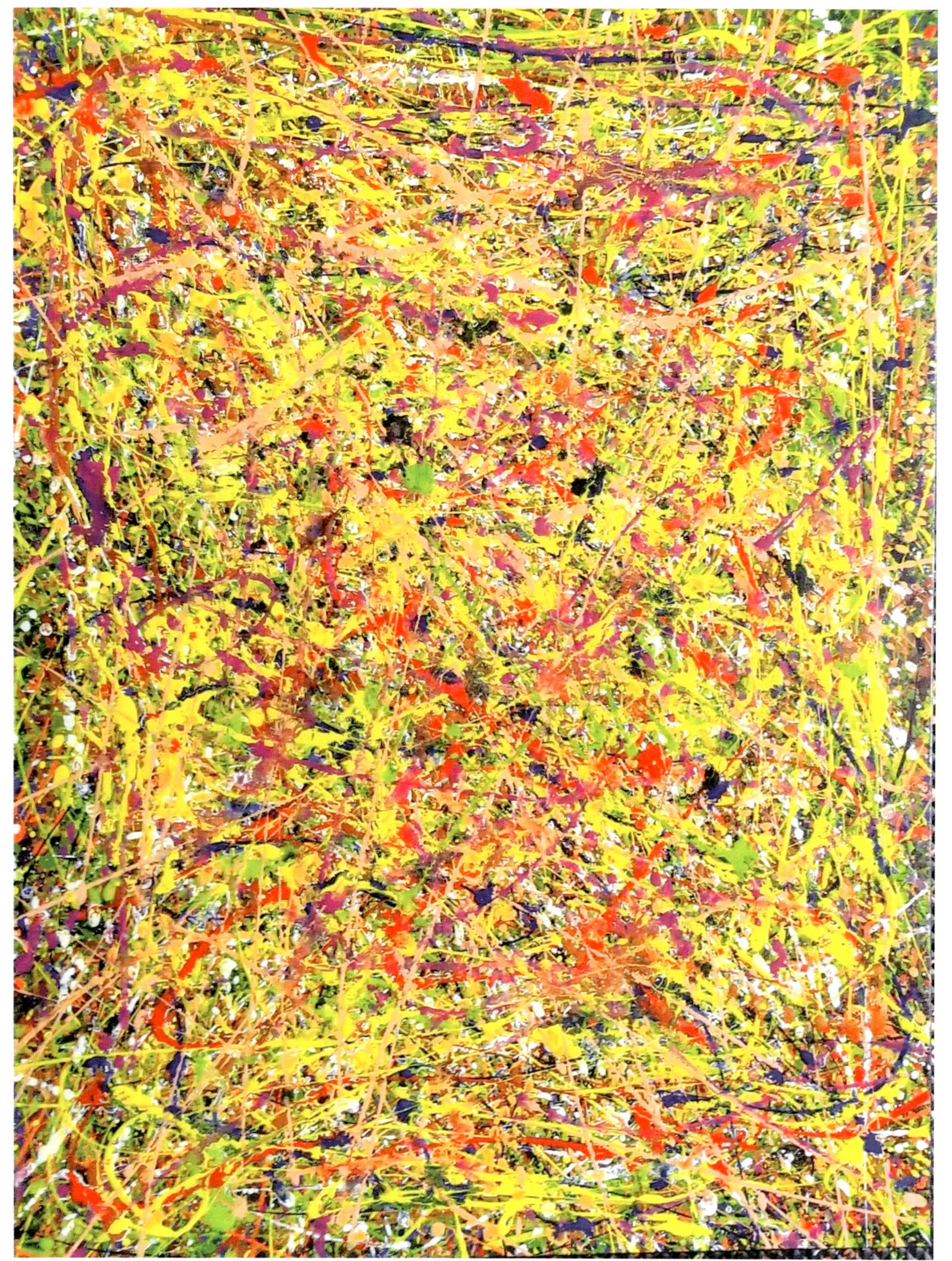

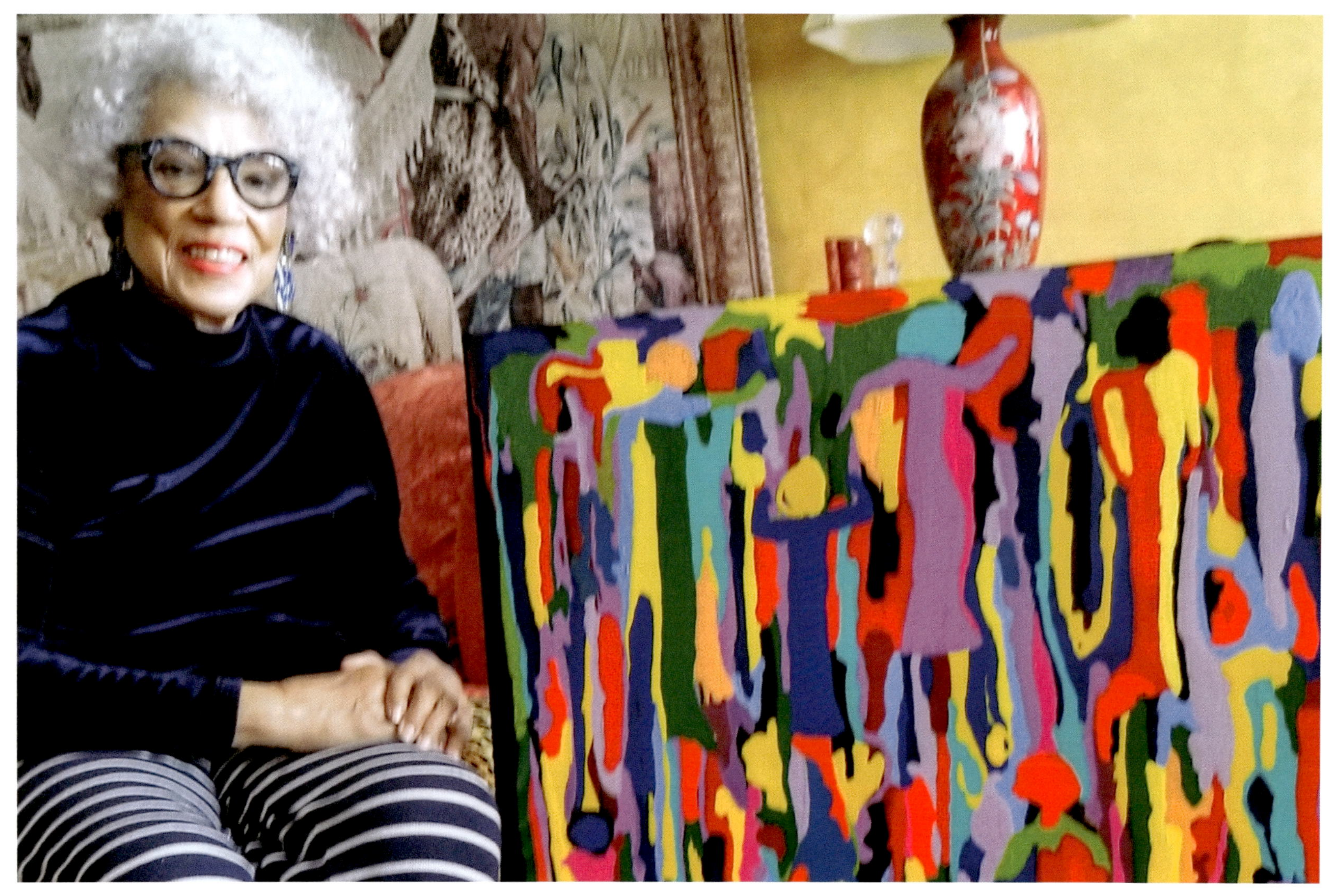

COLLECTOR:
THE HONORABLE TEOLA HUNTER

IF WOMEN RULED (36 X 36)
2020

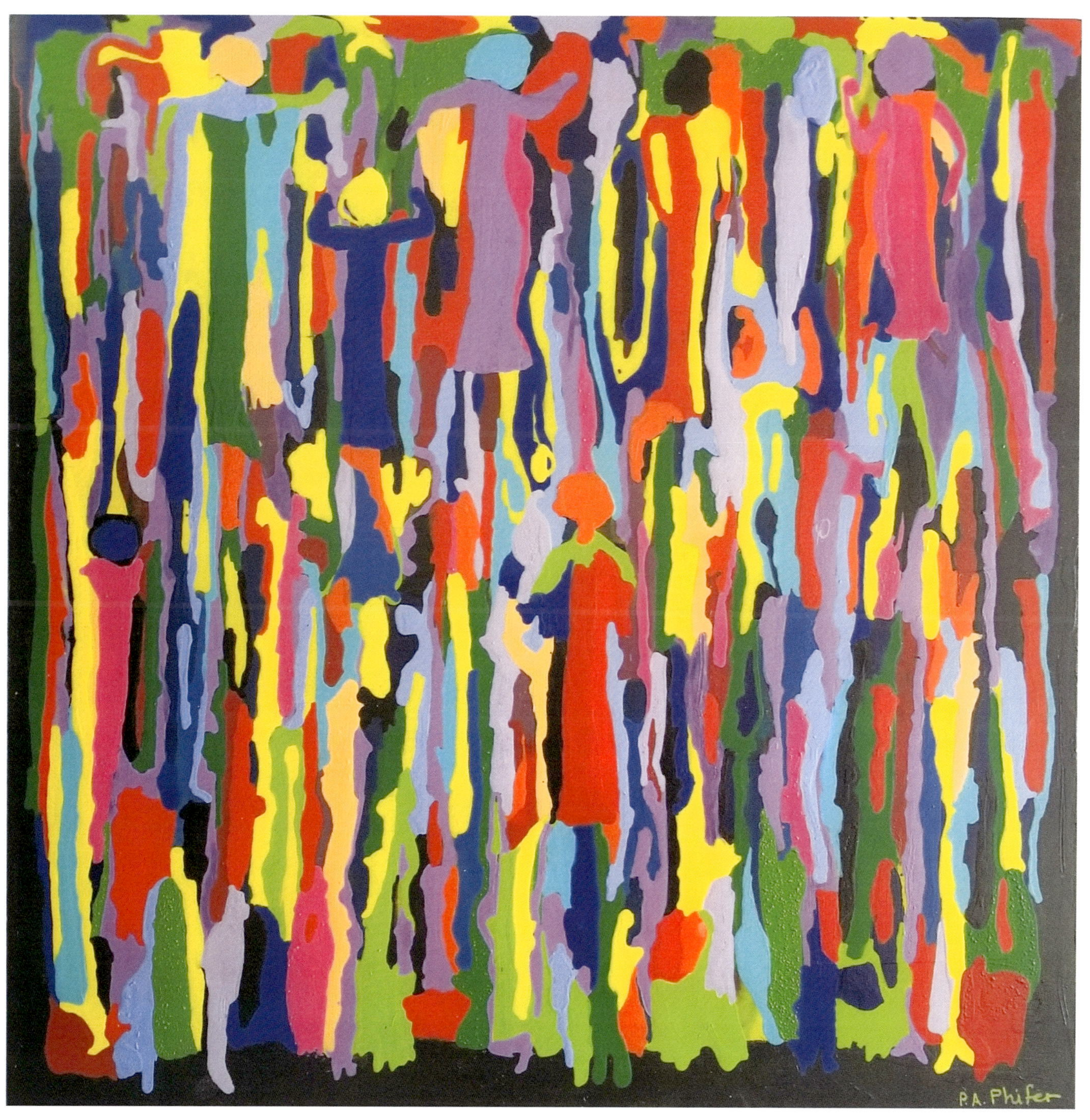
P.A. Phifer

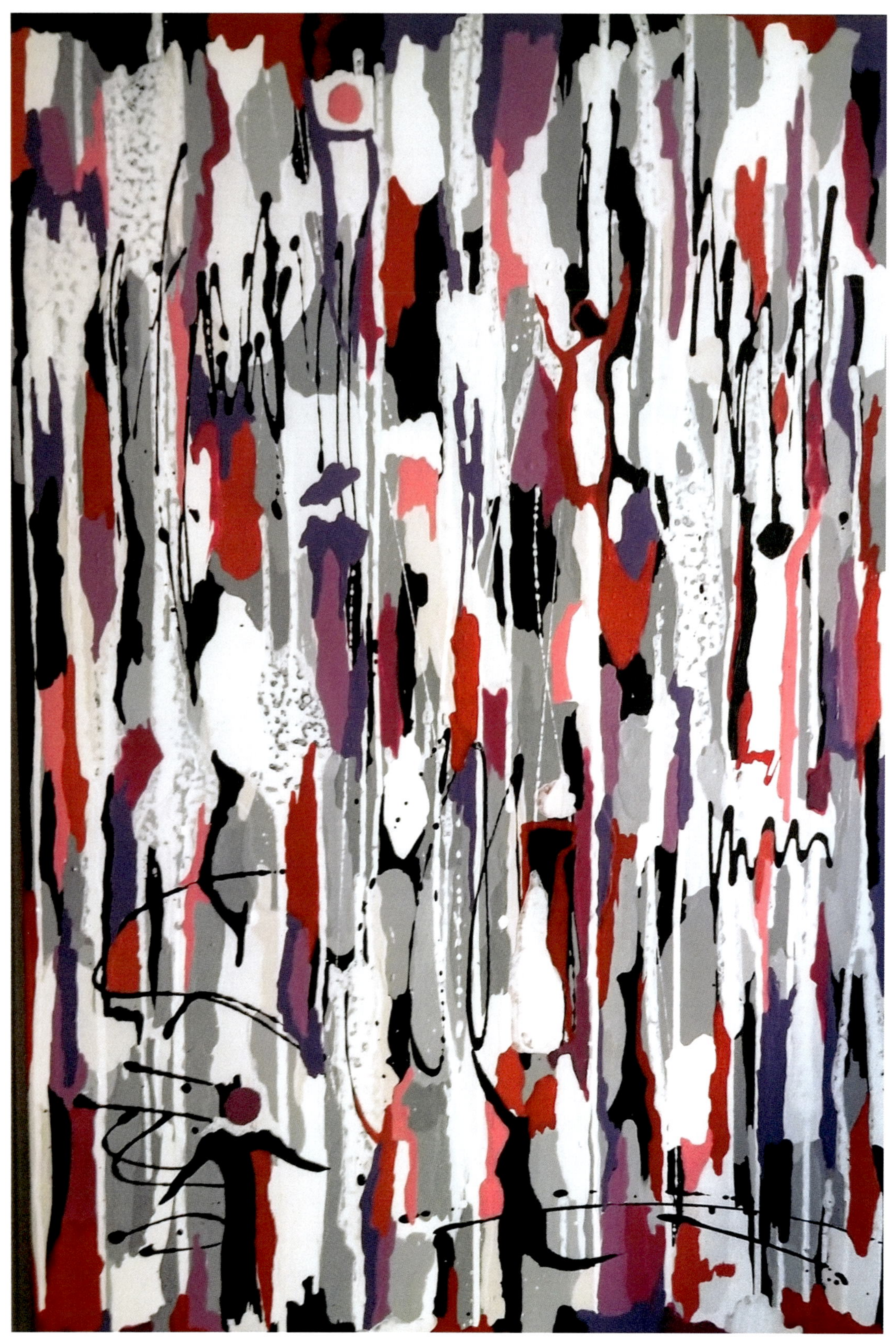

COLLECTOR:
IAN + TARANJI GRANT

FEMINISTS (24" X 36")
2020

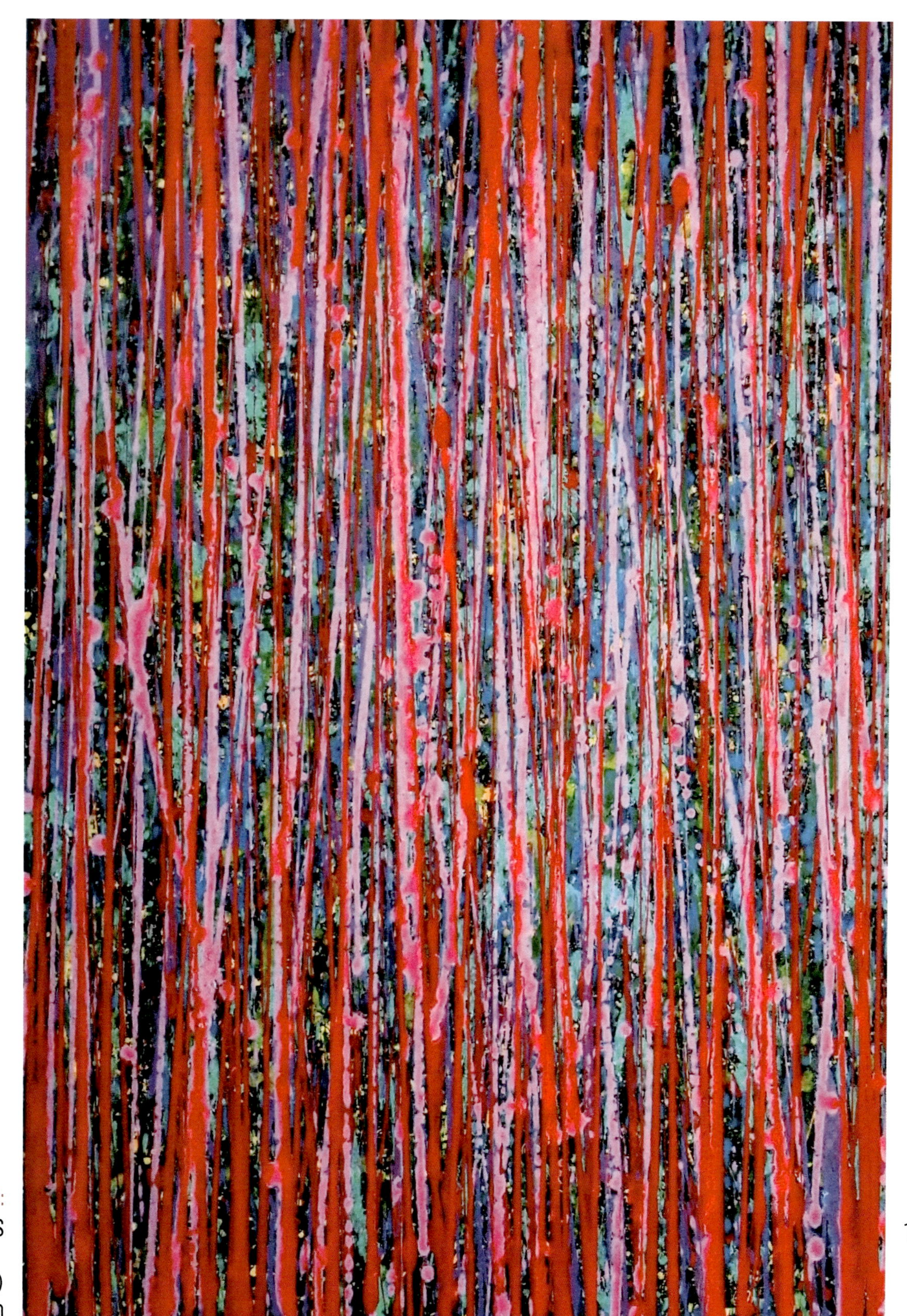

COLLECTOR:
THE HONORABLE SAMUEL BUZZ THOMAS

THE FOREST BEYOND (24X36)
2020

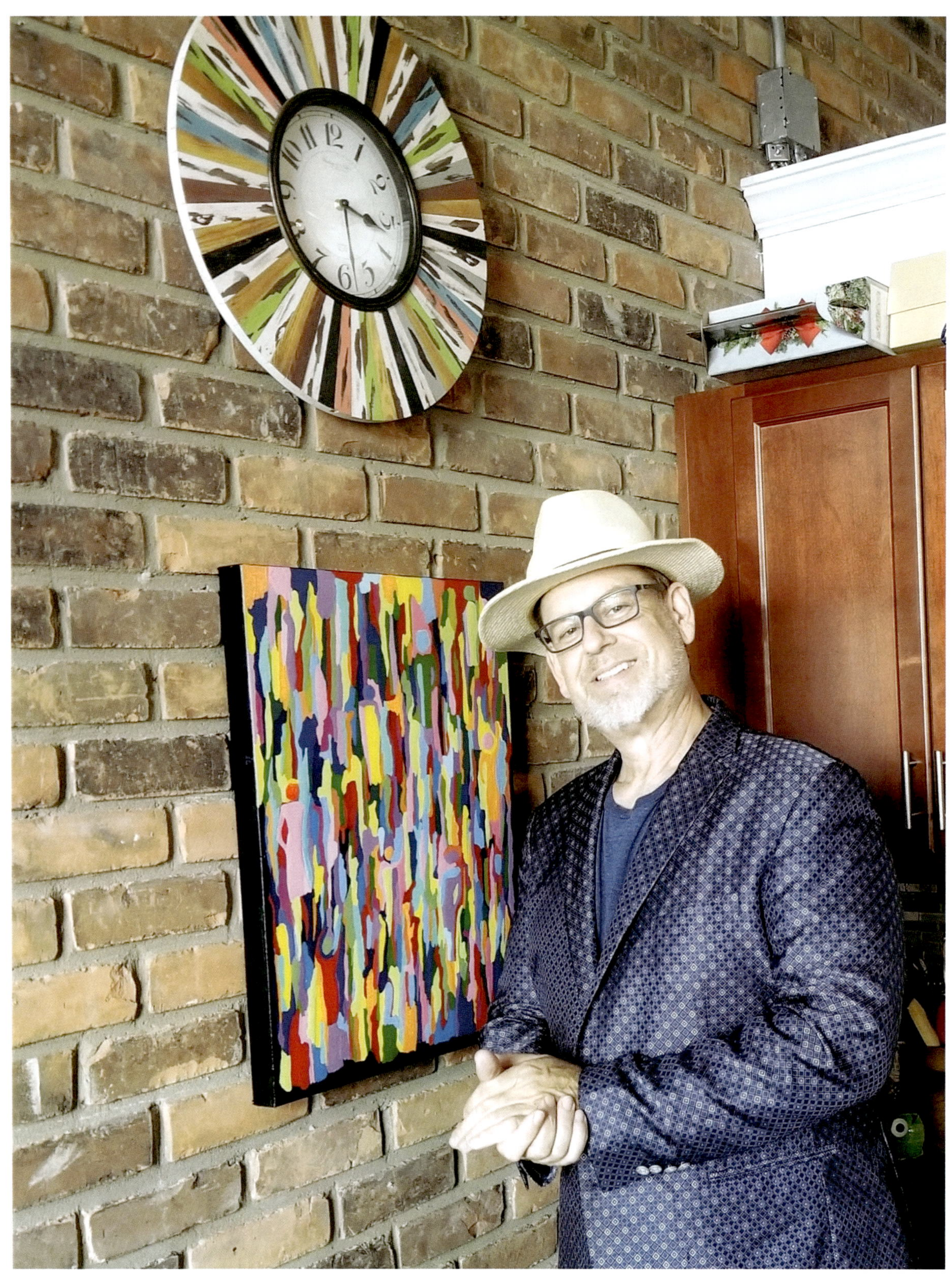

COLLECTOR:
SCOTT MCDUFFEE

IF WOMEN
RULED #4
(18"X 24") 2020

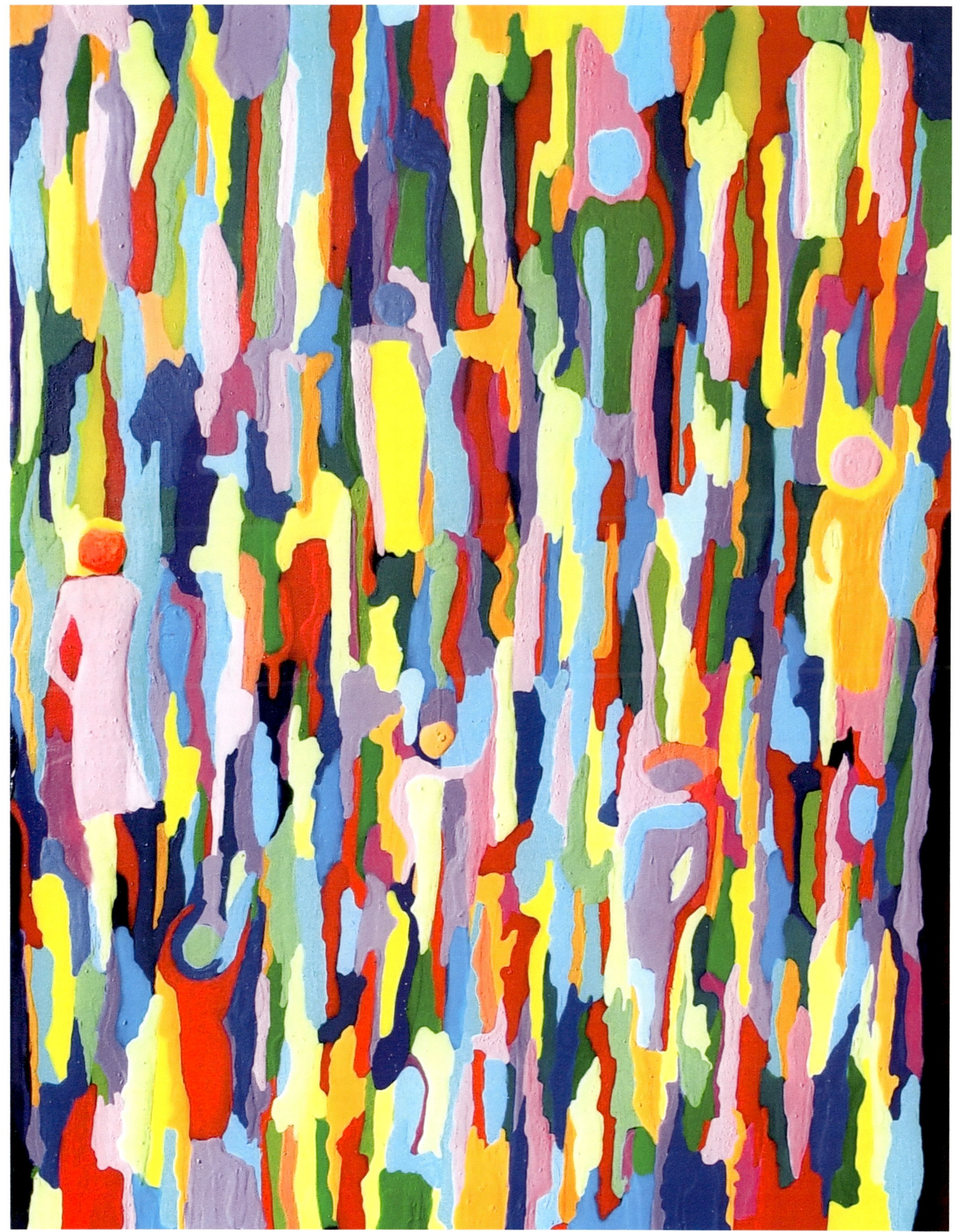

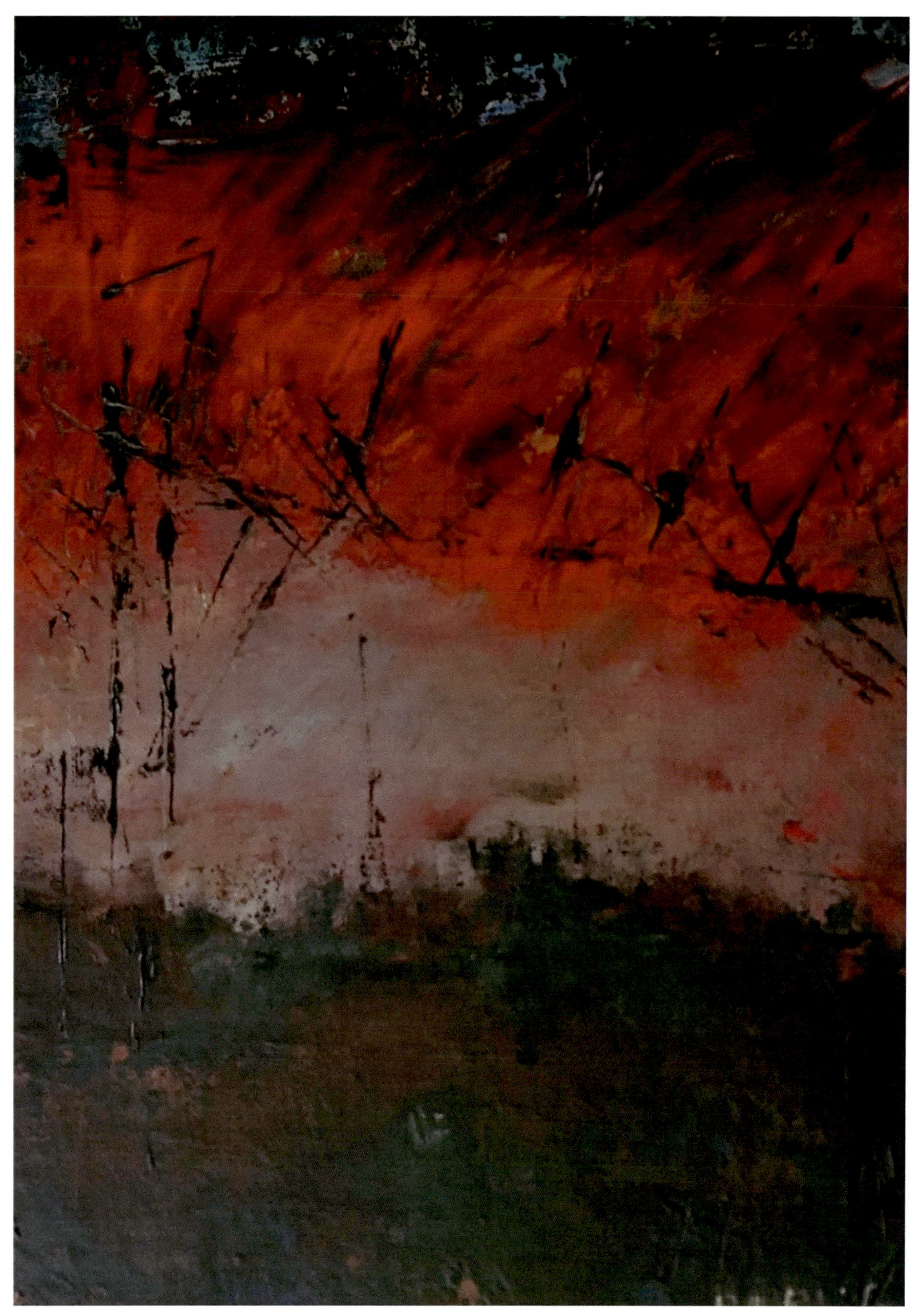

COLLECTOR:
STEPHEN BRAY

RAGING
(11" X 14")
2018

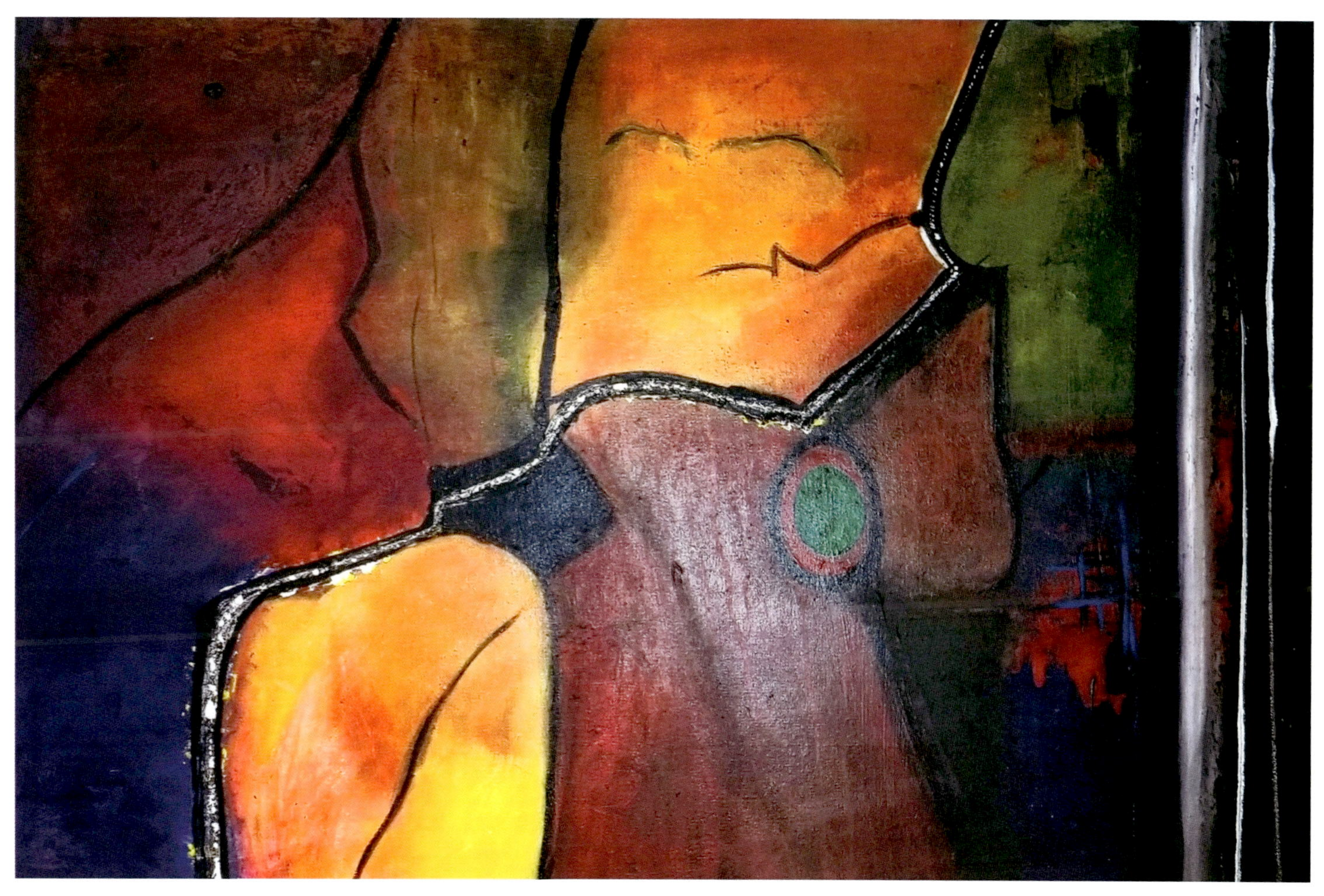

COLLECTOR:
ARLINDA CROSSLAND

TERRITORIAL (36" X 24")
2019

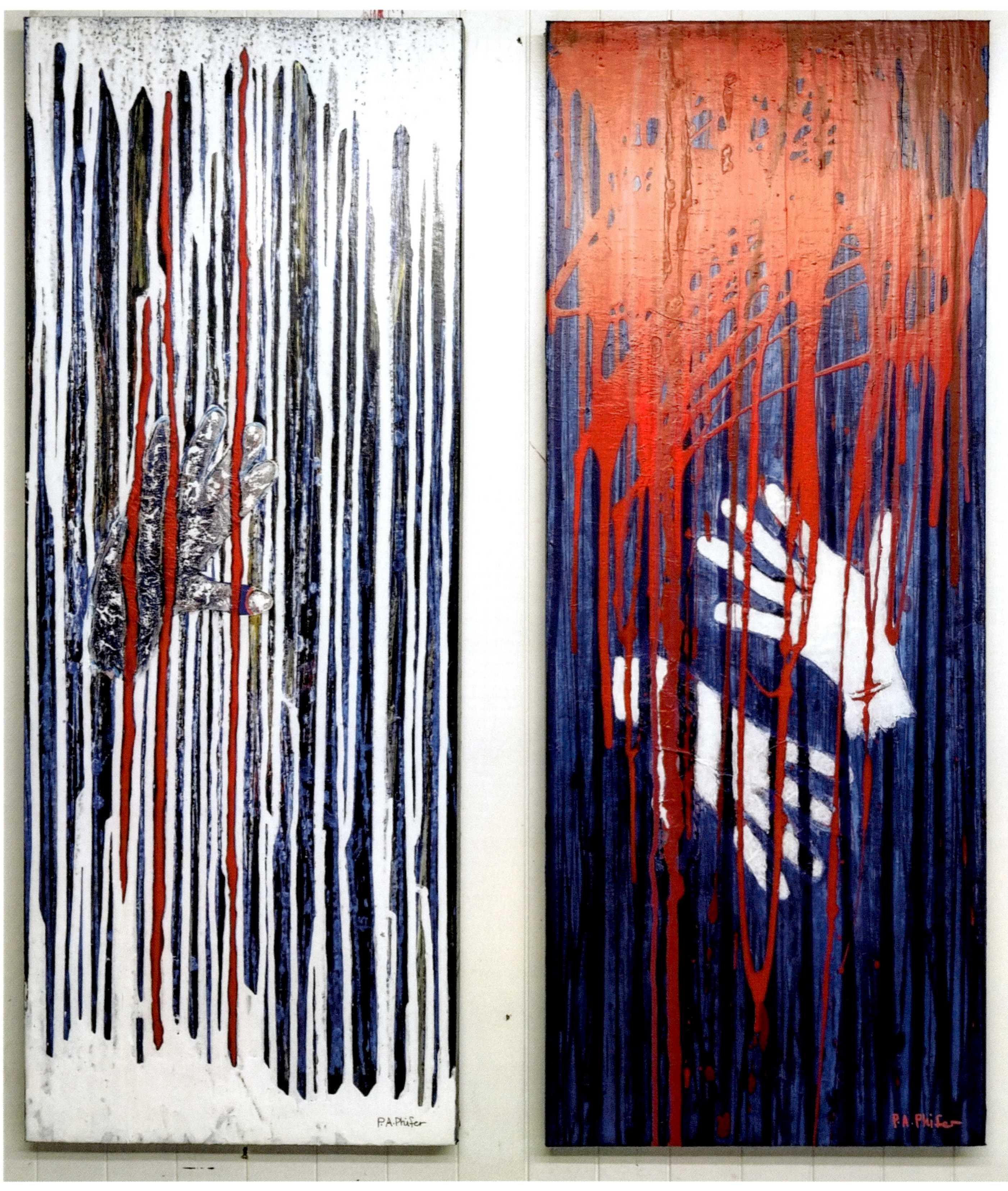
P.A. Phifer
P.A. Phifer

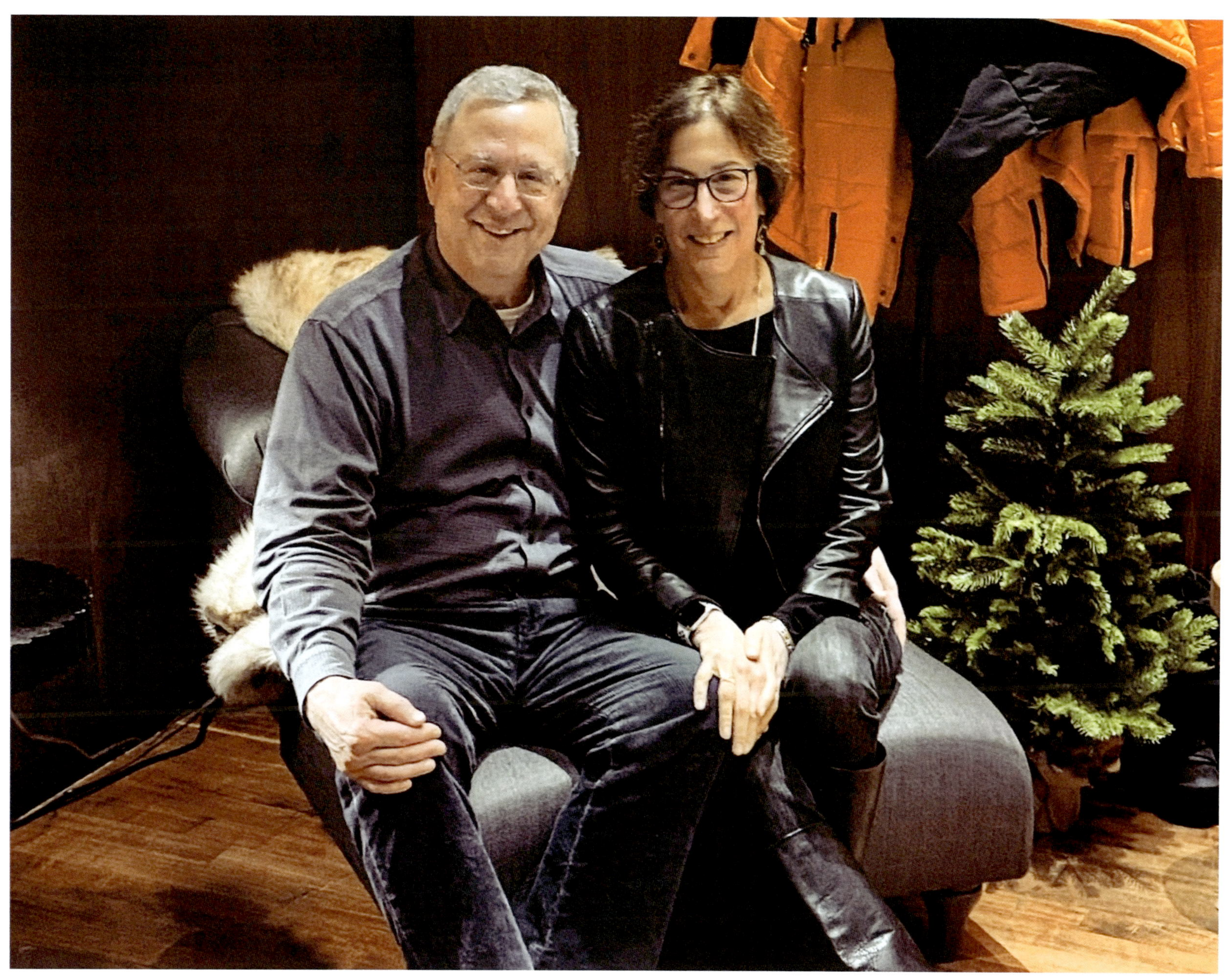

COLLECTOR:
PETER AND BARBARA SARGENT
(NEWTON, MA)

THE HAND WE WERE DEALT
BLOOD ON THEIR HANDS (BOTH 16 X 40)
2020

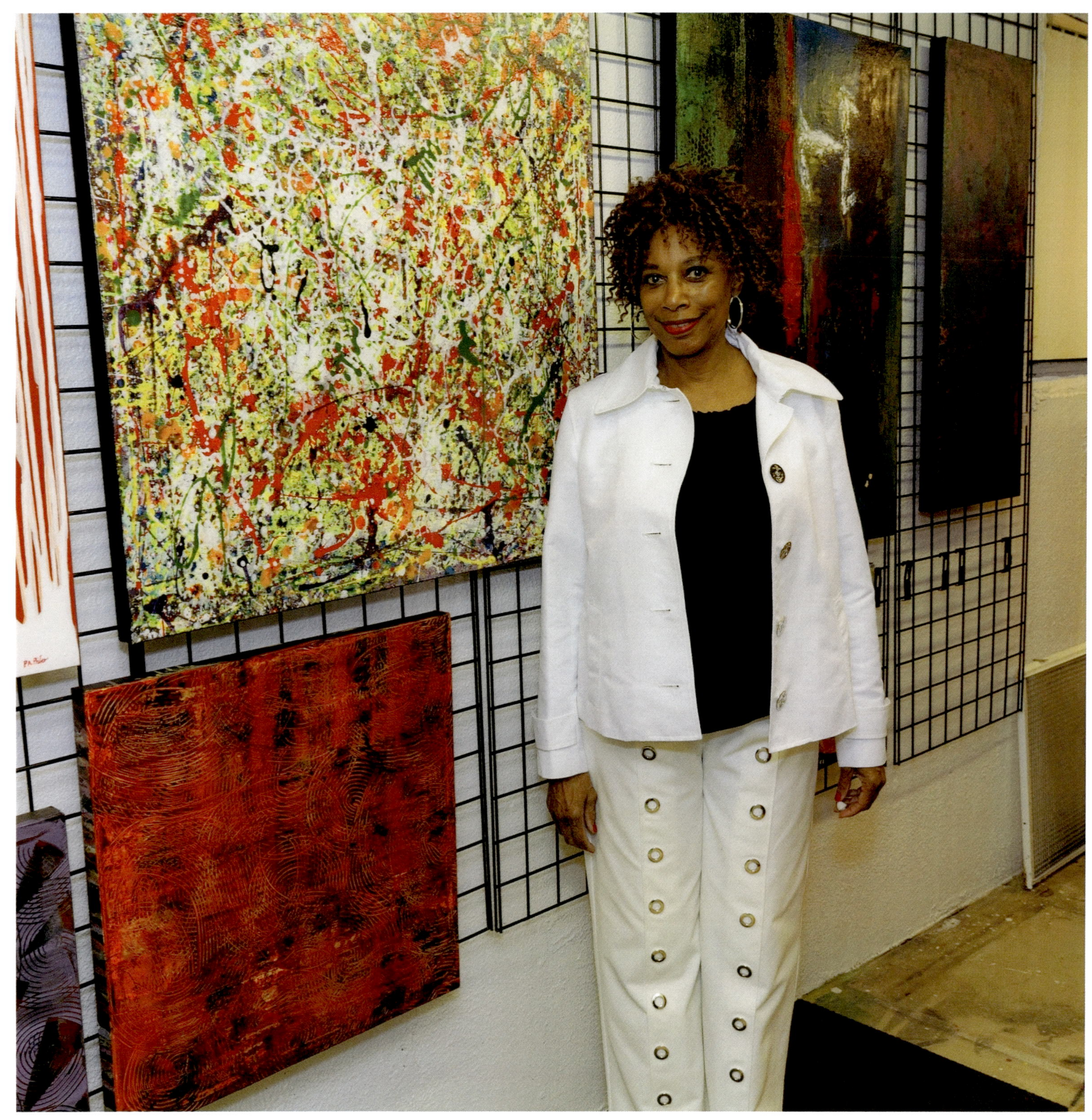

P.A PHIFER

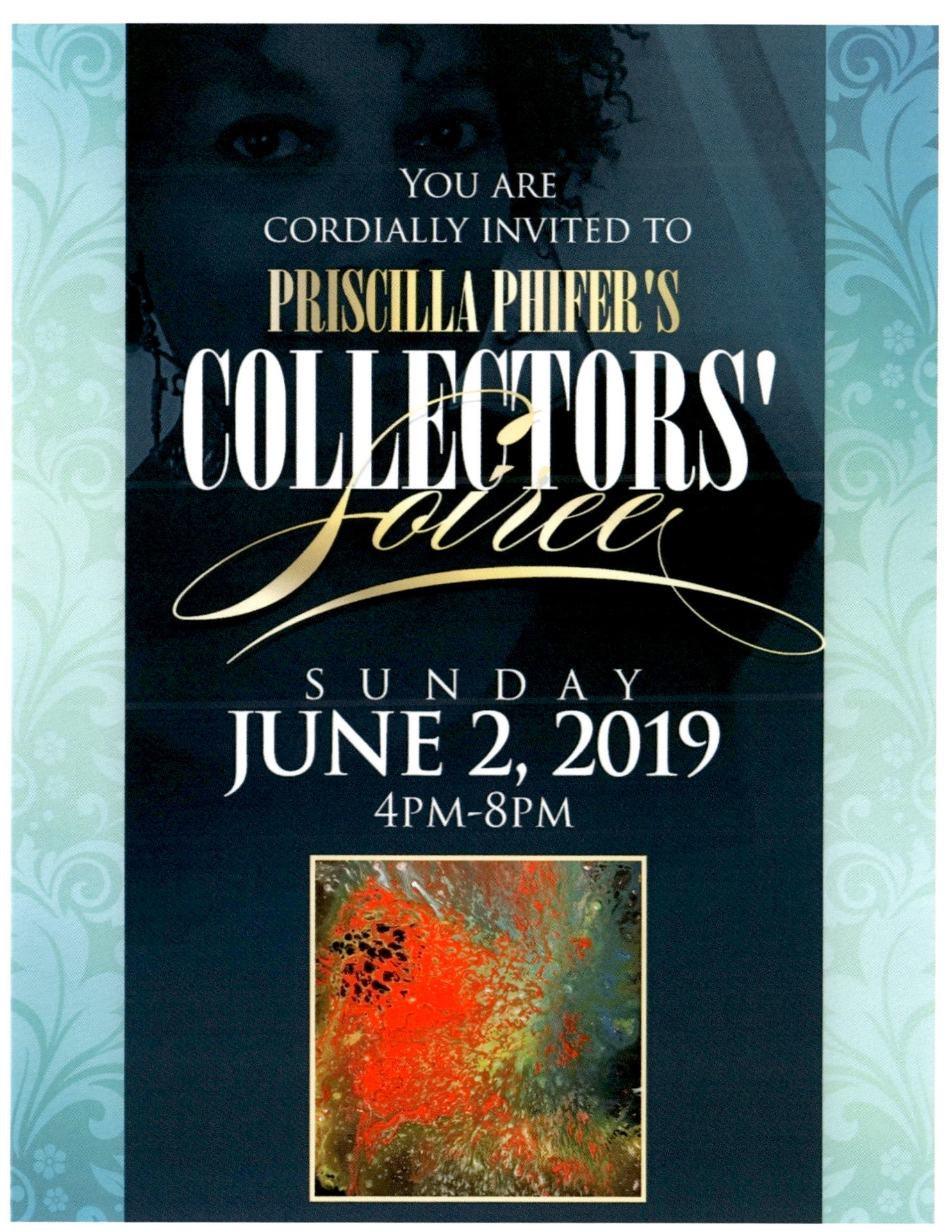
You are
cordially invited to
PRISCILLA PHIFER'S
COLLECTORS'
Soirée
SUNDAY
JUNE 2, 2019
4PM-8PM

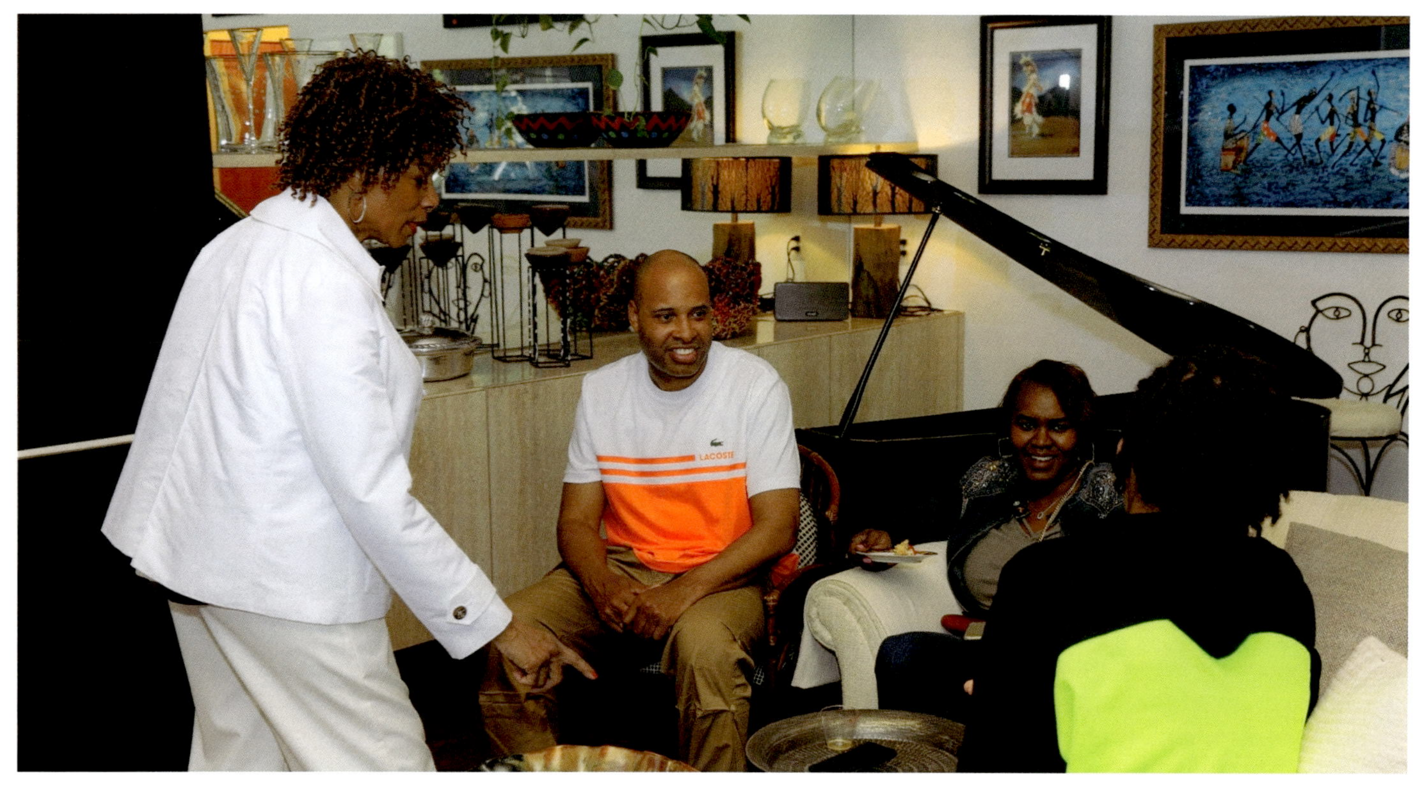

PRISCILLA + EUCLIDES + YOLANDA DURFIELD

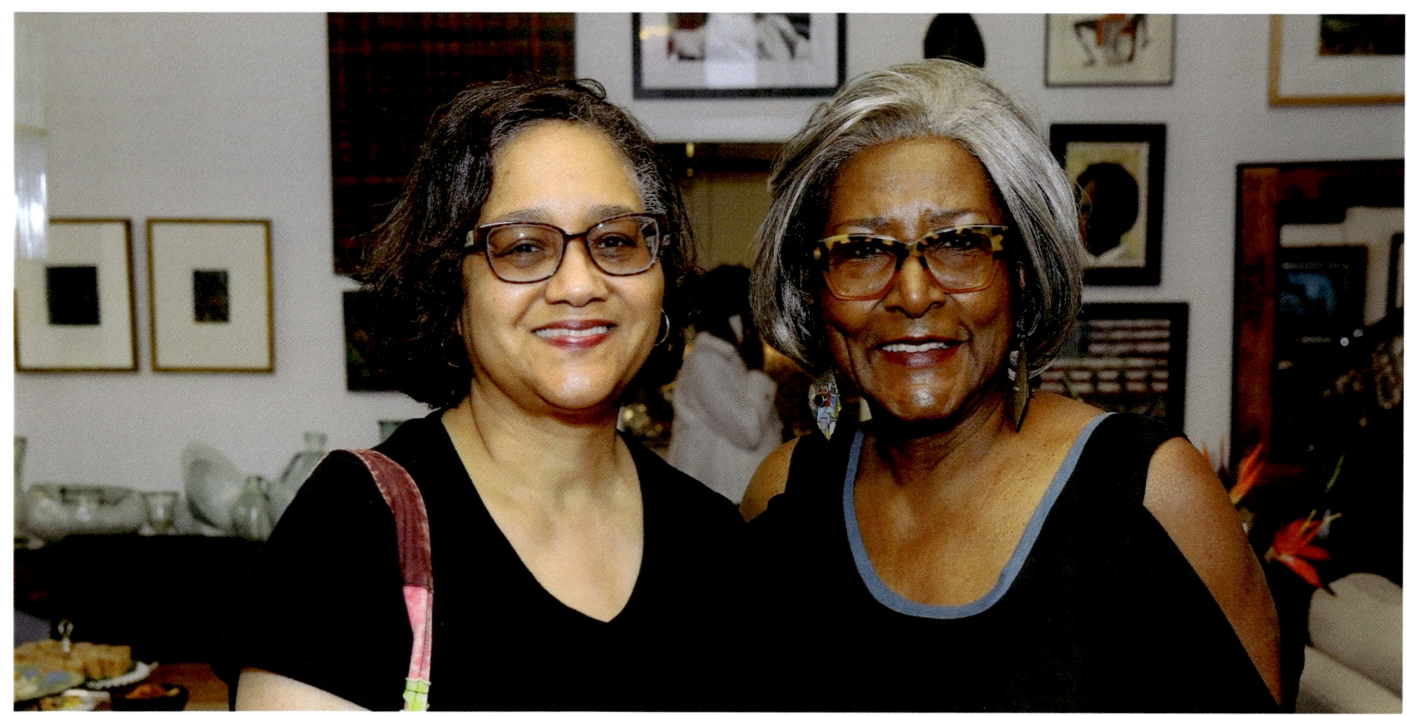

ROBBIE BEST (RIGHT) WITH DAUGHTER, ROBIN

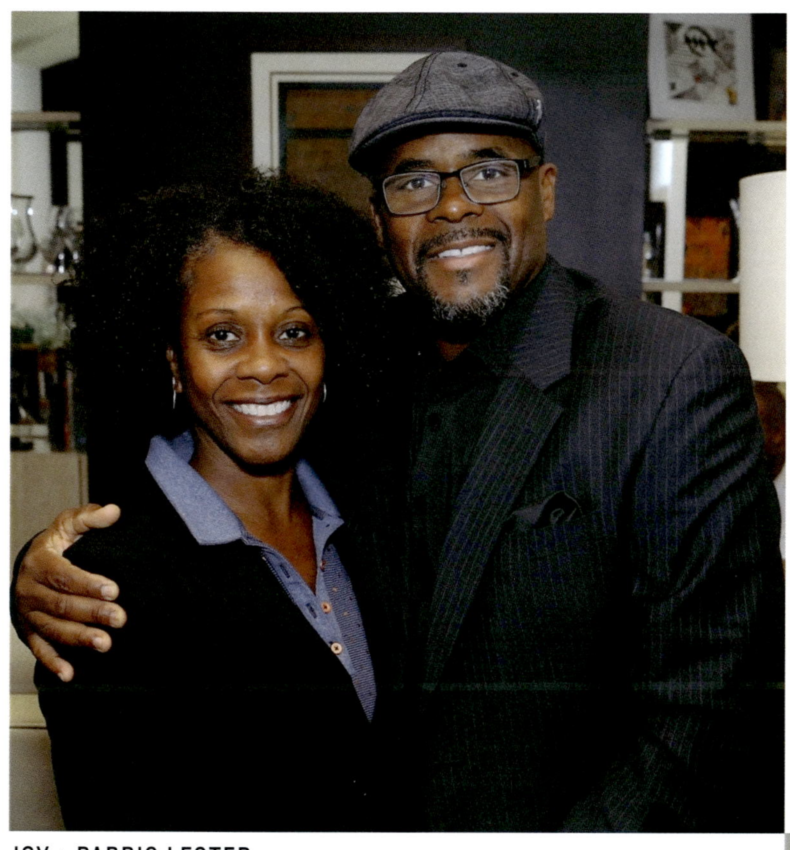

JOY + PARRIS LESTER

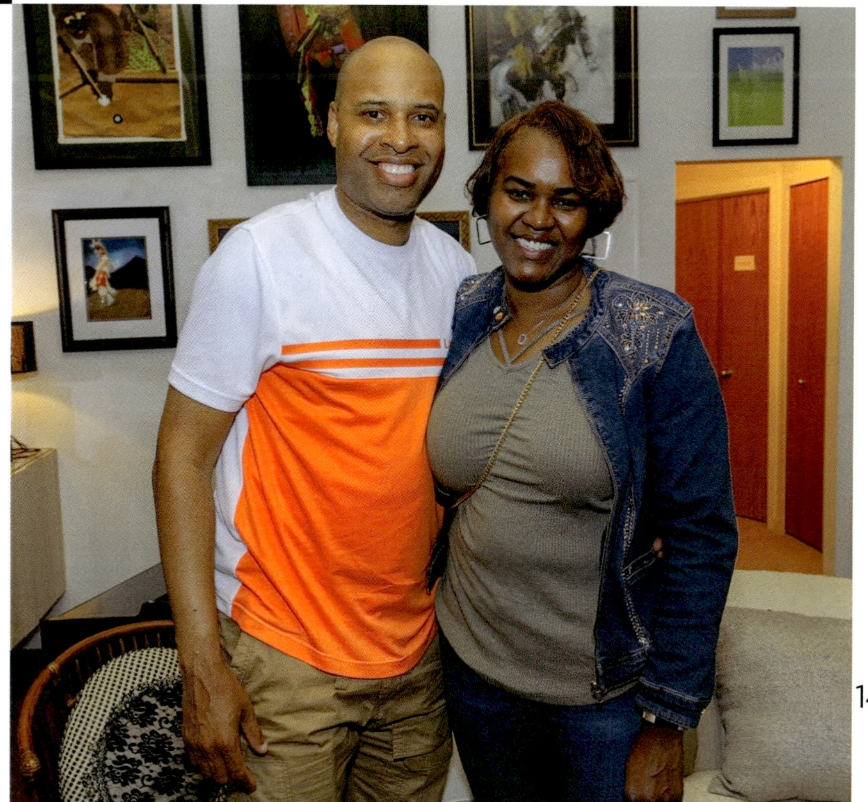

EUCLIDES + YOLANDA DURFIELD

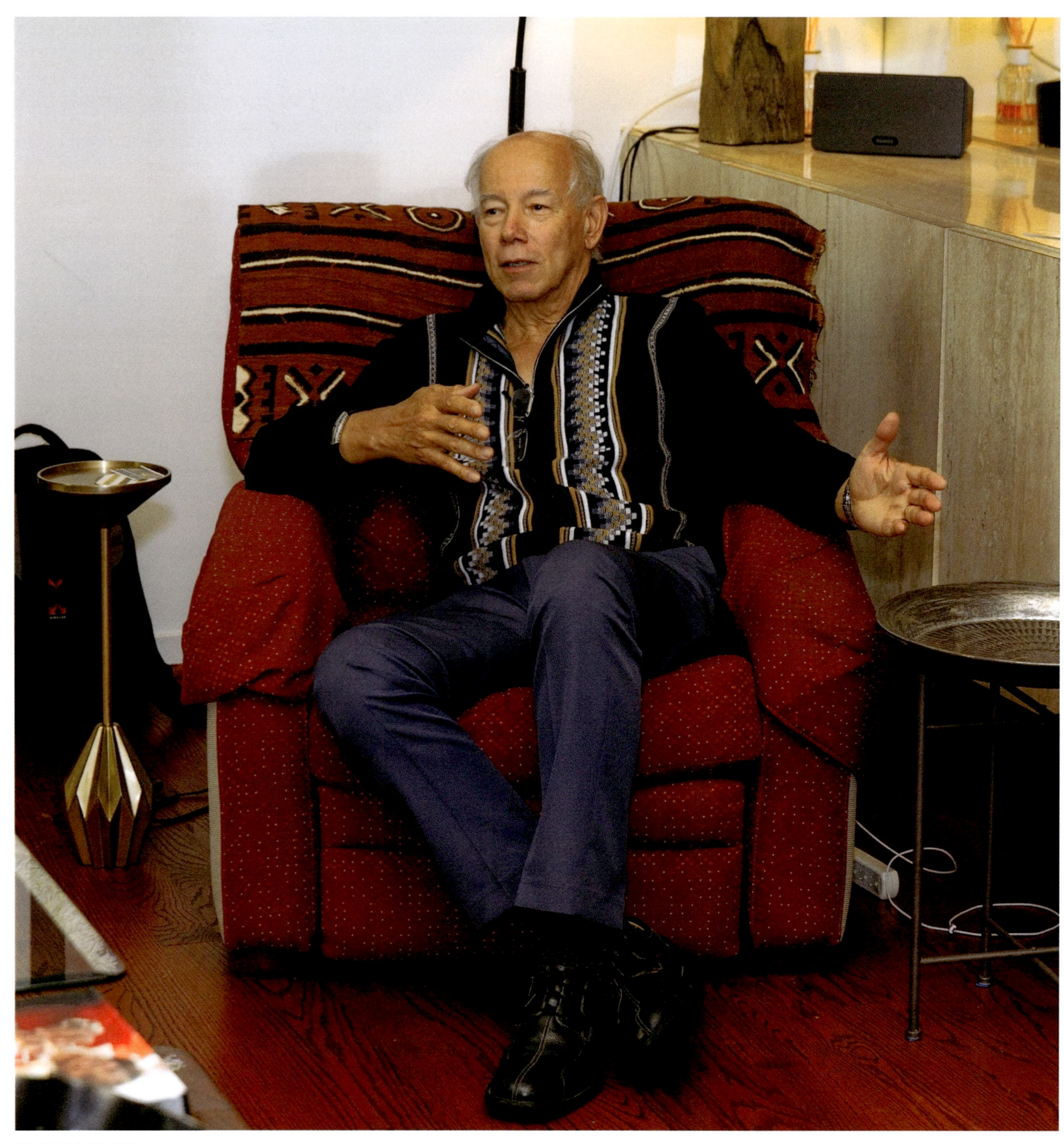

SIDNEY JONES

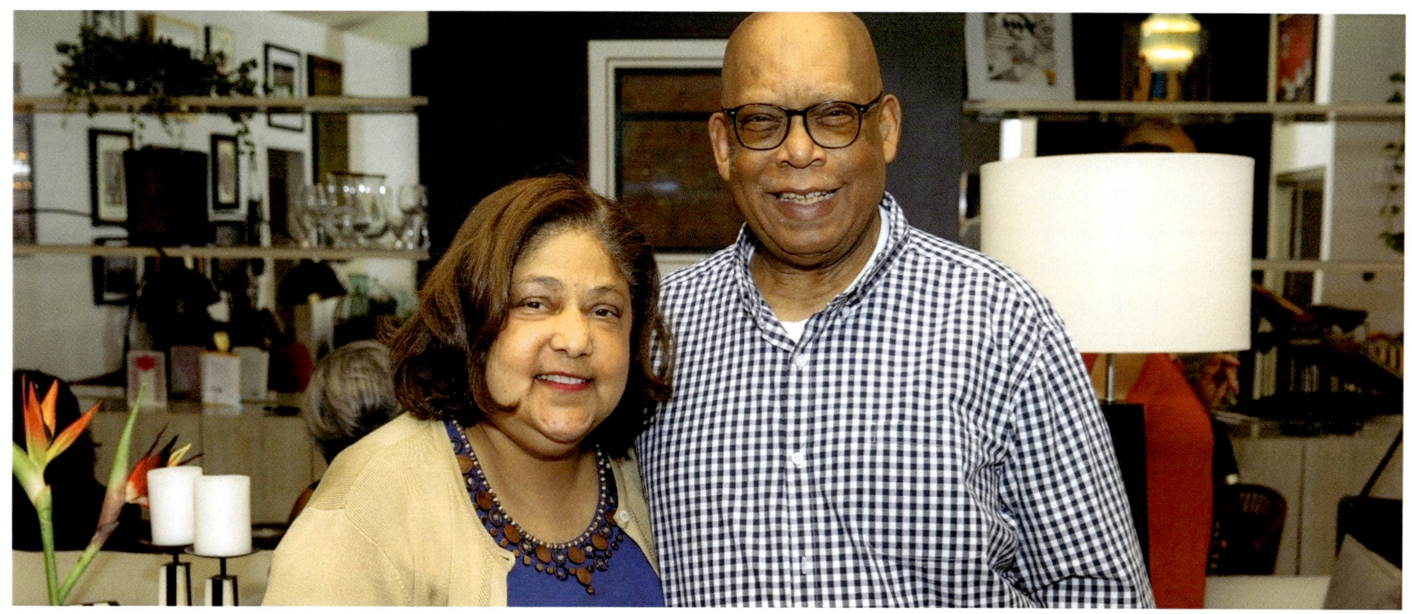

JACQUI + STEPHEN KEMP

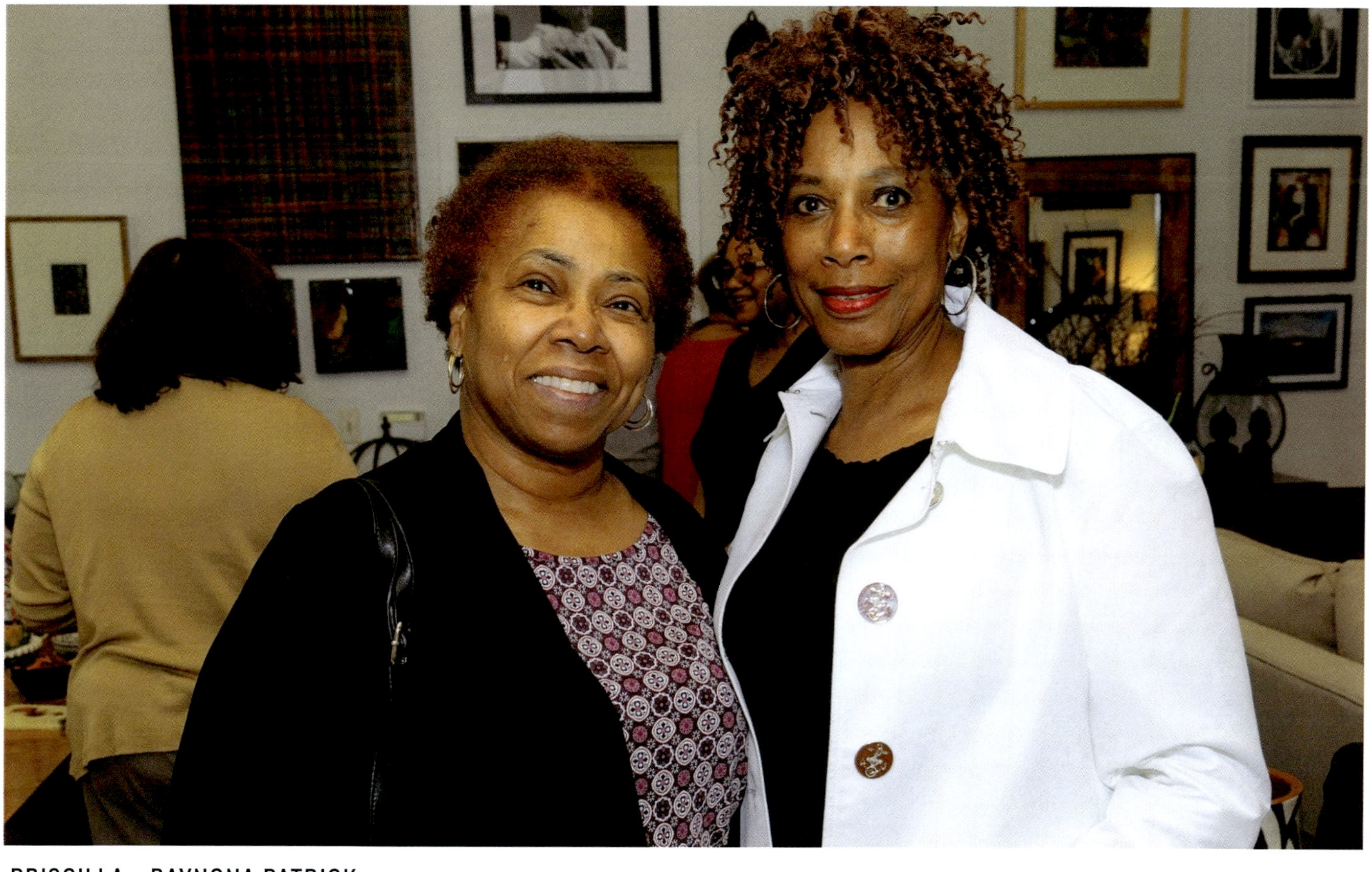

PRISCILLA + RAYNONA PATRICK

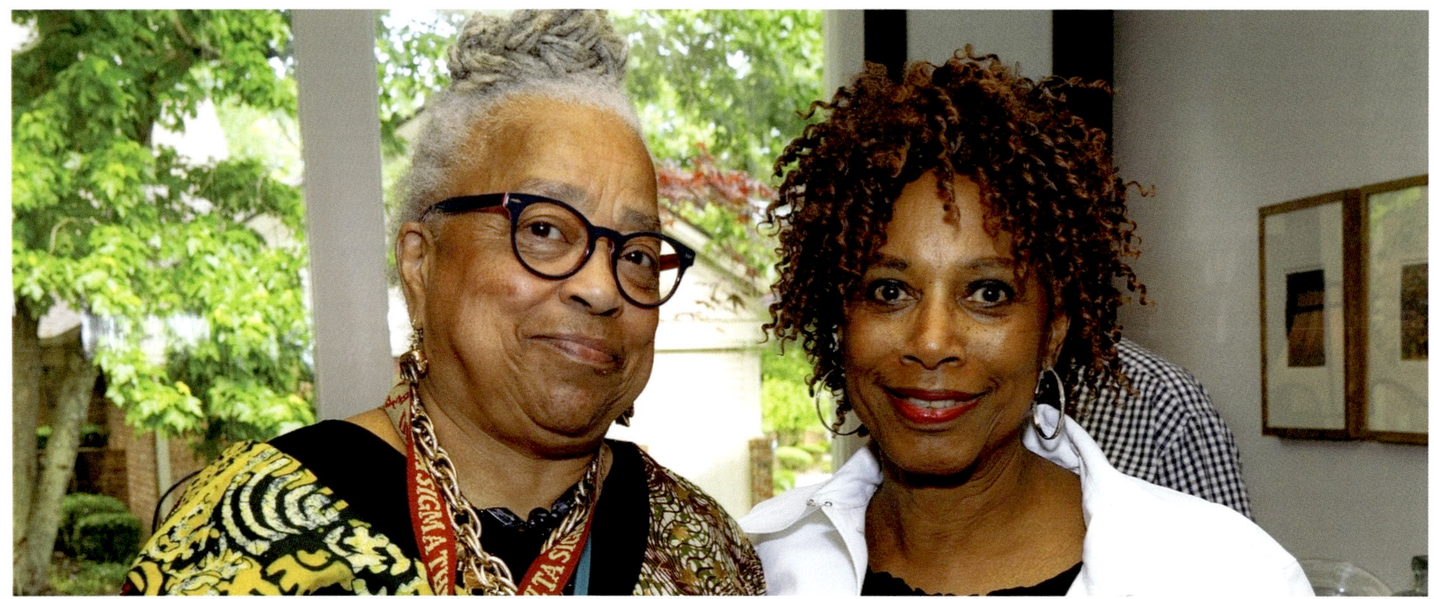

MARGARET TUCKER

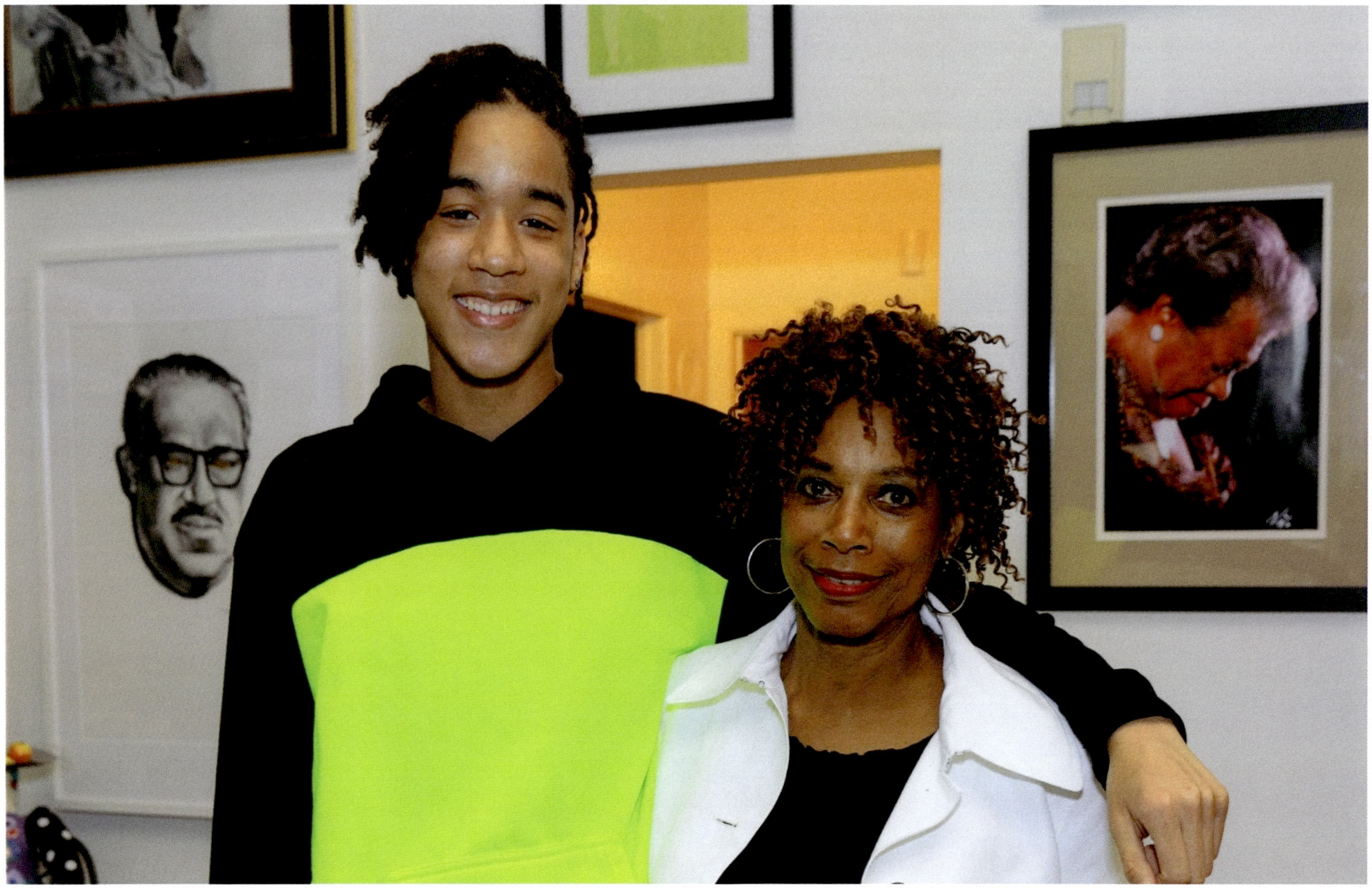

WILL BROOKS

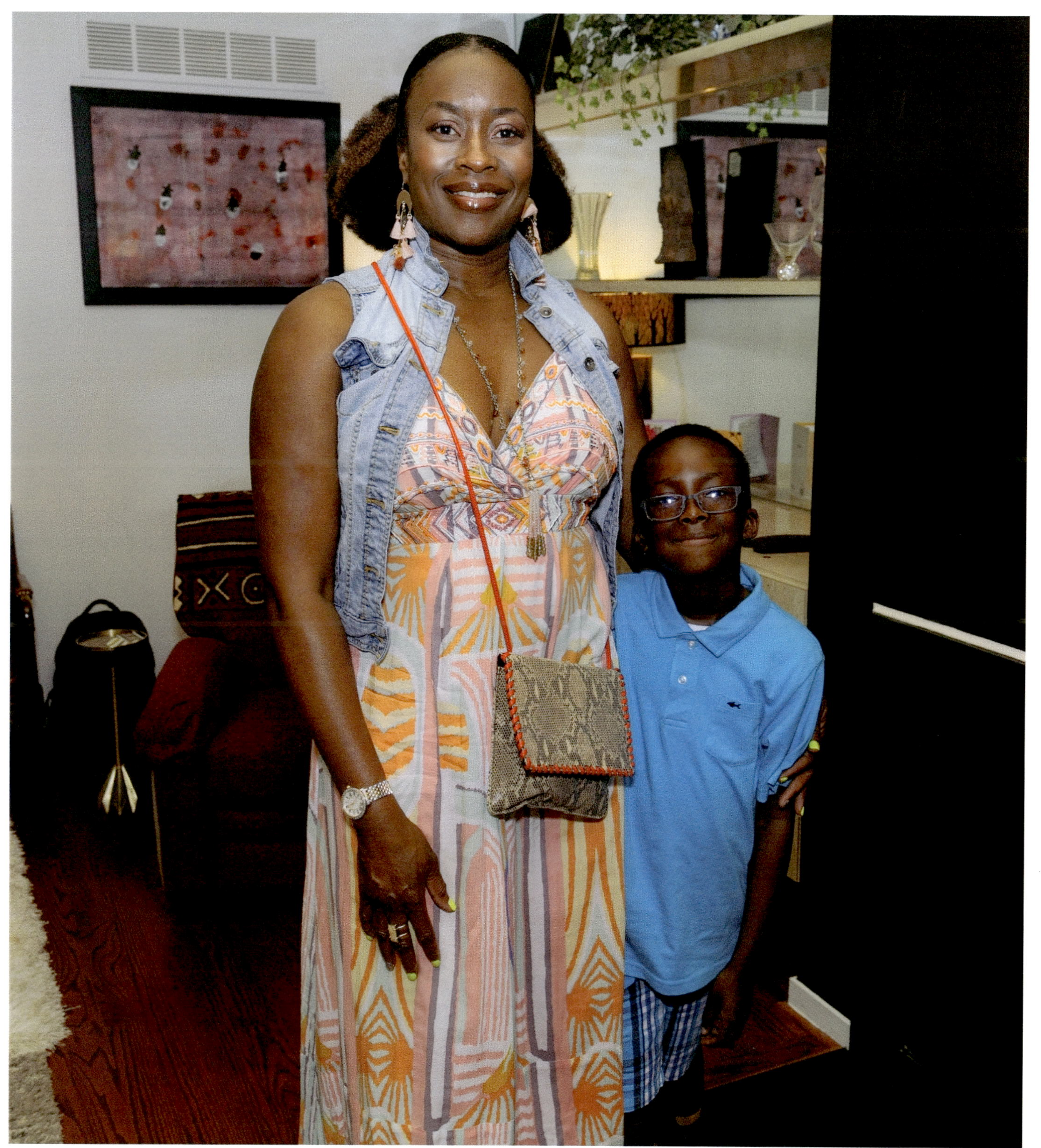

TIANA BAKER + SON, AJ

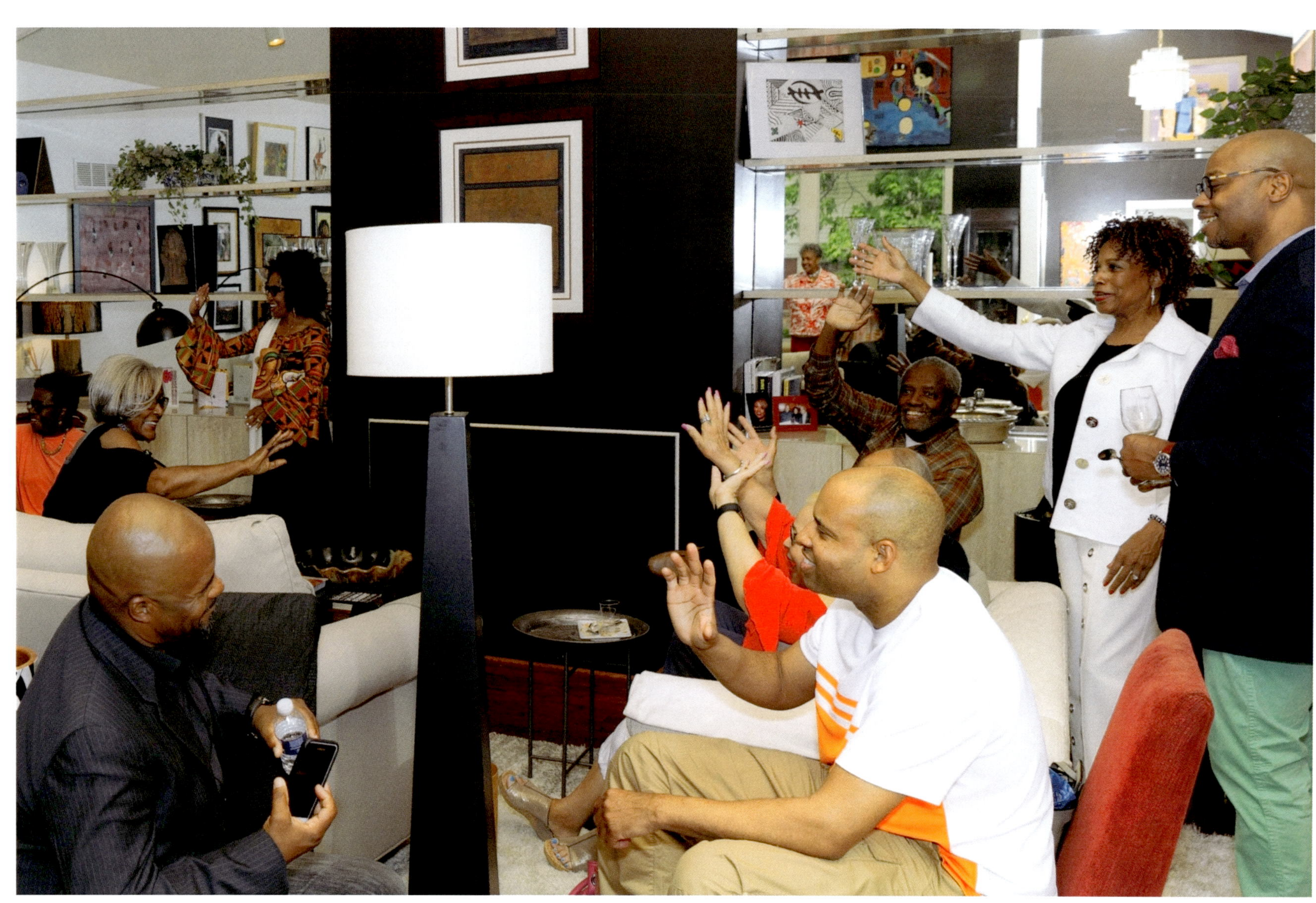

PARRIS LESTER , ROBBIE BEST, JACKIE BURDELL, HENRY HARPER + DRAKE PHIFER

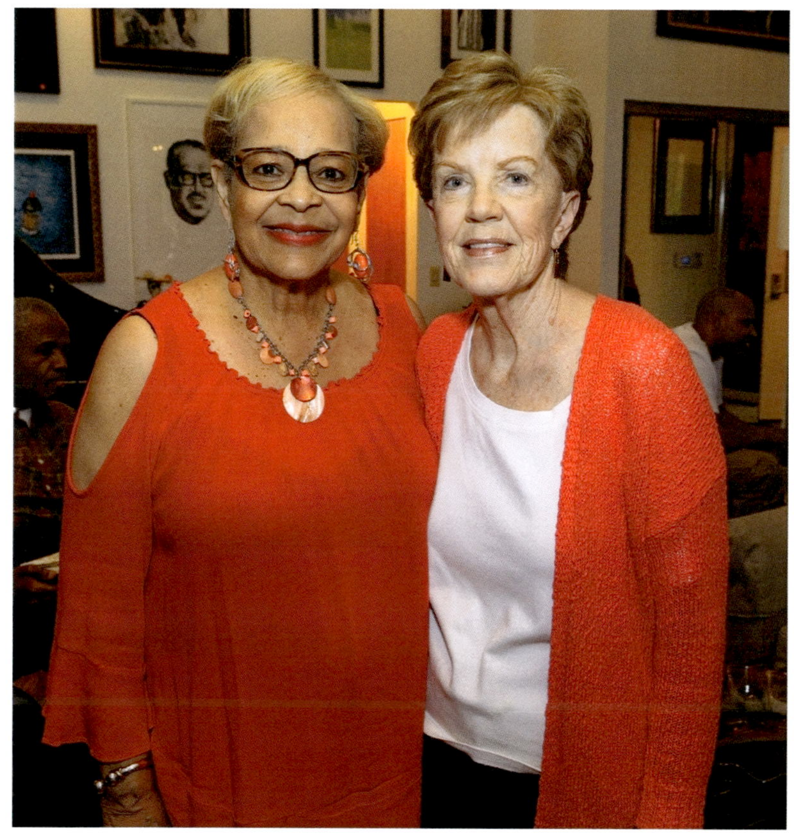

JOAN BRITTON + LYNN MYERS

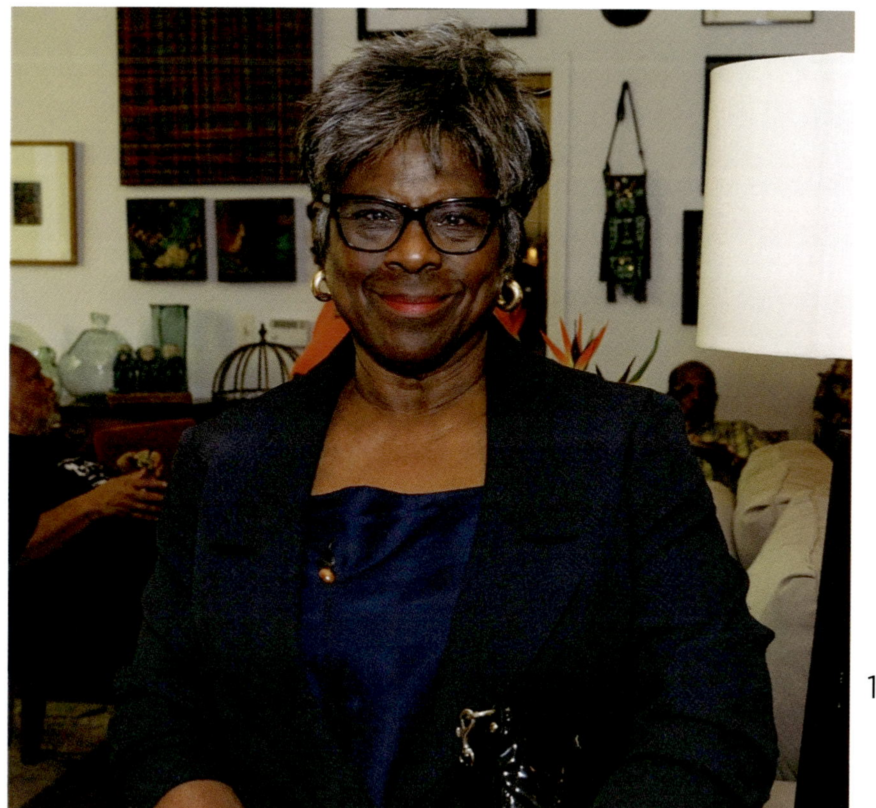

DORIS WITHERSPOON

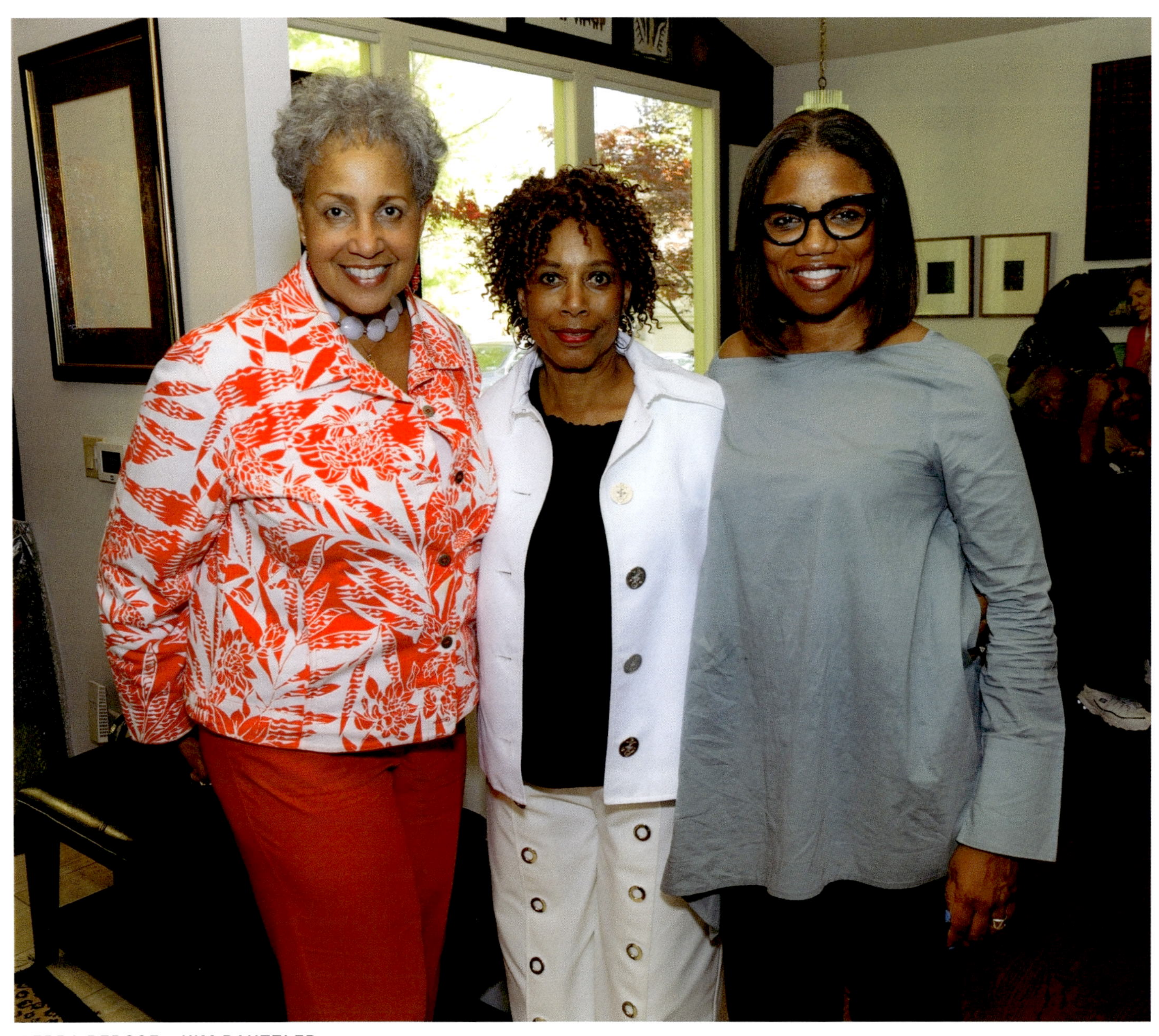

DEBRA DEBOSE + KIM DANTZLER

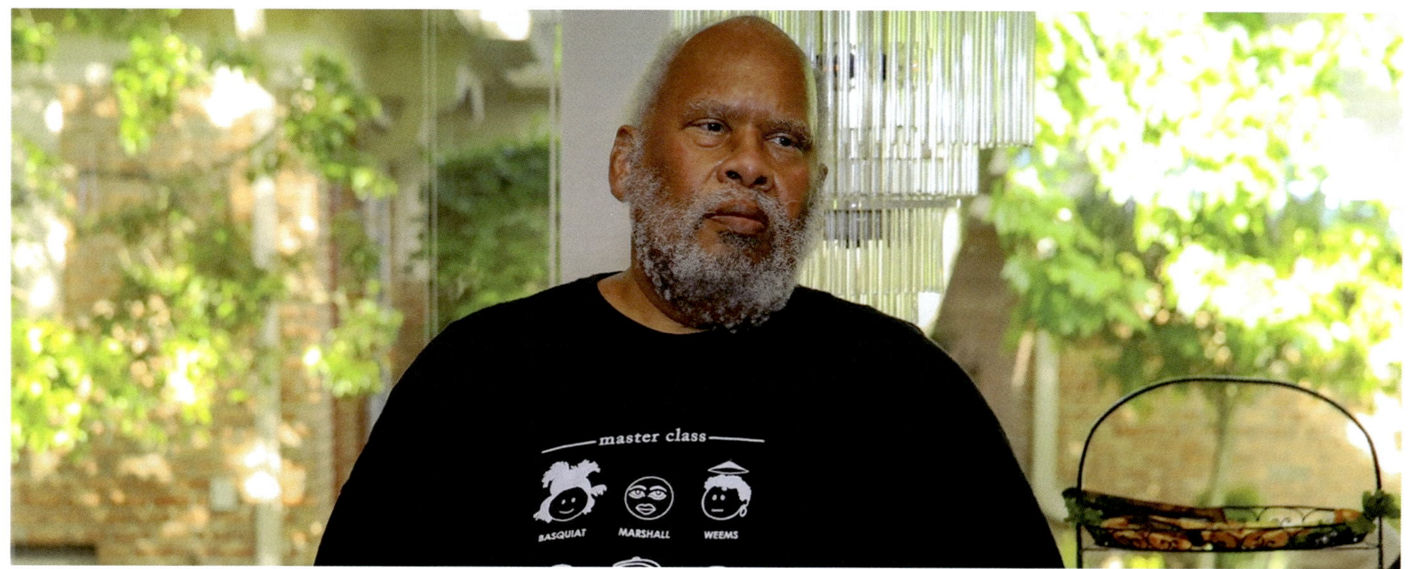

JAMES DOZIER

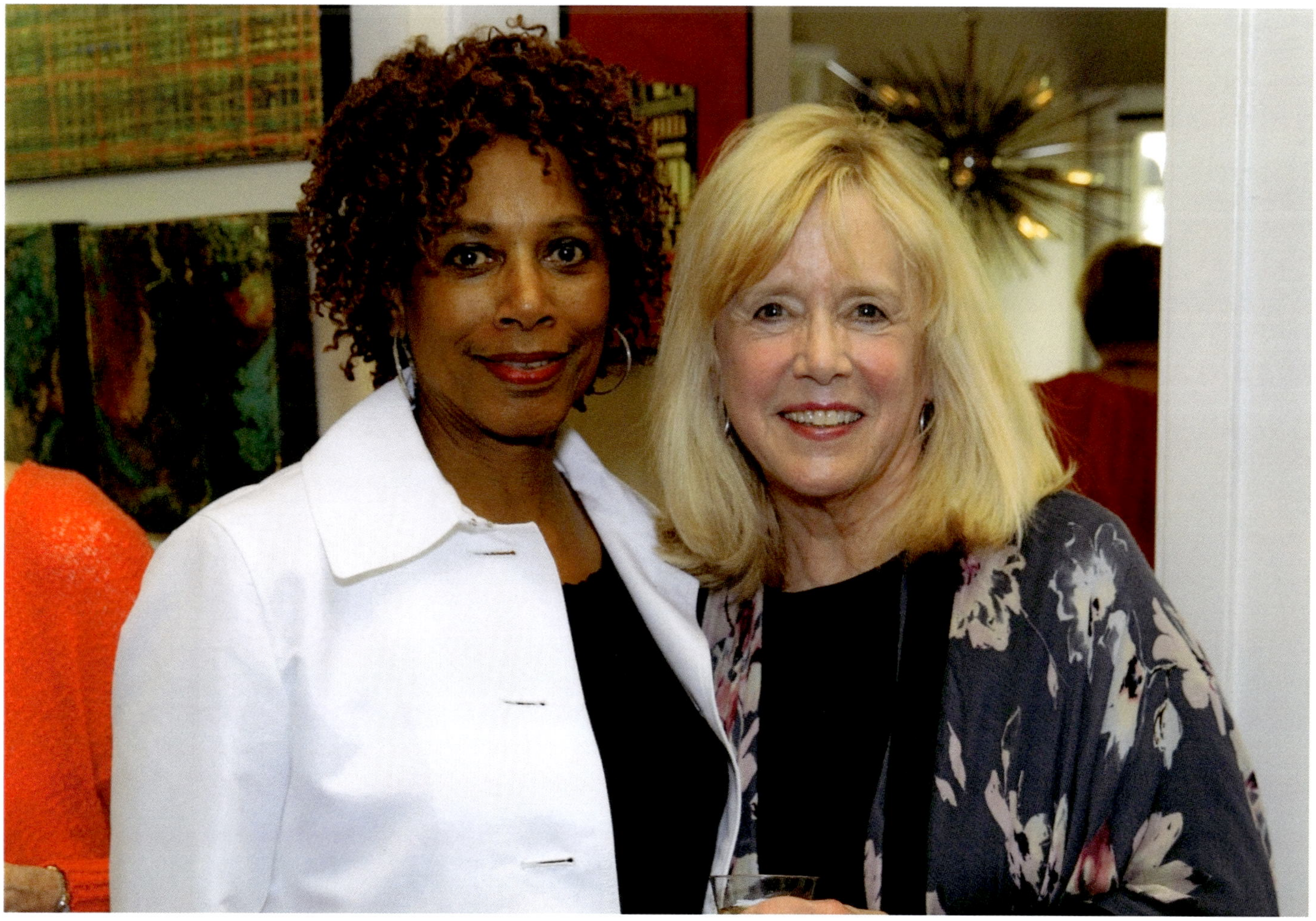

LAURIE MUELLER

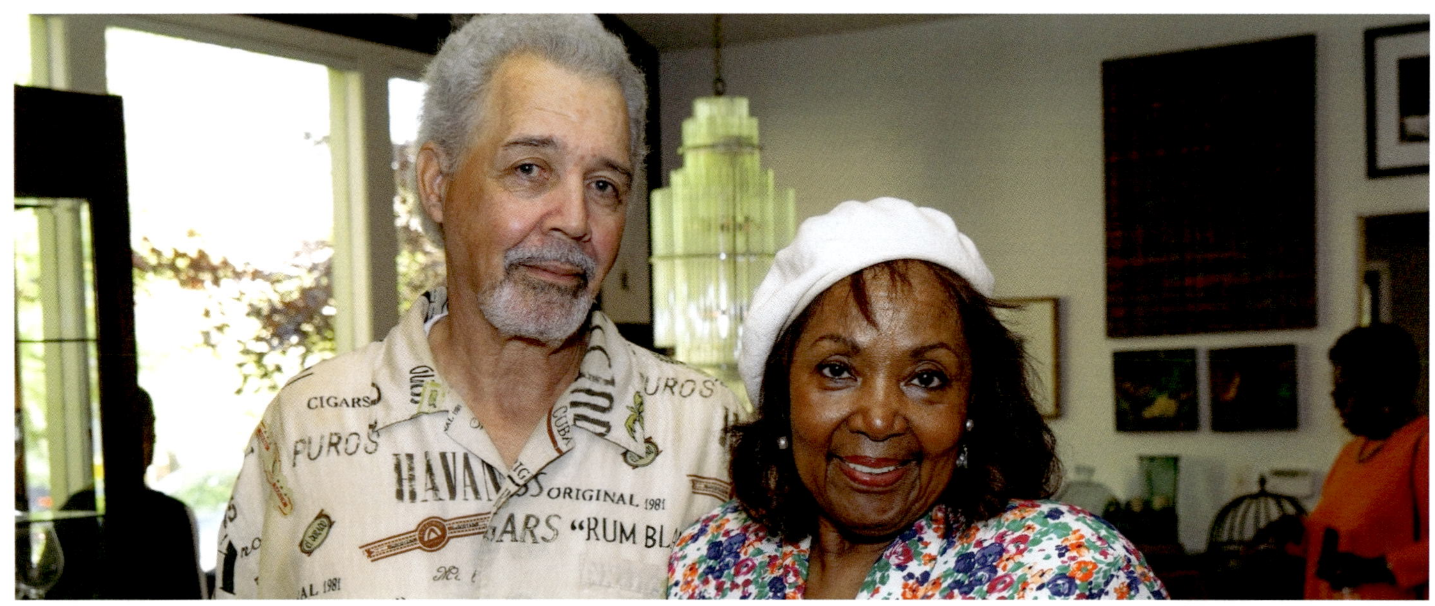

SANFORD + SHIRLEY WOODS

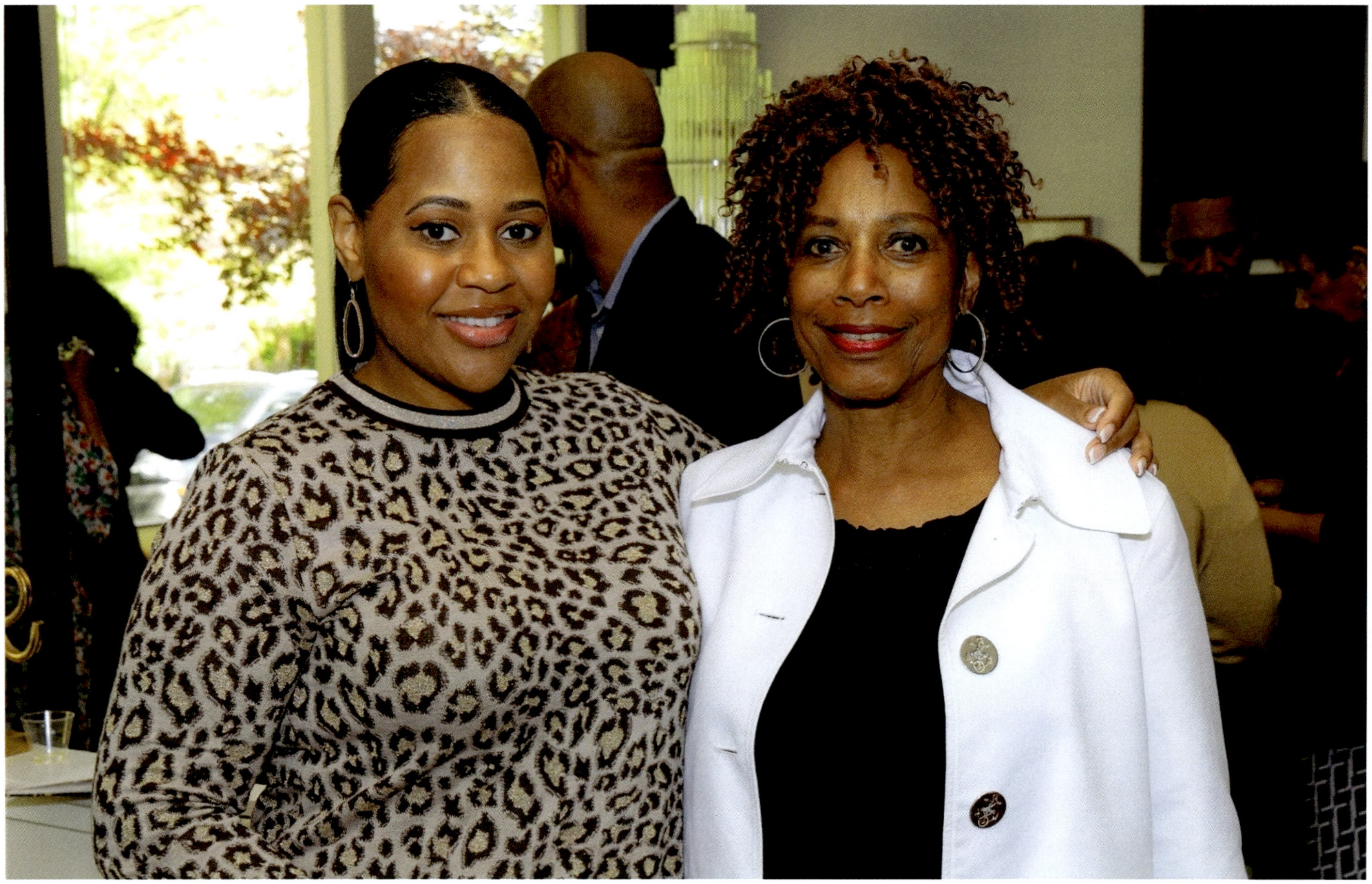

WHITNEY GRIFFIN

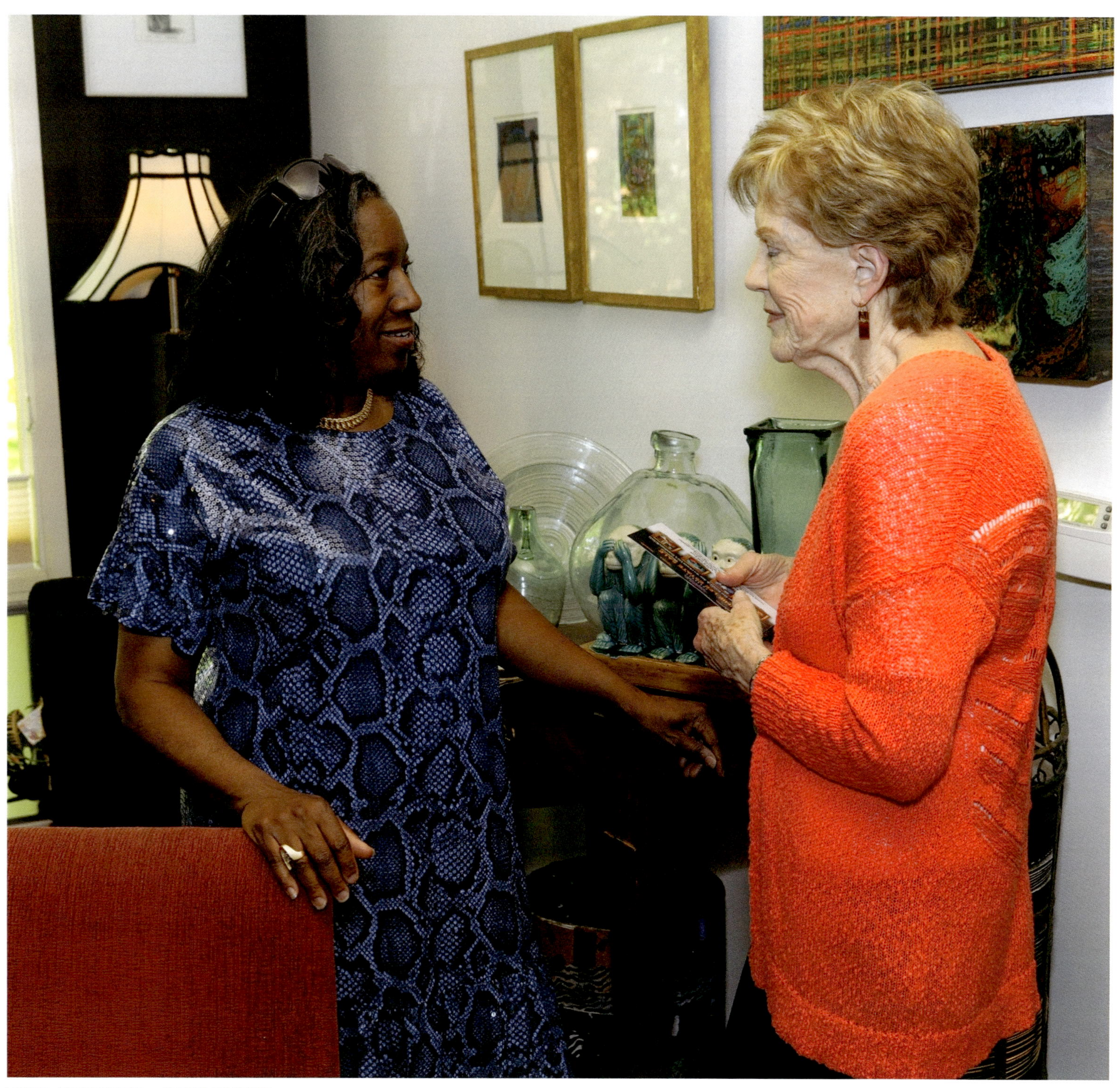

LINDA WHITAKER + LYNN MYERS

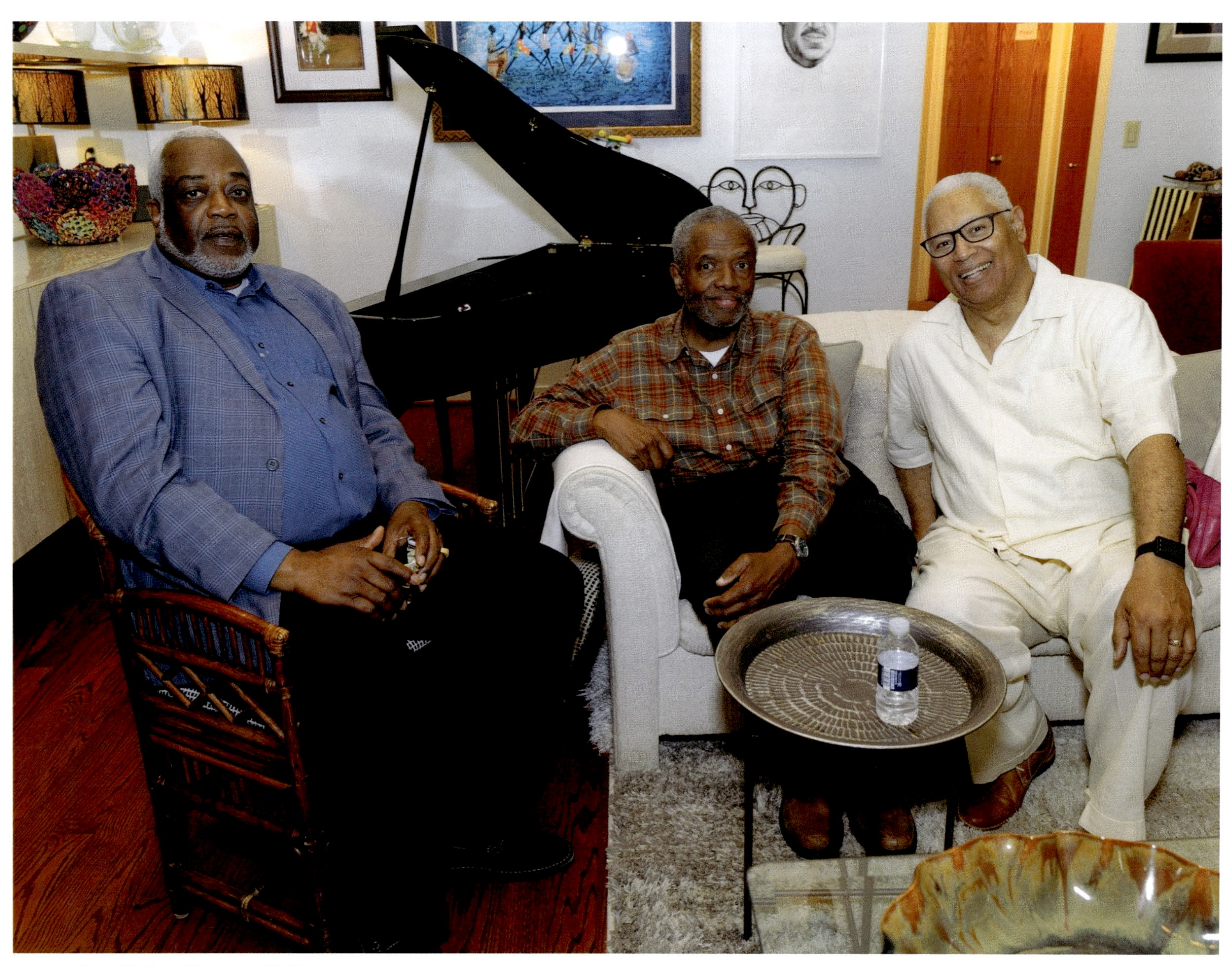

DAVID WHITAKER, HENRY HARPER + DEXTER MAYS

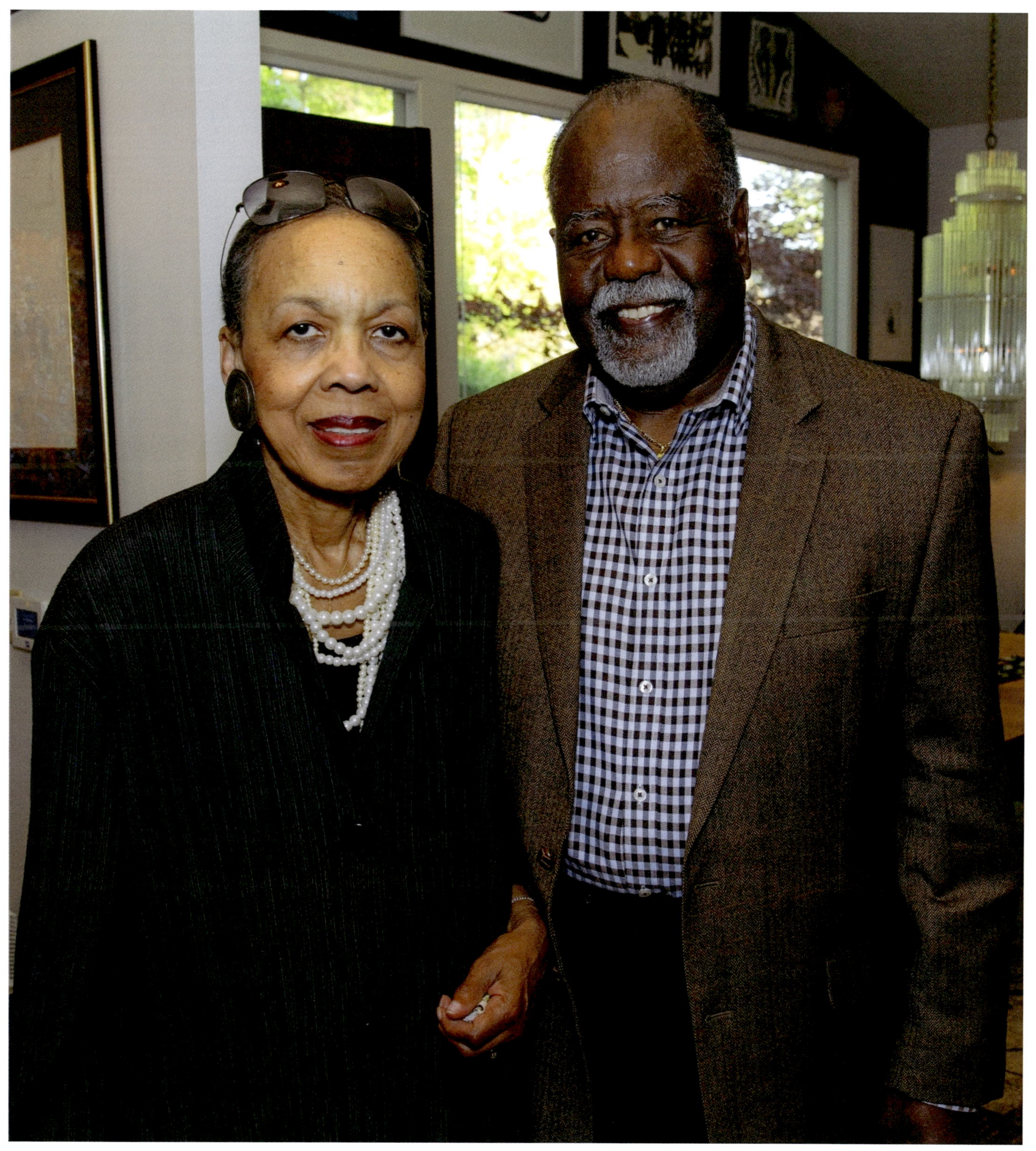

ERNEST + DE RETLAND

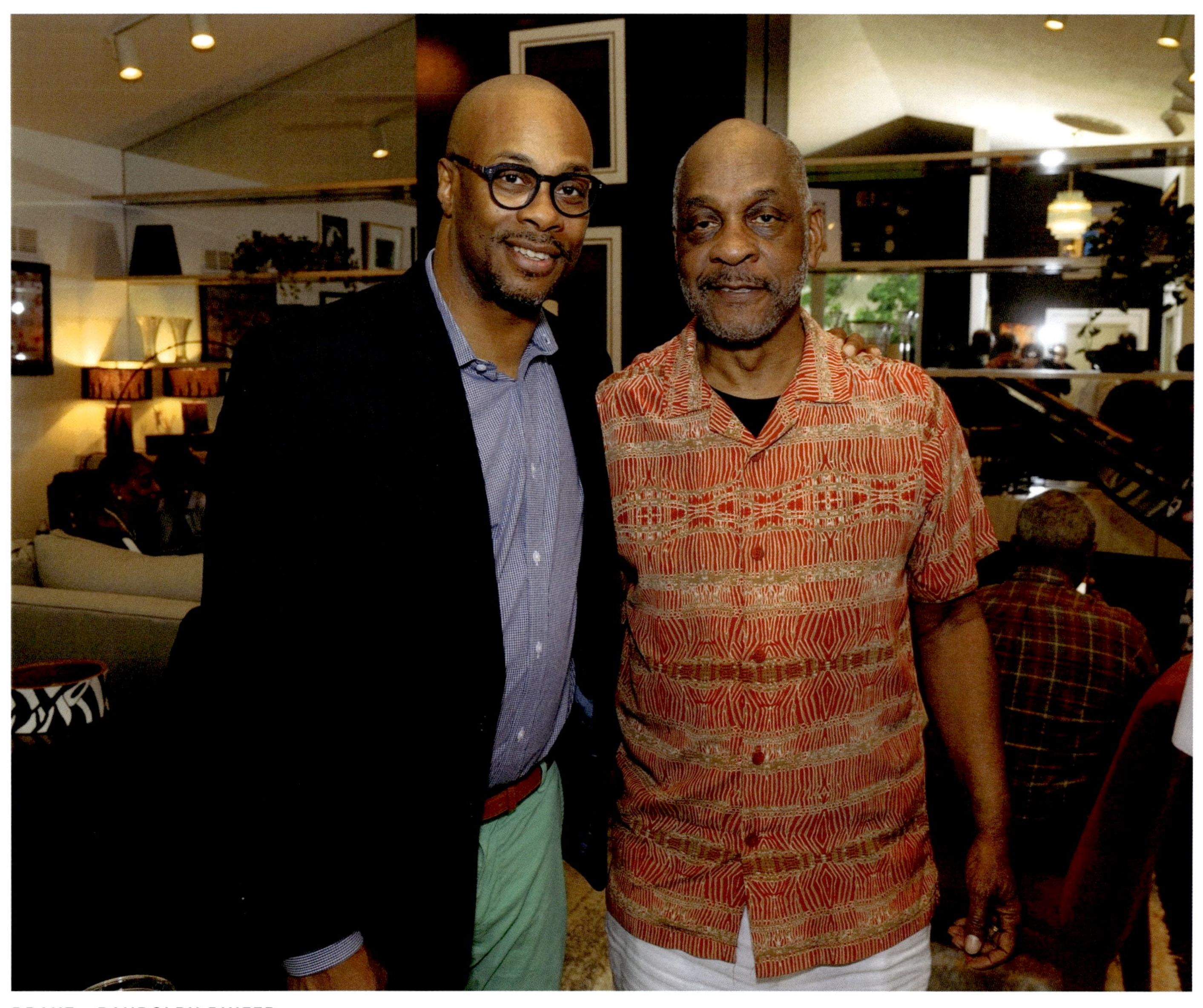

DRAKE + RANDOLPH PHIFER

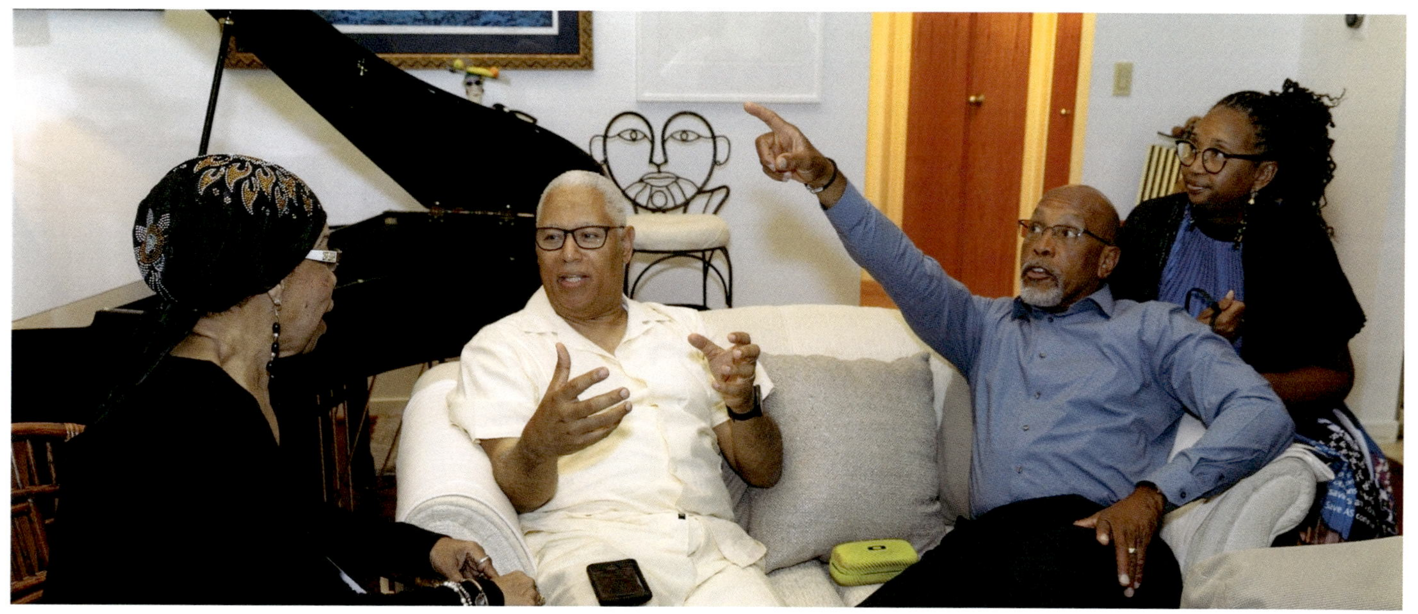

PATRICIA BAKER, DEXTER MAYS, ROBERT + BEVERLY ALLEN

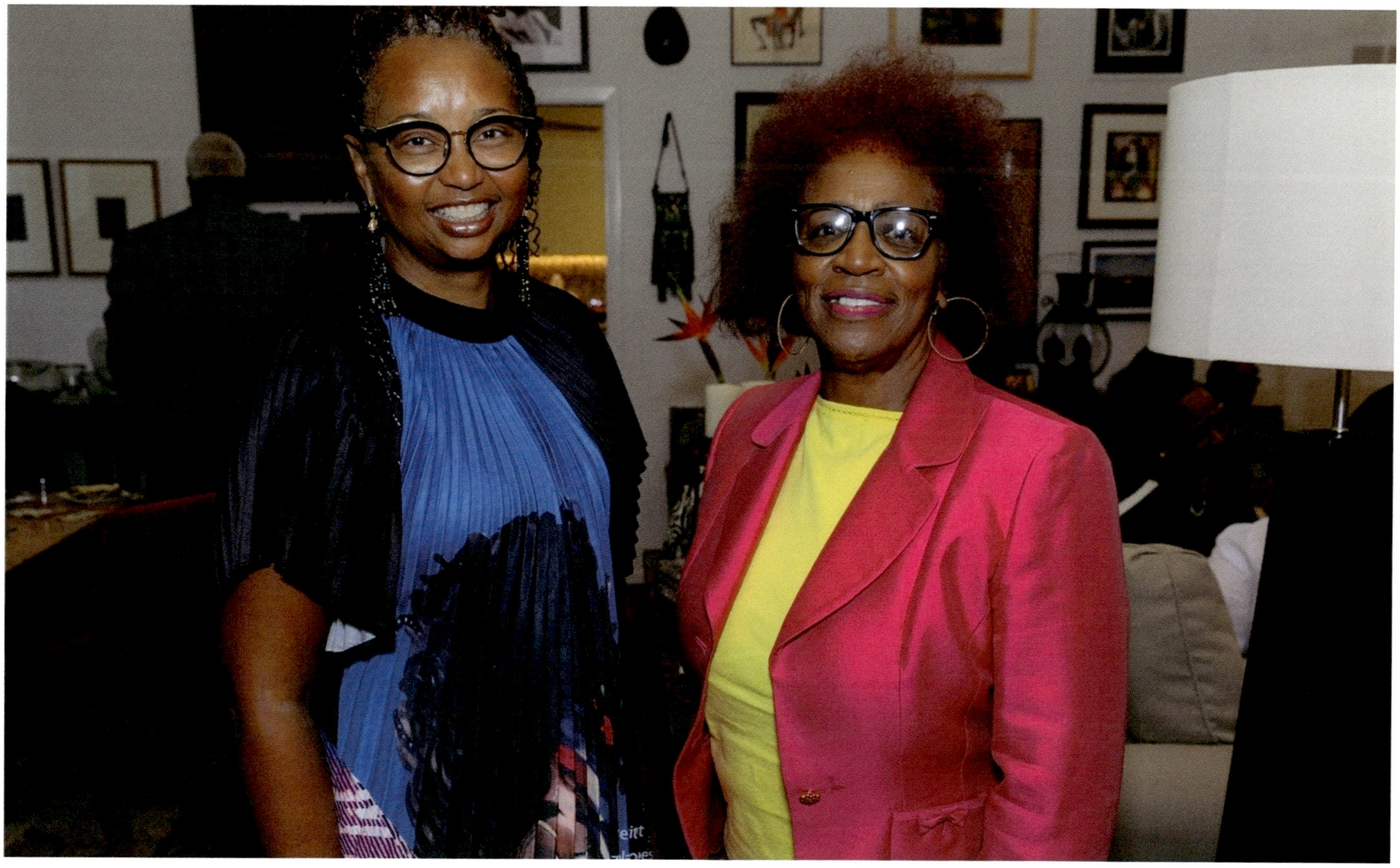

BEVERLY ALLEN + RUBY WHEELER

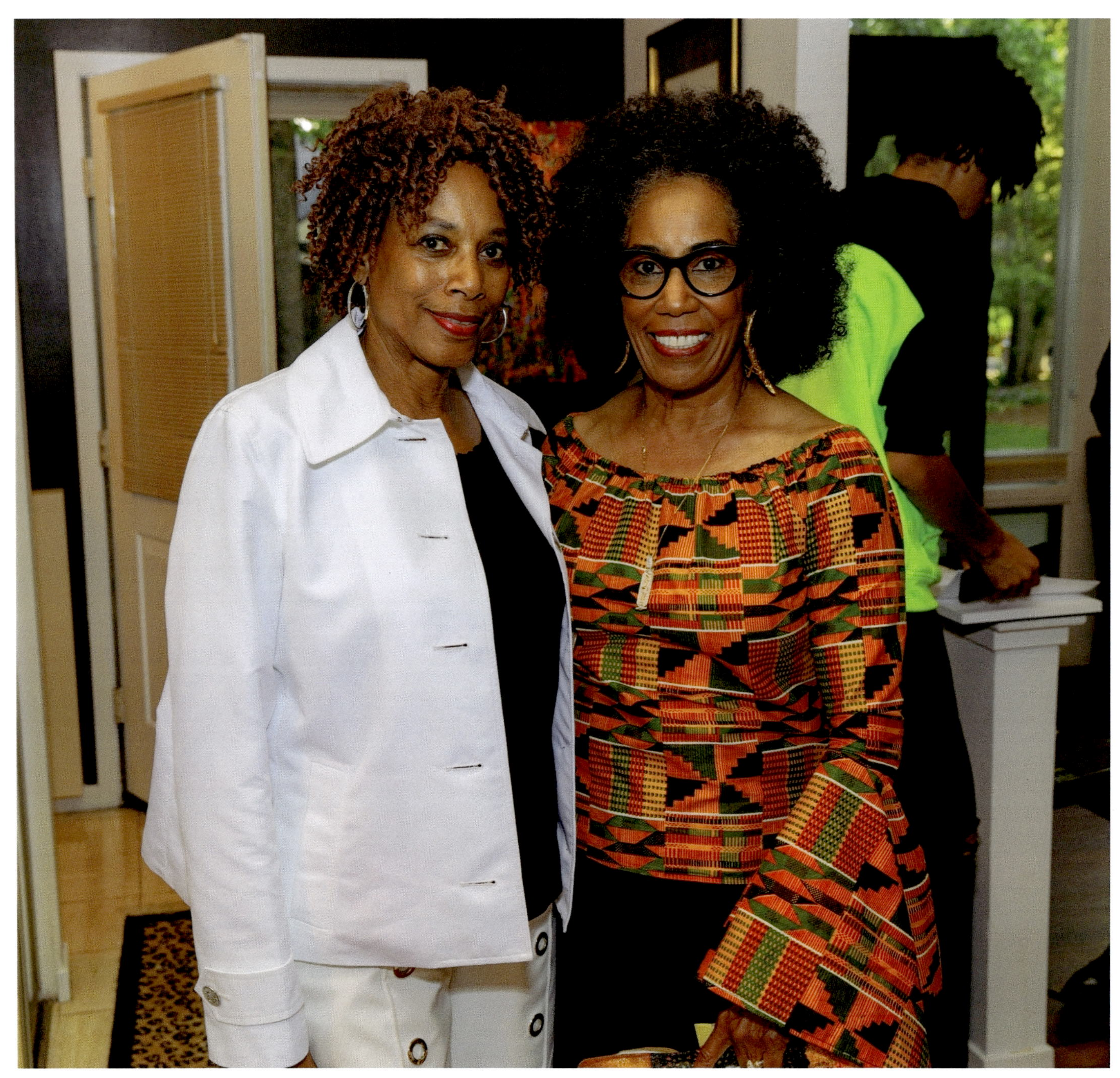

JACKIE BURDELL

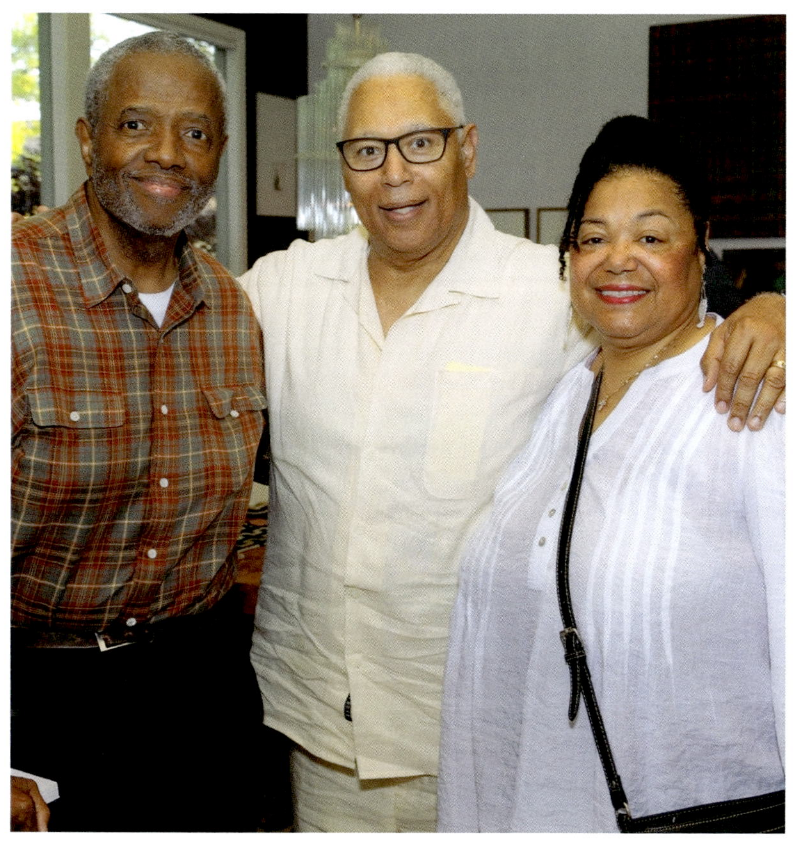

HENRY HARPER, DEXTER + HELEN MAYS

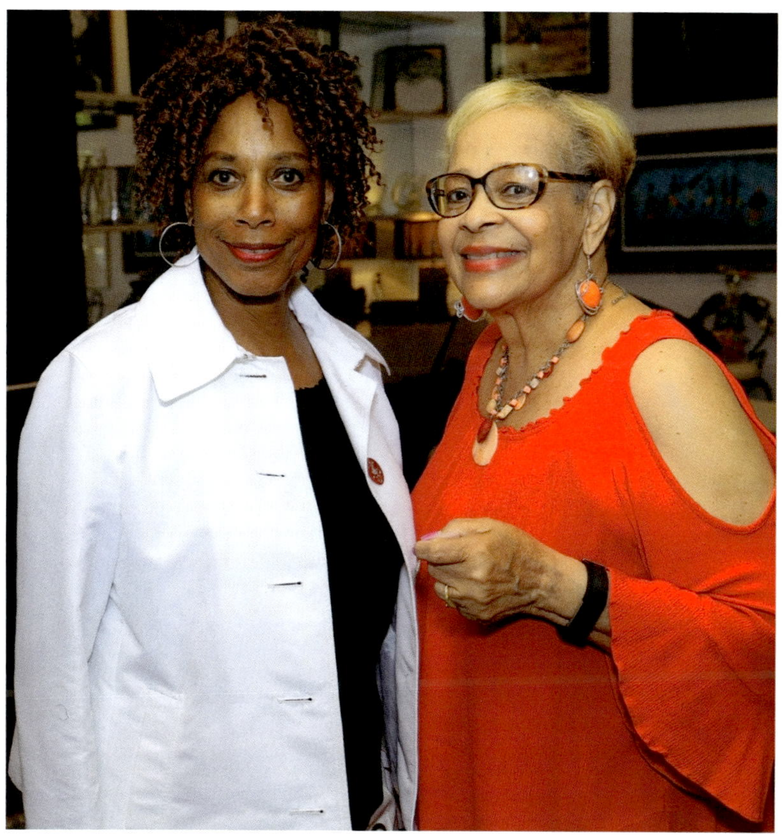

JOAN BRITTON

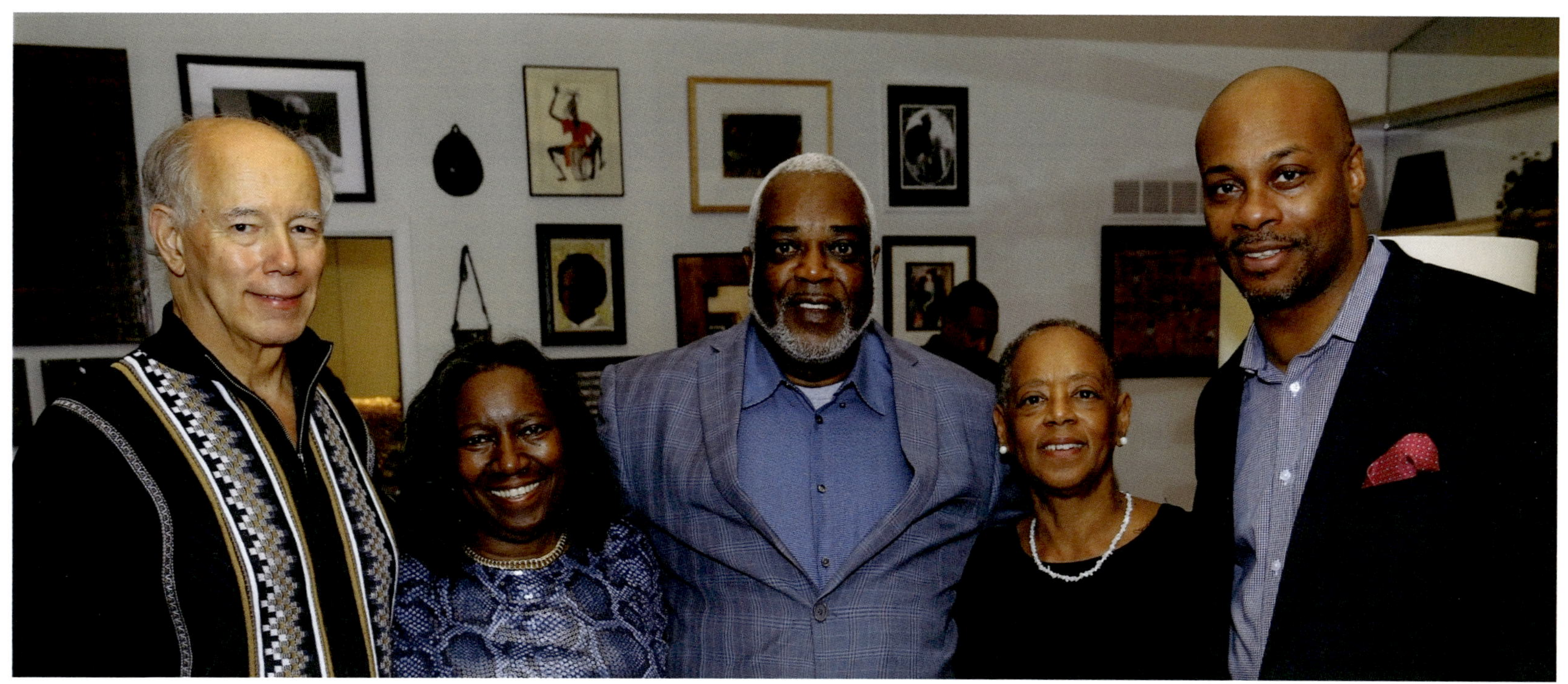

SIDNEY JONES, LINDA WHITAKER, DAVID WHITAKER, LINDA JONES + DRAKE PHIFER

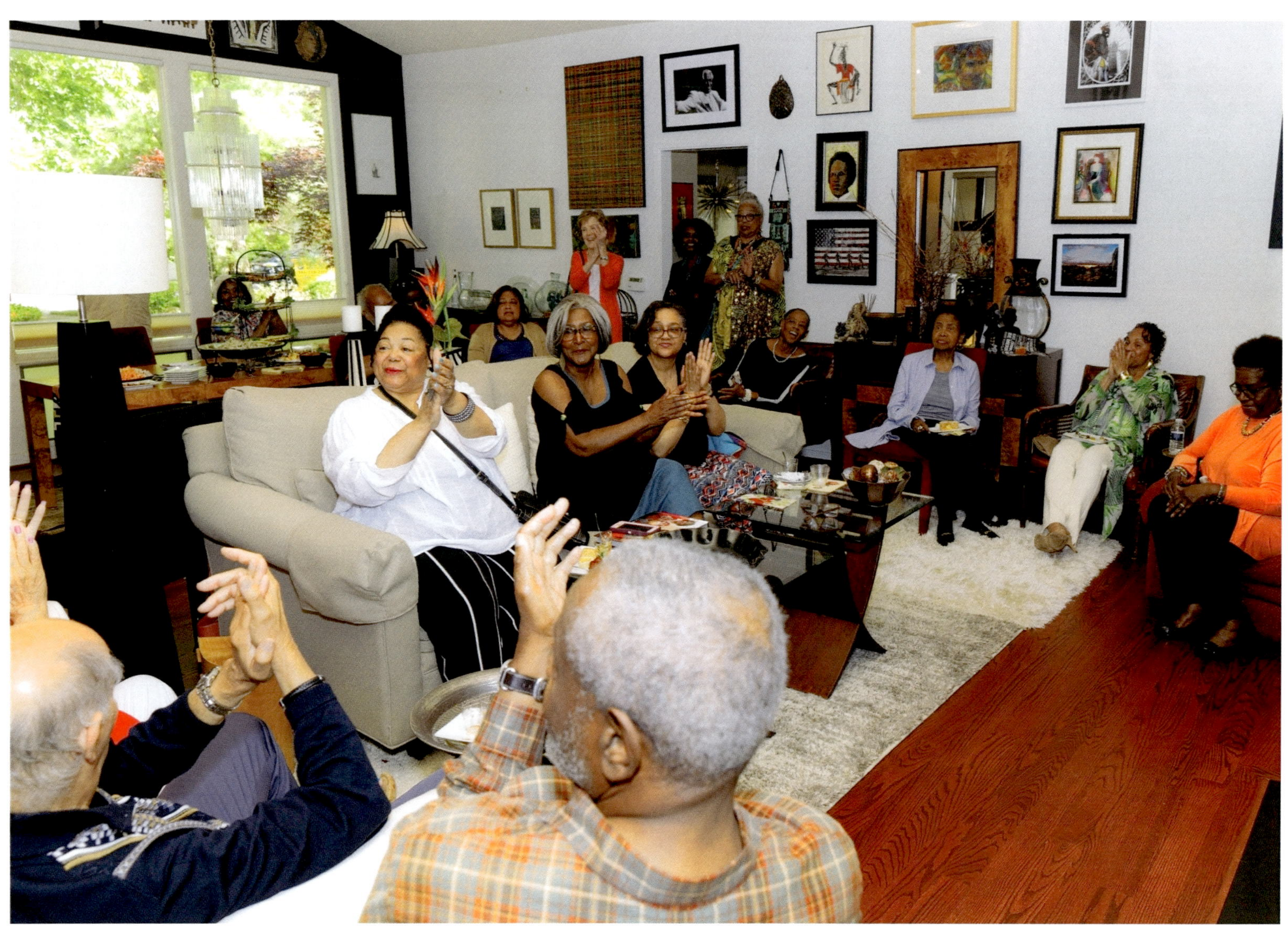

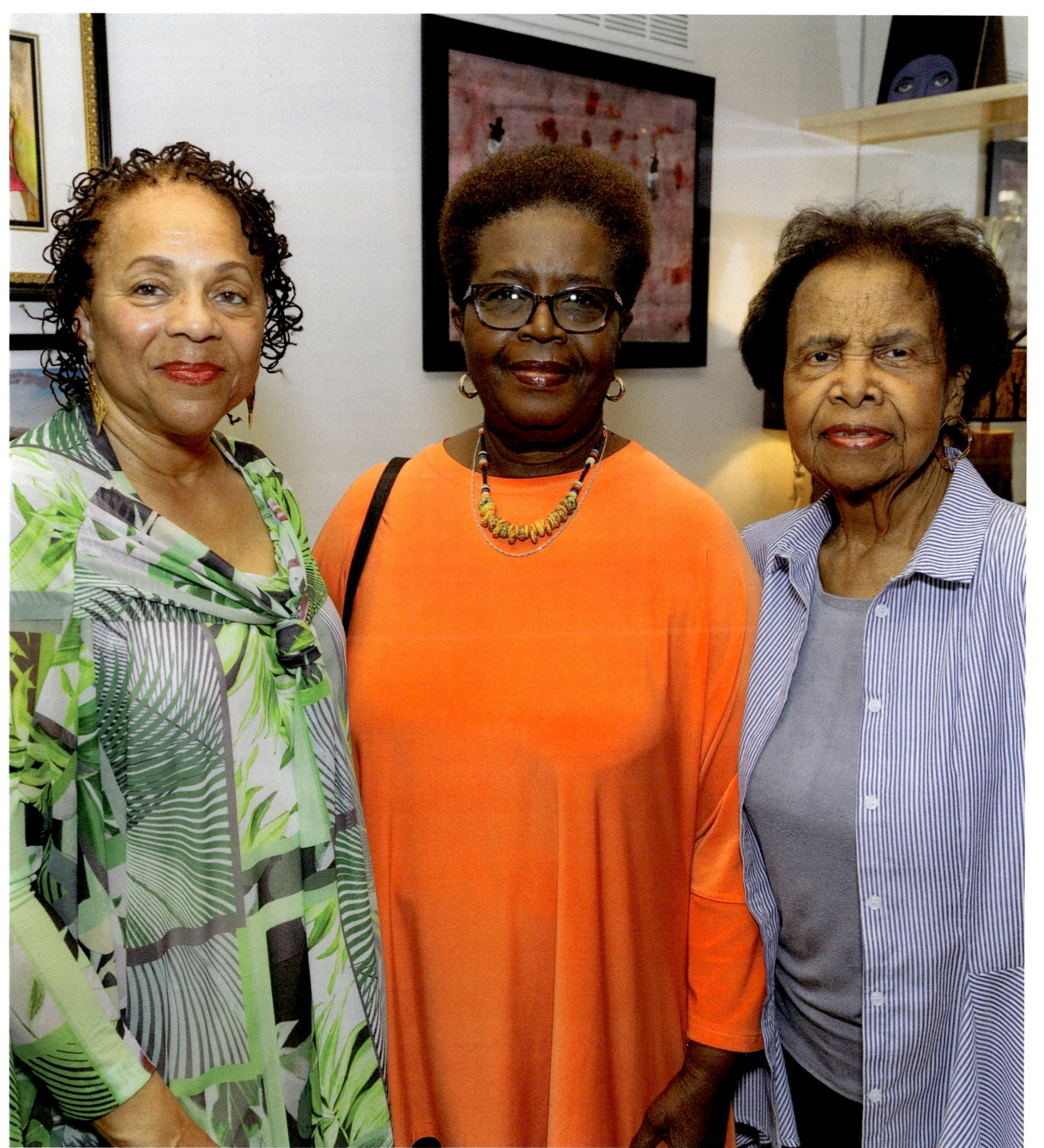

SHARON GAMBLIN, VELAROSE CLAY + SHIRLEY WOODSON REID

ACKNOWLEDGMENTS

This unplanned art journey would be impossible without the tremendous support from immediate family, extended family, special friends, mentors, instructors, gallerists, various organizations, media and, of course, collectors.

Immediate family: Husband Randolph Phifer, son Drake, and bonus daughter, the late Monique Parnell Phifer. They planted the seed to explore transferring my decoupage skills to painting on canvas, even finding a class to get me started, and they established the best marketing team, ever! Monique's absence is often deeply felt on so many levels. They along with daughter Tara Blackshear, who was living overseas or out of state for much of my journey, have given moral support encouragement and love. They were also first family to collect my art as were cousins Linda RM and Sidney Jones of Chicago.

Extended Family: Bernard Wilson, formerly of the Charles Wright Museum and currently with the Henry Ford Museum, for installation of art at each solo show; Will Brooks, exhibit assistant; Jessica Brown of Charles Wright Museum, art consultant, who assisted in pricing, critiquing and for participating in those fun "naming parties," which also included Drake, Tate Foster, photographer Mark Morden, Monique and Randolph. Photographers: Gary Washington of Mr. Washington Gallery; Rogers Foster of Rogers Foster Photography, and Kennette Lamar of Annistique Photography. Julie Constantine, for administrative work and for purchasing canvases using her Michael's discount card. Andrea C. Williams for her tireless efforts and patience for the graphic design of this book.

Special Friends: After an unfulfilling experience at the BBAC, I was on the verge of quitting. However, two sorority sisters, Debra DeBose and Marcia Griffin, each emailed that I might consider classes at The Community House (TCH). They pointed me to the right place at the right time because it was there that I met an artist who became the instructor on the second day when the original instructor left suddenly at the end of the first day. Paulette Boggs, who was the first person outside of family to purchase my decoupage and painting before I became a professional artist. Paulette also sponsored my membership into the Pierians Inc Detroit Chapter, an organization for women who support the fine and performing arts

Mentors: George N'Namdi of the N'Namdi Center for Contemporary Art; Henry Harper; Co-Founder of the DFABC; Harold Braggs, co-founder of the DFABC, and Shirley Woodson, of National Conference of Artists Michigan.

Artist Robbie Best, who took me under her wing, introducing me to the Detroit Fine Arts Breakfast Club of art enthusiasts, collectors, and other artists, an organization that would be one of my life-changing moments. I found my voice, my place, my purpose. Because of her, I am also a member of the Farmington Art Foundation where artists meet monthly and exhibit a few times a year. Robbie also led me back to the NCA, reacquainting me with the organization from when I held membership in the 80s. She and NCA president Shirley Woodson-Reid, an internationally acclaimed artist, invited me to present to the NCA at its monthly forum, affording more exposure to collectors and artists. That was quite an honor.

Instructors: Much is owed to Laurie Mueller, who was the instructor at The Community House (TCH) in Birmingham, MI, where I took several of her classes. She shared several techniques and encouraged me to apply for juried exhibitions. On my first try, I was juried into the annual TCH Art Exhibit and Sale. She also critiqued most of the 30 paintings for my inaugural solo show, saying to sign my name as no further work was necessary. Laurie is someone who goes above and beyond to push students to be their best and to gain confidence. I am where I am in large

ACKNOWLEDGMENTS

part because of her nurturing, patient, creative way of teaching. Clinton Snider, Birmingham Bloomfield Art Center (BBAC), who showed a different way of dripping and other techniques. Unbeknownst to me, his class was a mistake as it was for established or advanced artists, but I persevered for not only one of his all-day classes over several weeks, but two! Raymond Wells, National Conference of Artists, for his drawing instructions in 2019.

Galleries and public places exhibited: Dell Pryor Gallery (Dell Pryor), the first gallery that exhibited my work; N'Namdi Center for Contemporary Art (George N'Namdi); Blossoming Artists Gallery in Midtown (Peter Gahan); NCA Michigan Gallery (Shirley Woodson); The Carr Center (Oliver Ragsdale); Arts Extended Gallery (Dr. Cledie Taylor); Hannan Center (Richard Reeves, Vincent Tilford); Farmington Hills Library; Farmington Library; the City of Farmington Hills "for being exhibitor in its two-year public art program; Detroit Institute of Art (Salvador Salort-Pons) for the opportunity to exhibit with the DFABC artists; "Mackenzie Hall Cultural Centre Windsor, Ontario, Canada (Dennis K. Smith); Costick Center; Detroit Artists Market (Matt Fry); Allee Willis Wonderland; and the Franklin Grill, Franklin, MI

Julian C. Madison Building in downtown Detroit (Sharon Madison), Mash Detroit (Marlowe Stoudamire and Brandon Christopher) and the Torch of Wisdom Foundation (Yolanda Durfield), first three solo shows, 2015, 2016, and 2018, respectively.

Media: Munson Steed of Rollingout.com for three interviews; the late Brenda Perryman of the Brenda Perryman Show as guest; Terry Martin, Morning Toast Radio show and Tirrea Billings of Reflct Media.

If I have omitted anyone, please charge to my head and not to my heart.

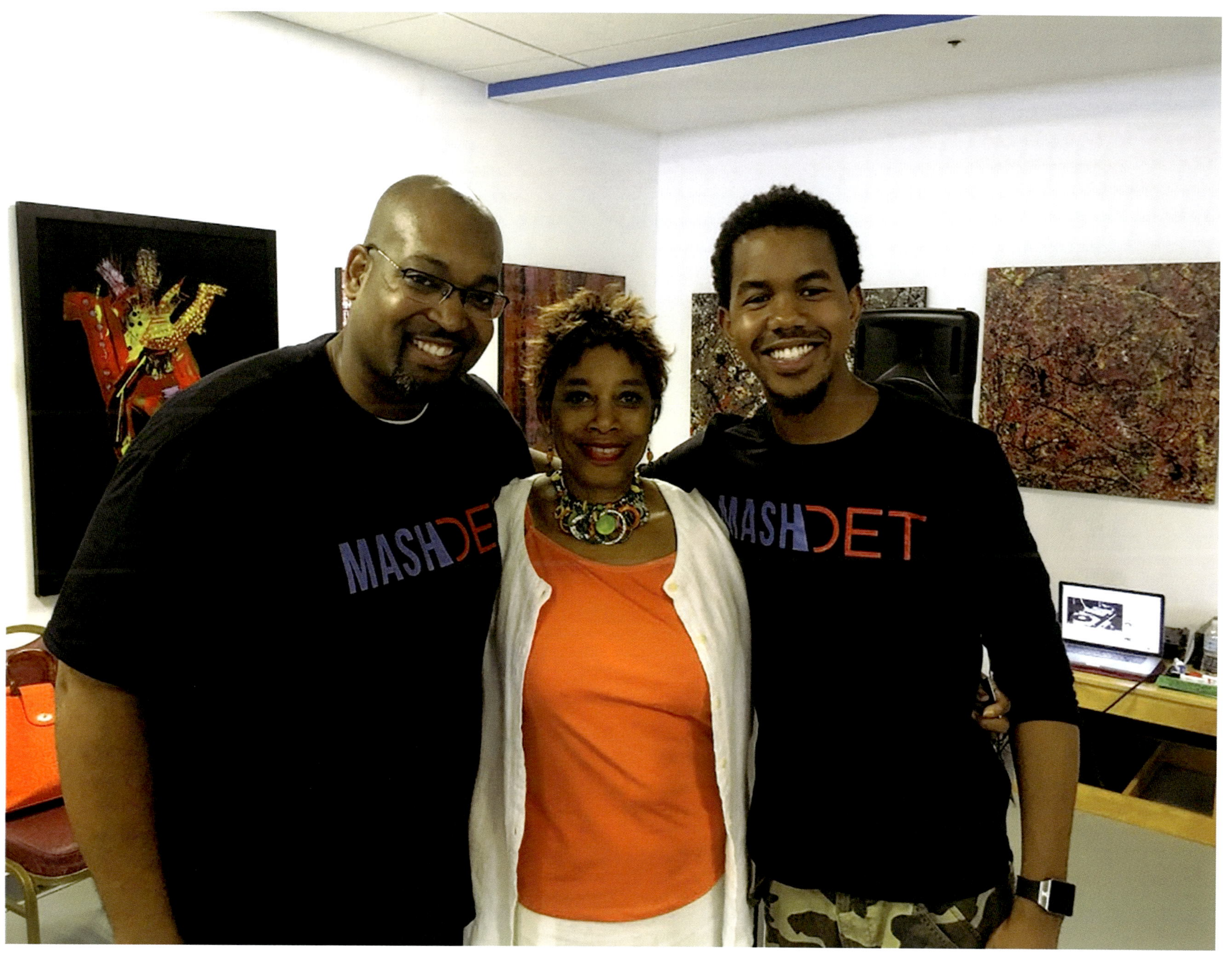

THE LATE MARLOWE STOUDAMIRE, PRISCILLA A. PHIFER AND BRANDON CHRISTOPHER

ROGERS FOSTER OF ROGERS WM. FOSTER PHOTOGRAPHY

COLLECTORS*

Mr. Robert & Mrs. Beverly Allen
Ms. Nikhol Atkins
Mr. Geoff & Mrs. Kate Baker
Ms. Patricia Baker
Ms. Tiana Baker
Mr. Jerome Basser
Mr. Arnold & Mrs. Robbie Best
Dr. Margaret Betts
Ms. Paulette Boggs
Mr. Stanley & Mrs. Judy MacReynolds Bowman
Mr. Lionnell Bradford
Mr. Harold & Mrs. Joann Braggs
Ms. Callie Bradford
Mr. Stephen Bray
Dr. Oscar & Mrs. Joan Britton
Mr. Andrew & Mrs. Loretta Brown
Mr. Ulysses & Mrs. Jackie Burdell
Ms. Schera Byas
Mr. Joseph & Mrs. Velarose Clay
Mrs. Arlinda Crossland
Atty. Paul & Judge Daphne Means Curtis
Ms. Kimberly Dantzler
Ms. Debra DeBose
Ms. Mary Duncan
Mr. Euclides & Mrs. Yolanda Durfield
Mr. Everett & Atty. Joan Everett
Ms. Karen Ferrell
Dr. Nicole Fields
Mr. James & Mrs. Joan LeMahieu Forster
Mr. Byron Tate & Mrs. Tracy Foster
Ms. Johnnie Fox
Ms. Sharon Gamblin
Mr. Ian & Mrs. Taranji Grant
Mr Grant & Mrs. Edythe Friley
Dr. Derrick Harper
Atty. Wyatt & Dr. Eleanor Harris
Mr. Dannon & Judge Brigette Holly
Mr. Larry & Mrs. Doreen Hunter
Hon. Teola Hunter
Dr. Keturah Jeffries
Ms. Carol Jenifer
Dr. Charmaine Johnson
Judge Sydney & Linda Jones
Mr. Chip & Mrs. Dora Kelley
Mr. Bernard & Mrs. Ruth Kelly
Mr. Stephen and Jacqui Lewis-Kemp
Ms. Ingrid LaFleur
Dr. Dawn Laws
Mr. Cleveland Leatherwood
Mr. Eddie and Mrs. Carole Lenton
Mr. Charlie Lewis
Mr. Jeremy & Mrs. Whitney Lewis

Ms. Domeda Macauleys
Mack Alive Permanent Ambassador Collection
Mr. Dexter & Helena Mays
Mr. Scott McDuffee
Ms. Sharon Merritt
Mr. Paul & Mrs. Laurie Mueller
Ms. Lynn Myers
Ms. Toney Natt
Dr. George R. & Mrs. Carmen N'Namdi
Ms. Kemba N'Namdi
Mr. Ed & Mrs. Karen Ogul
Dr. Taft & Dr. Sherida Parsons
Atty. Lawrence & Mrs. Raynona Patrick
Ms. Tamiria Perkins
Mr. Drake Phifer
Atty. Randolph Phifer
Dr. Tara Phifer Blackshear
Dr. Ernest & Mrs. De Retland
Mr. Brian & Mrs. Gloria Rhodes
The Honorable Dr. June Ridley
Mr. Paul Rogers
Mr. Peter & Atty. Barbara Sargent
Dr. Darryl & Mrs. Nicole Adams Sawyers
Mr. Charles & Mrs. LaRuth Shepherd
Ms. Patricia Solomon
Mr. Marcel & Mrs. Cynthia Stewart
Mr. Alfred & Mrs. Rosemary Summers
Mr. Brian & Mrs. LaShawn Taylor
Mr. Kevin Thompson
Mr. Patrick & Mrs. Margaret Tucker
Ms. Charlene Uresy
Mr. James & Atty. Katie Van Dyke
Mr. Walter & Mrs. Harriet Watkins
Judge Deborah Bledsoe Ford Watson
& Atty. Jerome Watson
Ms. L. M. Coz Watson
Ms. Ruby Wheeler
Atty. David & Dr. Linda Whitaker
Atty. Caryl Williams
Mr. Dennis & Mrs. Wendelin Williams
Ms. Allee Willis
Mr. Freddie & Mrs. Margaret Wilson
Dr. Doris Witherspoon
Ms. Shirley Woodson Reid
Mr. Sanford & Mrs. Shirley Woods
Atty. Barbara Wynder
Ms. Shanna Young

*Unknown by name are some collectors whose art was acquired at auctions or by agents.